A HISTORY OF

ART

An introduction to painting and sculpture

For Sylvia

20287

Published 1981 by Warwick Press, 730 Fifth Avenue,
New York, New York 10019.

First published in Great Britain by
Kingfisher Books Limited 1981

© Kingfisher Books Limited 1981

Library of Congress Catalog No. 81-51792.

ISBN 0-531-09188-0.

Design by John Strange
Colour separations by Newsele Litho Ltd., Milan, Italy
Printed in Italy by Vallardi Industrie Grafiche, Milan

A HISTORY OF
ART

An introduction to painting and sculpture

Norbert Lynton

WARWICK PRESS

Contents

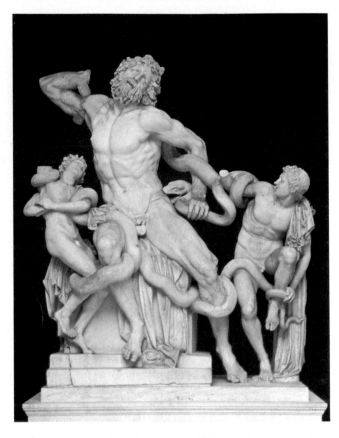

Laokoon, page 21 (left)
Detail of Fra Angelico's *Annunciation*, page 48 (above)
Detail of Cézanne's *Bathers*, page 131 (right)
Detail of Léger's *La Ville*, page 149 (far right)

This list is arranged to give a general idea of where art and artists come in time. Each heading refers to two pages. Dates are added here and there as appropriate, but sections dealing with non-western art have been inserted where they seemed most relevant – indicating a climax of activity, the discovery of a particular civilization or art, and the impact of that art on western art.

About Art and Us, and this Book

Art is very like people: always different and always much the same. Human beings make it, and they make it for human beings. We have got into the habit of thinking of art as something that keeps on changing, and of artists as people particularly intent on showing how different they are from each other. Some of the excitements, the adventures that come with art relate to this, but so also do many of the misunderstandings that get between art and us. It is time to stress that art has its constant aspects and its recurring interests and themes.

It is partly a question of what terms we like to use about art: these too change over the centuries and need questioning from time to time to see whether anyone really means them. In Renaissance times, artists and their patrons wanted to replace medieval conventions of art with others they claimed to be older, not newer. Medieval art was modern art; they wanted to bring back the art of the ancients, the Greeks and Romans. They emphasized their links with the distant past. They did in fact study Antiquity as much as they could but their knowledge remained very fragmented. They really knew very few examples of ancient art and sometimes they were wrong about what those examples represented, who had done them and when. They used what they had with enthusiasm and they invented the rest.

In modern times – more and more over the course of the last two hundred years – we have come to speak as though every artist had to rebel against the art he found when he arrived on the scene, and also to steer away from the art of his contemporaries. Art is praised in terms of being unique, new, revolutionary, shocking even. We like to think of the shocks suffered or imagined by our forefathers, in the case of, say, Impressionism. We feel good about admiring the artist whose work no one appreciated a hundred years ago, like Vincent van Gogh or Cézanne. But when we get to the art of our own day, we are frightened away by and in much the same terms, and say that an artist has gone too far, that what he does can no longer be called art. Or, rather, the media say it for us. And, on the whole, we agree because we expect to be puzzled by art's insistent newness – so much so that we do not notice the old themes, methods and also virtues that the art of our own century is full of.

So people's attitudes to art change, especially their attitude to artists. We require artists to be separate from the rest of us, figures with special talents and drives so big that conventions cannot contain them. They are not concerned with the rules and traditions that make up these conventions, and when they do something we speak as though they had worked in total isolation, mental as well as physical: they have 'expressed themselves', we say. We explain the result in terms of their personality,

their illness if possible – would we like Van Gogh so much if he had not suffered mental breakdowns and committed suicide? Previous ages went to artists with commissions: people needed art for specific purposes, they knew how and where to get it, and it was part of their ordinary life. Today we leave artists to their own devices and get rather cross with them if they want to come down out of the clouds.

A lot of modern artists do not want their art to be a personal display. They would rather meet us on common ground, address us on topics that concern us all and in terms that are not difficult to follow. They exist in the same world as us, and hate being kept out. It is us who insist on their separateness, condemning and ignoring many of them while treating a few of them like stars. It is us, pushed along by an art dealing system and by the media, that make the art world function like show business.

It is difficult to know how to stop it. Most of us grow up having little or no contact with art, old or new, let alone any real intimacy with it. When the media refer to art it tends to be about everything but the art itself: record prices at auctions, thefts, works by geniuses discovered in attics, or supposed works by geniuses – found not to be by them at all.

When we encounter art – real works of art, not reproductions – it is usually in art galleries. Some of these are rather pompous places, palatial prisons into which works of art are herded for their own protection. Protection they certainly get, against thieves and against the ravages of pollution and time. But they are also made to seem remote. We can see the objects there much more clearly than we ever could in the places they were done for. Also the galleries are good at gathering information about their possessions, and at arranging them so that we get some historical insight into them. But it is all rather remote from our lives, and the objects themselves are remote from their original functions and settings. Like the arts in general – drama, film, music, poetry, imaginative prose – art has become part of a special, separate corner of life.

There is no immediate way of rearranging the world so as to bring art back into the centre of our lives again. Yet people who want to can put it there for themselves. The first step is to accept that art is the human race talking to itself, across all possible frontiers of time and place and ideology. The second is to join in the conversation.

I said that art is like people. Getting to know art is very like getting to know people. Some are forthcoming, some less so. The same goes for art and it's not always the ones one gets to know quickest – people or works of art –

that are most worth knowing. But we don't get to know either sort unless we take some interest in them, give them a chance to open up and open up ourselves.

One way to start is to ask what they do and what they are interested in. Works of art are made for a variety of purposes. Some are like arguments or speeches; others are more like fond descriptions of places and persons. We may well find these more appealing than the more argumentative ones, but in the end the other sort may impress us more and matter to us more. Some works of art are very public – statues of rulers, sculptures on temples and churches, mural paintings in churches and town halls, all intent on making a particular point and driving it home. Others are much more intimate in their manner and intention. We obviously have to adjust our expectations to what kind of a thing the work is. We must not expect to be entertained by a painting that is speaking to us about grave matters, nor be made to think deeply about things by one that is intended to please our eyes and minds by showing something pleasant and simple. But most works of art intend both to please us and to make us think: they want to hold our attention by attracting our eyes and then to engage our minds in what they are telling us.

On the opposite page you see, at the top, part of two paintings dealing with a theme that concerns us all: death and what happens after death. More specifically, they were done for the Christian Church to show what will happen when the world ends, to those who have preferred sin to the service of God. They were painted within forty years of each other, one in Rome, the other in the north of Europe. The Roman example is part of a mural, a fresco painted with thin, watery paint into moist plaster. The northern example, done in the Low Countries (in part of what we now call Holland), was painted with oil colours on to a panel of wood.

Both are intended to bring home the horror of what awaits us unless we change our ways. They do this in very different ways. The Italian painter uses bodies almost exclusively, and better-than-natural bodies at that. He has enormous skill and imagination. He has studied anatomy closely. He has studied all he could of ancient sculpture, and learnt from it how to make the human image powerful and imposing, as well as how to charge it with expression. It is especially awesome to see such marvellous bodies in such a state of terror. The northern painter knows a lot about how bodies move and how people behave. He knows that his public will be interested to read the little scenes he uses and will recognize the actions and the sayings they represent: dice, cards, a backgammon board, the delights of music, the vanity of a pretty girl, the man beset by an amorous nun-sow, the fool behind them trying to balance two red balls on two boards.

Both paintings say 'repent now; tomorrow it may be too late' but they say it in very different ways to rather

different audiences. Each painter aims at his public's understanding, but each also means to stretch it and make people stand aghast. The problem was to make a strong impact but also to go on making it. They had earlier versions of the *Last Judgement* and of *Hell* to go by, but each treatment was also dramatically new, so the public would both know and be surprised by what it saw.

The lower pair of details on the opposite page show entirely different subjects painted for utterly different purposes. On the left, again, a mural in Rome, done in the same technique; on the right, part of a painting done in oil on canvas, a smallish object to be hung on someone's wall at home among other pictures. On the left, a gathering of the great philosophers of Antiquity; on the right, a party. Both, notice, are imaginary scenes; even the party was an invention of the painter's. The top pair shows what will come; bottom left shows what has been, bottom right a dream of what will never quite be and never quite was. Antique wisdom was painted opposite a fresco showing the central dogma of the Christian faith: the idea was to show the great thought of the past and the present in harmony. It is an intellectual theme, dependent on a learned public and one which suits the place it is in. The picture of a party does not ask for an educated response so much as a sympathetic one, to the charming details, the almost audible music, the elegant setting.

About two hundred years separate these two paintings. The mural is one of the most famous examples of what the art world called 'history painting' – a serious theme treated in a noble manner. The party scene is a very fine example of a type of picture much enjoyed but much less highly valued, the 'genre painting' – ordinary people doing ordinary things, usually produced for better-than-ordinary people. Here the painter showed not peasant but polite society, and so rather changed the relationship between the scene and its viewers. These viewers would have known at once that the people in the picture were not quite real: the picture is not a flattering portrait of a social group but something less certain, more needling.

Noting the differences is useful, but we should also do the opposite and look for basic similarities. Some of them perhaps we take for granted though we should not. All the paintings on the opposite page show figures in space. We are to look at these flat pictures as though they were slices of reality. In the lower two, space is handled in very much the same way: it is clearly described by the architecture and made navigable for us by the way the figures in it are grouped. There is space too for the figures in the *Last Judgement* mural, but most of them

Detail from page 64 (top left)
Detail from page 68 (top right)
Detail from page 62 (bottom left)
Detail from page 104 (bottom right)

are hanging in front of it, a veil of figures before a blueness that may be space or sky or the universe. We are not invited in; it comes at us. In the *Hell* panel figures and objects seem further back as we look up the picture, but we are more interested in surprising changes of scale, when things are shown much larger than we expect them to be, and so the reality of this careful account turns out to be an unreality, a nightmare. Again, we observe from outside.

All four paintings are basically naturalistic: they show us things more or less in the way they appear to us in real life. Yet we do not for a moment think of these scenes as real in the sense that we expect to meet them every day. These painters would not have thought it their business merely to imitate the world as closely as flat images permit, and that goes even for the painter of the party scene. His picture may well, in many respects, be the opposite of the *Hell* panel, but there is more than a hint, amid his jollifications, that every bit of fun will have to be paid for.

I have not yet said who the painter was in each case. Does it matter? Of course it matters, but I often think that our emphasis on 'great artists' gets in the way of our seeing their work. 'Who made you?' should not be the first, and certainly not the only question we ask a work of art. It is not very productive to go up to people, ask them their surnames and then walk away. You probably know by now who the four painters were, and perhaps that made you think of them, their other works and anything else you might already know about them. Knowing about them can certainly increase our understanding of what they did, but this should be added to our examination of the particular work we are confronting, not made to substitute for it. Were they expressing themselves? As far as we can tell, their personalities had an influence on their works, and they probably wanted to impress and satisfy their patrons, but the general aim was bigger than that and much less personal.

The other thing I have not mentioned is beauty. We all know what we mean by beauty, though we may argue about where it starts and finishes. But is beauty art's first aim and duty? Must all people be beautiful and would we appreciate it if they were? People can be marvellous in many ways, their appearance, the way they move or speak or behave, their expression, their character, their deftness in relating to others. If we accept all of these ways as being beautiful, then art too must be beautiful, but not in any shallow sense of being merely agreeable to our eyes or to our minds. The four examples on the previous page would all be called beautiful by most people – no harm in that as long as they realize that they are stretching the term to include scenes of terror and a taste of bitterness.

If we did not know what the paintings referred to we might well still admire them but they would be more distant from us and perhaps we would misunderstand them in some ways. Similarly, we can find it difficult to appreciate works of art produced for societies we have little knowledge of, even if they are explained to us. Yet the gap becomes surprisingly small if we persist, just as language barriers almost disappear when we like people enough. Conversely, we may make too little allowance for the gap between us and the fifteenth century Roman or Dutchman. What, for instance, was the world like when images were few and rare and very special, not a daily flood dazzling our eyes and our minds?

But it is important to realize that their public understood them pretty well. Roughly speaking, people knew the story, were willing to be told it again, and were deeply responsive to the way in which it was told. The painter worked to deliver the meaning of the story vividly and freshly. In the same way, a modern theatre director will strive to inject his production of *King Lear* or another well known play with new force and value. But the party scene does not offer much by way of a story. We can all recognize what is going on; even non-westerners would know that this is a picture about people having a good time. But we miss much of the point of the picture if we do not know that it is a fantasy and not a picture of an actual event.

All art relies on some knowledge, and some art demands quite a lot from us because we do not readily have the knowledge that the artists could take for granted in the people they worked for. In the last hundred years or so artists have often tried to make their art easy for everyone, by demanding little or nothing of the book-learning sort of knowledge, and appealing instead to our common experience of seeing and living, and they have been roundly cursed for it.

The Impressionists thought that everyone would be able to respond to the light and colour they saw when they looked at landscape. Putting that down vividly would surely produce in spectators the pleasure they themselves had felt. It didn't, not for a long time, though in the end they have been proved right. The abstract painters of the early twentieth century thought they could connect directly with us all by speaking through shapes and colours, rather like the composers of music use sound, to suggest something dramatic or comforting, anxiety or joy. They are still, seventy years later, a problem to many people.

There is no doubt at all that we can and do respond to shapes and colours, and also to marks that look gentle or aggressive, swift or slowly assembled. We are sensitive to them because we need to be: they relate to quite basic issues in our daily life, things we have been learning about since we were born – gesture, facial expression, sharp claws as against velvety paws, cold and warm, food that is appetising and food that is unpleasant. All this too is a form of knowledge, knowledge gained from experiencing and surviving.

Detail from page 124   Detail from page 138   Detail from page 146

The three details shown here all look rather abstract; none of them is so entirely. The one on the left is from an Impressionist painting, the one in the middle from a Cubist painting, the one on the right from an almost abstract painting associated with Expressionism. Labelling them with these terms has the effect of separating them out, but they have a lot in common. Most important is that we cannot read them the way we read more directly descriptive art. Yet the Impressionist painting is actually very much concerned with describing the scene, only the painter has picked a scene especially empty of clear forms and he has avoided imposing his knowledge of what he is looking at on what he is actually seeing. He knows what boats look like, but he painted what they actually looked like, at that misty moment.

The Cubist painter knows how to paint a bottle and a glass in a realistic way, and he could have painted them like an Impressionist, showing the way light falls on to glass and both reveals and hides its shape. Instead he chooses to give us information about the bottle and the glass in a diagrammatic way, almost as though he were telling us about them: 'You know, bottle: a tall thing that gets narrower near the top but is circular in plan . . .' Yet, at the same time, his gentle touches of greys and browns do suggest an atmosphere, and when we study the whole picture we find that it is the atmosphere of a bar. What he is doing is giving us a mixture of seeing and knowing, or even half-seeing and half-knowing, which is very much the way we experience things before we have decided what we want to focus our eyes and our attention on. In a sense this is very realistic, closer to experience than what we would accept as a straight picture of a bottle and a glass in a bar.

The Expressionist does not want to be real in that sense at all. He hints at particular objects in his paintings but it does not matter to him whether we can make them out or not. The paintings are not about them. The marks and the colours are his first concern and message: he wants us to listen to them like music, or read them like a facial expression, for the feeling they convey. And that process too, in yet another way, can be called real; it has to do with emotional experience. His painting – not done impetuously though he wants it to look un-rehearsed, and requiring a lot of skill and judgement – is his way of transmitting to us not external facts nor specific messages but something internal and personal. We expect this from music and also from some sorts of poetry; he asks us to receive his paintings in the way we receive them.

Art takes time. Attention is what counts, the essential thing. Remember, art is made by men and women for men and women. You don't get to know people by nodding to them as you go by. A book can offer only words and illustrations about and of a few samples chosen from the wealth available to us. But the best illustrations in the world can only hint at the character of the work they represent: only the real thing will do. The more actual works of art you give your attention to, the better you will be at using illustrations as informative substitutes. In the same way, the words I provide cannot bring art to you nor you to art; they can at best help in both directions. Perhaps they can provide some pointers and remove some misconceptions. If they fail to convince you that art is at once mankind's most wonderful and also most basic invention, then it's probably my fault, certainly not art's.

Prehistoric Art

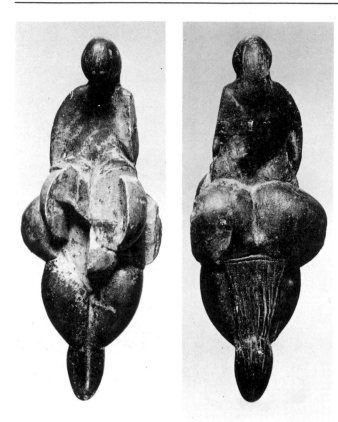

Venus of Lespugue
c. 25,000 BC
ivory
15 cm (5¾ in) high
Musée des Antiquités
Nationales,
St Germain en Laye

The cave paintings of prehistoric man, done 15 to 20,000 years ago, began to be discovered in the last quarter of the nineteenth century. A world gradually coming to terms with the shocking new art of Impressionism (page 124) learned that there was art before the dawn of human history. Before human beings learned to write or otherwise record their activities for posterity, when life meant living off whatever the environment provided, the plants that grew, the animals that could be killed (for tools made from their bones as well as for food), people had gone down into the bowels of the earth to paint large images of animals on to the walls and ceilings of natural caves, and paint them not like clumsy beginners but realistically, naturalistically.

We are still amazed at the quality of these paintings. They prove close intimacy with the beasts, but then hunting them ceaselessly could well bring that. They also prove an intimacy with a very sophisticated thing: with the process of turning a living, moving being, experienced at all sorts of angles and often in situations of danger, into a two-dimensional image composed of smears and rubbings in two or three earth colours. Today every child learns from its parents the trick of identifying the pictures it is shown in books with objects in the real world. Yet we all know that the difference between a pattern of inks printed on paper and a creature of flesh and blood on quite another scale is total, or very nearly so. It is because we see everyone else make the leap so readily, and because we enjoy making it, that we are quick to identify the cow on the page with the cow in the field and also to accept invented beings that we never see in real life as having a reality of their own, like Mickey Mouse and the Pink Panther.

Prehistoric people had to discover this trick, but the other way around: they had to get from the bison in the valley to the bison on the cave wall. We know neither how they did it nor why. The cave paintings show animals – horses, bison and oxen and also, much less frequently, mammoth, deer and ibex. Occasionally they show other things: crudely simplified human beings and signs for things that may be spears and traps.

It used to be said that these paintings were done to give the painter and the group power over the animals represented. There are still tribal societies where a lifelike image is thought to have power over the person whose image it is – carrying such an image away deprives that person of their power to live or, at least, makes them liable to attacks via their image. In the same way, prehistoric groups may have believed that a painting of a bison would give them power over the bison or deprive the bison of power over them. This is a satisfying explanation of why such lifelike images should have been painted deep down in dark places where they can hardly have been meant to be looked at, but doubt has been cast on it recently. For one thing, we know from other evidence that these hunters of long ago ate mostly reindeer meat and used reindeer bones as tools, yet they did not paint reindeer images.

So it may be that these painted images had a less direct, one to one role. Yet it was clearly important that they should be so lifelike (unlike the human images). The painters must have gone to enormous trouble to execute them with the means at their command: tufts of fur perhaps, dipped in ground earth mixed with animal fats, and sputtering grease lamps to work by. It must have taken time for them to develop this art, and it is more or less certain that the painters were specialists who passed the knowledge and the skill on to each other. Perhaps they were also the tool makers of the group, thus giving power to their fellows. They may even have been spiritual as well as practical guides, the prehistoric

Ceiling painting of horse
and three cows c. 15,000 BC
painting on rock surface
Lascaux, Dordogne

equivalents of the medicine-men of the American Indians or the witch doctors of Africa.

What we call art and associate with pleasure and interest was then a basic necessity, part of the struggle to survive. Did it give pleasure as well? Did the painters ever say to each other, or the others say to them, 'That's a good one' and 'That one is not so good'? Again, we can only guess. Some utensils were 'decorated', as we would call it. For instance a spear-throwing stick, consisting of a long bone with a little hollow at one end in which to lodge the end of the spear, has the cup around the hollow formed like a bird. To us, this is decoration; to prehistoric peoples. it was probably functional and power-increasing. It is hard to believe that something that had to be handled and used, like this object, would not develop in its maker and user a sense of satisfaction in the object, in the form as a form, to hold and to touch and to look at.

We cannot be certain. Prehistoric men also made many little figures of women, which we call Venuses. About 150 of them have been found, and they vary a

great deal, depending partly on the material they are made of. The one shown here is a marvellous example, even though parts have broken off. It was found in France, at Lespugue in the Pyrenees. Like many of the others, its forms stress breasts, buttocks and thighs. The head is small and without detail; the arms can scarcely be seen. But the shape of the whole also stresses symmetry. Perhaps that is because we are more or less symmetrical, but then the figure as a whole does not seem intent on being naturalistic. And she is not only symmetrical left to right; her forms are very satisfyingly almost symmetrical top to bottom. And her generous curves play rhythmically against each other, like a succession of phrases in music or waves in water. In other words, one feels that she has been composed, been given an interesting silhouette. We take pleasure in it. Perhaps prehistoric people, using such a figure to ensure the fertility of the earth, the animals and the women themselves, would have identified this pleasure with effectiveness – like we do with anything from a spoon to an aeroplane.

Egyptian Art

*King Mykerinus and Queen
Khamerernebty II from Giza*
c. 2530 BC
schist
142 cm (56 in) high
Museum of Fine Arts, Boston

The art and architecture of Egypt suggest permanence
and stability. The very shape of the Egyptian pyramid,
that mountainous version of the heap of stones or sand
under which many a body must have been buried then
and later, expresses solidity and excellence in equal
measure. A square plan; sides inclined at 45 degrees to
the base; a perfect meeting at the top in one stone, itself a
perfect pyramid. Think of the organization it must have

involved, as well as the labour. Think of the elaborate
chambers, passages and doors inside, as well as false
doors, false passages and traps designed to prevent
robbery of the precious objects put in there with the
body of the dead king or queen.

But think also of the mathematics. On such a scale a
slight deviation from accuracy would badly distort the
whole shape. The Egyptians inhabited a long thin
country stretching along both sides of the river Nile, kept
fertile by its regular flooding every year and also kept
together by communication and transport along the
river. On either side lay desert sands and mountains, and
for the rest there was the sky, with the sun born anew
every morning and travelling across the sky to die in the
west, and the lesser lights of the nocturnal sky and the
patterns they made. The Egyptians learned to measure
time and to measure earth and sky, and the common
factor in all this was what we call mathematics.

The sun and the Nile were worshipped as gods. The
king was a semi-god, an intermediary between men and
gods. When he died, his body and his spirit had to be
kept safe and supplied with all necessities so that he
could enter paradise and befriend the people he left
behind. For this the Egyptians made the pyramids and
the statues and also the paintings that went inside the
tomb – dignified, formal images of the king and those
close to him in standing, more informal images of
servants and animals. Here too mathematics was important, and to understand that we must try and see
mathematics not as a useful juggling with numbers but
as basic knowledge and necessary law.

The statue of Mykerinus and his wife delights us today
with its sheer good looks and optimistic air. It is an early
sculpture, of the time of the great pyramids at Giza, and
it is as perfect as they are. Man and woman stand
together, splendid specimens of young adulthood, serene,
strong and confident. We cannot help admiring them as
ideal human beings. That, strictly, is what they are: ideal.
They are not portraits but human beings shown in such
a way as to bring out all the perfection that humanity can
exhibit if we study the most perfect specimens and ignore
all imperfections. Perfection must have been a necessary
part of their equipment, essential if their spirits were to
reside contentedly in such man-made housing.

Like the pyramid, the perfect human image was
governed by mathematics. The dimensions of the whole
figure and of its parts were determined by means of a
grid of lines: so many squares for the height, so many
from foot to hip, so many from shoulder to elbow, and
so on. A drawing on a board could easily be transcribed
on a larger scale on to a block of stone by means of an
enlarged grid. Nothing would be left to chance. A more

detailed grid would control the drawing of the face and transmit that to the stone.

There was little or no concern with change or novelty. Egyptian art hardly changed at all as the centuries rolled by. What we call fashion hardly changed either. There was certainly no room for artistic self-expression or originality, but then there were probably no such people as artists – only those who knew the formulas and traditions and those who executed their instructions. No doubt there were master craftsmen, in charge of a team of variously skilled assistants, and perhaps they were the same men as those who saw to the building of the pyramids, temples and other buildings known to us. But control rested in the hands of the kings and queens, as did all military power, religious and civil law and communication with the gods.

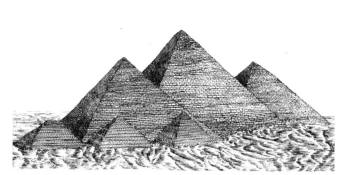

The great pyramids of Giza, (above)
built around 2600–
2400 BC

Banquet scene from the tomb of Nebamun c. 1400 BC
paint on plaster
95 cm (37½ in) high
British Museum, London

The painting of the Egyptians followed the same conventions. In many ways it is not very lifelike to our eyes: it does not attempt to suggest space and have figures moving and existing in it but spreads them out on the surface of the painting, combining a profile presentation of head, arms and legs with frontal treatment of shoulders and eyes. Eyes, more than anything else, give life to an image. Egyptian writing was a combination of abstract signs and simplified images, and no firm line is to be drawn between writing and image-painting.

In the example shown here, we see both the use and the setting aside of formulas. The guests seated at the banquet arranged for the entertainment of Nebamun's spirit follow the convention for the two-dimensional representation of three-dimensional persons. Their servants can be shown more freely and are able to serve more effectively because of the freedom of action that goes with the freedom of representation. But the musicians can be varied, it would seem, for variation's sake. It was very rare indeed for faces to be shown other than in profile, and it is difficult to believe that it was done here other than for the sake of variation and to show that it could be done. Is the painter demonstrating his power of invention? Perhaps, but we have to remind ourselves that when the painting was done, and the other preparations were complete, Nebamun's body would be placed in the tomb chamber, sealed up, and never – in theory – seen by human eyes again.

Early Greek Art

EUPHRONIOS
Sarpedon carried from the battlefield (red-figure vase: side A) c. 510 BC
painted ceramic
vase 46 cm (18 in) high;
scene 21 cm (8 in) high
Metropolitan Museum of Art,
New York

Red-figure vase *(Kalyx-Krater)* painted by Euphronios. Side B (above) shows five men arming themselves for battle.

The Greeks got many of their art ideas and methods from the Egyptians, but they had one interest or appetite which the Egyptians do not seem to have shared. And it made their art very different from the Egyptians. The vase painting reproduced here suggests what it was.

Pottery had often been decorated but the Greeks were the first to make pottery into a vehicle for painted scenes. The form of this particular vessel – a bowl in which wine and water would be mixed – allows for a broad and almost vertical band that gives very little distortion to painted images. One guesses that the form was developed in this way for the sake of the painting.

The vase shows the dead Sarpedon, slain in the fighting between the Greeks and the Trojans, being carried off the battlefield by the winged figures of Death (right) and Sleep. Hermes, the god, watches over this act. We know who they all are partly because their names are written close to them. There also, to the right of the head of Hermes, we can read the name of the painter, Euphronios. Clearly he wanted his skill at telling the story credited to him just as much as he wanted the story to be understood.

Those who looked at his picture of it knew the story of the Trojan wars: it was recited or sung at festivals and gatherings long before it was written down in the sixth century and ascribed to a poet called Homer. To us it is a famous story and a marvellous, and marvellously early, epic poem. To the Greeks it was history: the story of their forefathers and of their interaction with the gods.

Homer's poem is full of light and shade, colours and tastes, feelings and jokes as well as heroic actions. Euphronios does not have light and shade, only silhouettes and internal lines. There is no space, no ground for the feet to press on, no background. What there is in plenty is line, in black and red, and visual pattern and texture. Hair and clothes readily turn into pattern and so does anatomy itself, as we can see especially clearly on Sarpedon's stomach where natural form has been turned into a satisfactory abstraction. And there is lots of movement. The faces are formulas of the Egyptian type, but the way the figures move expresses something more than what they are doing. We have a sense of why they are doing it, of sympathy for the dead warrior, of the piety that goes with caring for dead.

Hermes' two-way movement, looking this way and rushing that, is almost funny, or pathetic, to our eyes: pathos, the exciting of pity and fellow-feeling in the beholder, is very much what Euphronios was trying to achieve. The moment he chose to represent on this side of the bowl is perhaps more likely to engage our feelings than Sarpedon's slaying by Patroclus would have done. On the other side Euphronios painted five men arming themselves for battle.

I have used the word 'scene' for the representation of the group: the interaction of the figures there invites it whereas the five figures on the other side, together yet separate, do not. 'Scene' comes from the Greek words for stage and also for shadow. Magnificent as the Greeks' art and architecture were, their greatest art form was drama, especially tragedy – the retelling of an important event combined with the re-enacting of it. The same spirit that led them into that awesome invention is also the spirit that produced their painting and their sculpture. It was the urge to tell and retell, and in telling again give value and meaning to stories that were important because they helped them to understand the world of the present.

The Greeks learnt the art of making monumental figure sculpture from the Egyptians, but rapidly developed it in ways the Egyptians would not have considered. The Greeks had harder tools and, in the several forms of marble to be found in the Greek islands, they had a material which, though durable, was much more responsive to metal tools than the granite and schist used by the Egyptians for their most important statues. So the Greeks set up a great number of statues in public places, especially around their temples, and these stood there for all to see.

The statue of the man carrying a calf on his shoulders as an offering to the gods follows Egyptian prototypes. The formality of the figure, his left foot a little forward (though now lost), the serenity of his face and the smooth falling of the thin cloak over his shoulders – all these things suggest Egypt. Even the marvellously effective device of having the man's arms and the calf's legs form a cross on his chest recalls an Egyptian way of showing kings holding sceptres. But this man was no king, merely a citizen of Athens. It is partly in this dignifying of the ordinary man and his devotional act to the level of a model action portrayed in lasting form that we recognize the Greek spirit: as the act was intended to speak to the gods, so the statue addresses itself also to men. And lifelikeness is part of the mode of address. Formal though the sculpture is, it is charged with human feeling and presence. The animal's head next to the man's has something to do with that, but also the delicate carving of the anatomy. Compare, for example, the treatment of the man's stomach with that of Sarpedon: an acceptable pattern has become flesh and blood.

Moschopheros (calf-bearer) from the Acropolis c. 560 BC marble 165 cm (65 in) high National Museum, Athens

Classical Greek Art

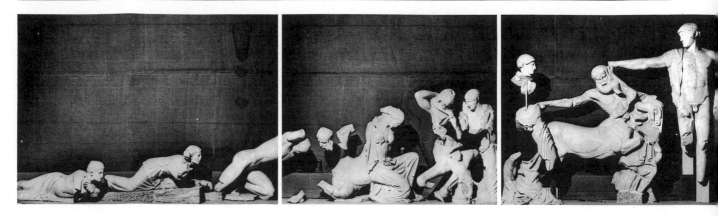

Every four years, from 776 BC on, people came from the several city-states on the Greek mainland, from the islands and from further afield, to participate in athletic events at Olympia. Today the Olympic Games are contests between nations, political events that sometimes smell of war. Then they were religious practices, accompanied by other acts such as processions and recitations, all dedicated to the honour of the king of the gods, Zeus. Olympia itself was not a city-state; it was the chief sanctuary of Zeus in Greece, not a human dwelling place.

The Temple of Zeus was its focus. It shows us, in a fully developed form, the typical Greek temple. A rectangular building, clearly a man-made shape among the rough forms of nature, consisting of a shallow pitched roof resting on a rectangle of large columns, and, inside that, an enclosed space in which the statue of the god, here a vast sculpture faced with ivory and gold, was housed. The perfection of the building is relaxed by the columns and the steps on which they stand. This object can be penetrated and used; it is not an inviolable solid, like a pyramid.

The harmoniousness of the form of the temple was not achieved by accident, nor was it achieved merely so that it should look good. The Greeks learned measurement from the Egyptians but pursued mathematics as a form of philosophy, investigating how forms and numbers work both in the abstract, as numbers and forms, and in real experience. This matter of numbers in actual experience may seem odd to us. But when we look at a sphere or a cube or a double cube we feel in our bones that the strength of the form has something to do with its simplicity, that is with the simple number-relationships it depends on. The sphere is just one dimension, call it 1, rotating from the centre; the square is 1×1; the cube $1 \times 1 \times 1$; the double cube $1 \times 1 \times 2$. Let us take an example that starts from something not visual but aural. Pluck a note on a stringed instrument; then pluck a note on a string half as long, and you get the note one octave

above the first – the same note at a higher pitch. So the ratio of 1 to 2, which can describe a double square, describes also that particularly clear and clean interval, the octave. Ratios almost as simple, and measured the same way along the string, give us the other main intervals in music: a fifth is 2:3, a fourth 3:4.

What has this to do with art, or with Greek architecture? The Greek system of architecture, with its columns with capitals and sometimes bases, with calculated spaces between the columns, and with carefully shaped beams and cornices lying on top of those capitals, depended for its harmony on the relating of the parts to the whole, each in due proportion. A similar concern is revealed when we measure whole buildings. If we measure the Temple of Zeus using the Olympian foot (about 32 cm – $12\frac{1}{2}$ in), we find that the building is 200 long, the columns are 32 high, and the distance from the centre of one column to the centre of the next is 16. That gives a ratio of 2:4:25. It looks orderly, but what was important to the Greeks is that it echoed the order they saw in the construction and functioning of the universe and of humanity itself.

Notice that they were concerned with the relationships between numbers, that is with proportion, not with absolute measurements. They took over from the Egyptians the idea and the process of making large stone sculptures, but they soon abandoned the Egyptian grid (which only works when the figure represented follows the verticals and horizontals of the grid) in favour of a system of proportions. Whatever the position the figure is in, the proportions apply.

The sculptures in the west pediment or gable of the Temple of Zeus could not have been conceived without such a system. They show a drunken brawl at a wedding feast. The Lapiths are having a wedding. They have invited the half-horse, half-human Centaurs who, being uncivilized, do not know how to hold their wine. They get drunk and attempt to carry off the bride and the other girls at the wedding. The Lapiths fight back.

Temple of Zeus at Olympia: sculptures of west pediment
c. 460 BC marble
central figure about 300 cm (118 in) high
Archaeological Museum, Olympia

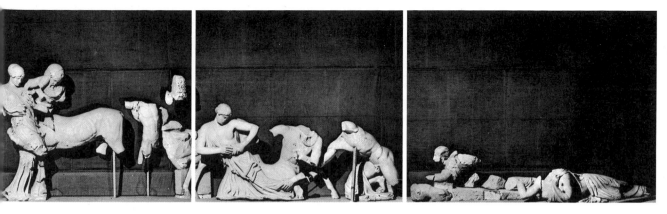

Apollo, the god, descends to take control. The point of the legend was that the Greeks identified themselves with the Lapiths and their enemies, the Persians, with the barbaric Centaurs. The sculptor has made the story into a scene, into one moment in a re-enactment of it, the moment when order triumphs over disorder.

A century or so later, the much admired sculptor Praxiteles carved his figure of Hermes with the little Dionysus. Hermes is probably dangling a bunch of grapes just out of the boy's reach. Now Praxiteles invented neither the theme, nor the arrangement. What people admired was the ease and grace he brought to the subject, the way he overcame the technical problems involved in making a large stone sculpture, and the subtle surface he gave to the bodily parts of the sculpture. Apollo, in the earlier sculpture, has much of the formality of Egyptian sculpture, but he has it for an expressive purpose: he commands peace and embodies peace. Praxiteles' theme is a god at rest, playing with his little half-brother. He combines a marvellously relaxed pose and an expressive face with the dignity and beauty of a god. The proportions of Apollo and Hermes are the same.

PRAXITELES
Hermes and child Dionysus
c. 340 BC (left)
marble
215 cm (84 in) high
Archaeological Museum,
Olympia

Plan and east elevation of the
Temple of Zeus at Olympia,
built about 460 BC.

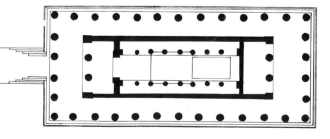

Art of the Greek Empire

Venus de Milo c. 100 BC
(Aphrodite of Melos)
marble
203 cm (80 in) high
Louvre, Paris

With change comes choice. When art changes noticeably – and it developed very rapidly in Greece from the sixth century on – artists and their patrons can have preferences. Change becomes a matter of discussion and for encouragement or discouragement. The Greeks, who of course valued their storytellers very highly, came also to value their artists in much the same way and were pleased to notice differences between the work of one and

another – what we would now call personal style. So both change over time and distinctions between one artist and another became matters of conscious concern.

The two sculptures shown here belong to what is often called the Hellenistic period of Greek civilization. 'Hellas' is the Greek word for 'Greece', so Hellenistic means Grecian, and the term is used to point to the spreading of Greek taste and influence around the Mediterranean and into the East. About the time when Praxiteles was carving the *Hermes*, the young king of Macedonia was making himself the leader of a federal union of Greek city-states. He was Alexander; we know him as Alexander the Great. He formed a big army and marched into the Near East and into Egypt to subdue the Persians and their allies once and for all. Tempted by cultural curiosity as much as by military prowess, he pressed on all the way into India, bringing Greek ways with him but also absorbing much of what he found on the way.

The *Venus de Milo,* discovered on the island of Melos in 1820, used to be thought a sculpture of the time of Praxiteles and done under his influence. The grace that he showed to be possible in monumental marble sculpture encouraged the production of images of Venus and other goddesses. He himself carved some famous Venuses, and we can credit him with making the female body prominent in sculpture once again, as it had been in prehistoric times. In fact the *Venus de Milo* is much later than Praxiteles; probably as late as 100 BC, though the date is still argued over. The fact is that she is difficult to date because the sculptor was adopting the ways of earlier sculptors.

She has in her pose something very like the relaxed turning of the Hermes. Her right arm probably came across her body, her fingers lightly touching the drapery at the top of her left thigh. So the arm moved against the turn of the body, producing a small answering phrase to the main statement of the body. Her left arm rested on a column, placed there not to support her form – which supports itself well enough, thanks to the draperies – but as a recognized way of identifying this particular Venus, or Aphrodite as the Greeks called her, with a particular place. She was the goddess of love, but above all of beauty and of generation throughout nature and the cosmos.

The date of the *Laokoon* is also uncertain. We know that the group was carved on the island of Rhodes and that it came into the possession of the Roman emperors. Then it was lost. It was found in 1506 in a vineyard not far from the Colosseum in Rome. It caused tremendous excitement, being by far the most complete sculpture-in-the-round (i.e. not relief) known to the Renaissance. In

Laokoon c. 160 BC
marble
242 cm (95 in) high
Vatican Museum, Rome

Theatre at Epidaurus, built about 350 BC. The theatre uses the slope of a hill to provide seating for 14,000 spectators on a circular plan 118 metres (387 ft) in diameter. The level circle is the *orchestra* or dancing area. The stage was framed by an elaborate architectural set, now in ruins. The acoustics are excellent.

its painstaking display of muscular activity as well as facial expression it became a model for anyone wishing to be at once classical and dramatic. Michelangelo watched as it was dug up.

Today we value the sculpture less highly. Michelangelo himself in the end turned against this kind of art, having used it so forcefully. It represents one extreme in sculpture: sculpture as a triumph over matter, making movement and life where there had been a lump of stone. The other extreme is that of stable sculpture, echoing the inertness of stone and deriving some of its force from that, as in Egyptian sculpture and in some modern works (page 140). Dramatic sculpture can be very exciting, as Bernini showed (page 92), but it can become too noisy, too theatrical and in consequence rather cold.

This is the common complaint against the *Laokoon*, but in view of the ancients' and earlier moderns' very high regard for the piece we should keep an open mind about this and test our own response to the sculpture itself in Rome. The scene it represents comes from the story of Troy but it is not an episode told by Homer: the prince-priest Laokoon has argued against taking the wooden

horse into the city of Troy. So Apollo, who is of course on the side of the Greeks, sends serpents out of the sea to kill him and his sons. Again, a complex story that has to be told through one telling moment; again, too, the representation depends for its effectiveness on the audience's prior knowledge of the story. We witness here a late stage of what we saw in a much earlier stage in Euphronios' painted vase: narrative art, now in a highly developed form and, oddly, rather more artificial than the more primitive example.

Note, though, the sympathy given in both instances to the vanquished. It is not just the formal adaptability and the narrative power of Greek art that made it so influential then and since, but also its markedly humane character. As the short-lived political empire of Alexander broke up after his early death in 323 BC, the influence of its literature, learning and arts pervaded the western and Near-Eastern world and instructs us still.

Roman Art

Ara Pacis: Mother Earth between air and water 13-9 BC
marble 156 cm (61½ in) high
Lungotevere in Augusta, Campus Martius, Rome

The great historian Edward Gibbon, writing in the eighteenth century, had no doubt at all which was the age when 'the condition of the human race was most happy and prosperous'. It was the second century AD. Here is how a Greek addressed Rome at that time:

> You have demonstrated the universal saying that the earth is the mother of all and the common fatherland of all . . . . You have measured the whole world, spanned rivers with many kinds of bridges, cut through mountains to make level roads for traffic, filled desolate places with farmsteads and made life easier by supplying its necessities amid law and order . . . . Cities are radiant in their splendour and their grace, and the whole earth is as neat as a garden.

We think of the Romans as the practical people who came after the Greeks, the organizers after the idealists. There is some justice in this. The Romans were brilliant planners of war, law and cities. Their contribution to art was secondary to this and is in most respects a continuation of Greek practice – often in fact the work of Greek artists in Roman employment.

This was certainly so with the relief sculptures set up around the *Ara Pacis* in Rome. This 'altar to peace' was set up in Rome by the Emperor Augustus after he had ended the civil wars that followed the murder of his adoptive father, Julius Caesar. Some of the reliefs show Augustus, his family and a few other eminent men and women, in religious procession. They are life-size figures at once dignified and positively lifelike and, as that might itself suggest, modelled on Greek sculpture of the fifth century. The relief illustrated here is a symbolical panel befitting the theme of the altar. It shows the figure of Earth, as a mother with children, together with farm animals and fruit. Either side of her are representations of Air, with a swan, and Water, with a fish. Again the style, the proportions of the figures, their positions, draperies and faces are clearly Greek of the fifth century. Augustus obviously wanted all the grandeur that the art of the past could offer for this monument to his taking command of the world.

Equestrian statue of Marcus Aurelius c. AD 170 (left)
bronze
508 cm (200 in) high
Piazza del Campidoglio,
Rome

The Colosseum, Rome, built
AD 70–82 (the top storey was
added in the 3rd century).
The amphitheatre holds up to
50,000 spectators. The tiers
of seats are supported on
rings of arches – an
architectural invention of the
Romans.

Fragments of these carvings were found in the fifteenth century and taken into the Medici family's collection of ancient and modern sculpture in Florence. Their influence can be seen in many paintings as well as sculptures of the Renaissance. Renaissance painters had hardly anything in the way of ancient paintings to study and, in their attempt to achieve a re-birth of the great art of the ancients, they were avid for such remains. They also knew Roman copies of some famous Greek sculptures, and did not try to distinguish between the two.

Among the Roman works they knew were several portrait sculptures, often in the form of busts – that is, head and shoulders only. This type of sculpture had been invented by the Greeks but the Romans greatly developed it, varying the form and above all bringing an extraordinary degree of realism to it. The Greeks would not have thought it sensible to use art to show a wrinkled old face merely for the sake of likeness; they would have argued that the temporary appearance of a face was not its true reality. But the Romans delighted in it, and portraiture as we know it, as a matter of producing a recognizable likeness and giving it artistic value, is their chief contribution to art.

The portrait of Marcus Aurelius on horseback is an outstanding instance, one of the most magnificent of many portraits on a monumental scale set up to celebrate successive emperors. He was one of the great men of the second century, a warrior but essentially a man of peace and a philosopher whose *Meditations* are in print today and valued for their essential goodness.

The equestrian statue shows him as a leader, though a plain man amongst leaders, not bedecked with ornamental armour nor accompanied by symbolical figures of victory or anything of that sort. A man on a horse and a commanding gesture – that is all. It is the fact of his existing in this bronze form at all, well over lifesize, that shows him to be an emperor. The sculpture is a great feat of bronze casting as well as a fine piece of modelling. It survived the dark ages that followed the collapse of Rome as the hub of the empire because it was thought to represent Constantine the Great who re-established the empire with Constantinople as its centre. Many other bronze works of antiquity were melted down to make arms or to make more art, but this one survived, and it was Michelangelo who gave it its present fine place in Rome.

The Art of the First Christians

The man in the painting has turned and paused on his way, and seems to speak to us. There are sheep beside him, and there is a sheep on his shoulders. We half recognize him: he must be a descendant of the Athenian calf-bearer of 800 years earlier. Yet in some fundamental ways he is not. He is not bringing his animal as an offering to the gods, nor does his image mean to be a unique record of his act. He is an image of the God of the new faith in the person of Jesus. He is the Good Shepherd. The sheep he is carrying is the one that was lost, and there will be great rejoicing in heaven because it is found. Those who see the image recognize it not because of the Athenian but because it is a standard image, a familiar visual sermon on repentance and the goodness of the Christian God.

The first Christians were converted Jews and pagans, not newcomers from another world. They had no new language nor did they feel the need for one. In many cases, they were members of the suppressed and relatively voiceless part of society, poor people and slaves. The more educated among them may have wondered whether Christianity would be contaminated by contact with the imagery used for the cults of the Greeks and Romans. Certainly there was a widespread feeling that the official religion was too official – a state ritual – and also too earthy. There was a hunger, not only among those who became Christians, for more detachment from material affairs, for greater spirituality – not processions and public sacrifice but prayer and meditation. No more images of gods in the faith of the true God, some would have said. The Jews had outlawed such imagery for fear of breeding idolatry, the image being mistaken for and treated as the real thing.

It might well have happened that Christianity like Islam later (pages 102-103), might have rejected figurative art as part of religion, and deprived the western world of that wealth of devotional images that makes up so much of European art history. That this did not happen says much for our ancestors' appetite for figures. For actors, even. We know that the man carrying the sheep is not a *portrait* of Jesus. We will see, and probably have already seen, other images of him that look quite different – dark haired, perhaps, and bearded. So each image is like an actor taking the role of Jesus. We are confronting again, though in an even clearer situation, the Greek appetite for re-enactment – for the re-enacting of already known and valued narrative.

This painting of the Good Shepherd, on the ceiling of a chamber in the Catacomb of Priscilla outside Rome, is not a major work of art. It is a typical product by a typical painter of the time, one who had probably used his brush in the same way to put decorative scenes into the houses of well-to-do Romans, Christian and non-Christian. The catacombs were burial places carved out of the ground, not for secrecy but for security. The Romans cremated their dead, but Christian belief looked to the physical resurrection of the dead at the Last Judgement. And that day was coming soon.

The day did not, after all, come soon. Instead of Christianity remaining the religion of the few, it became the official religion of the state. Rome remained the religious centre of Christianity, but the political centre of the new Christian Empire was much further east, in Constantinople, formerly Byzantium, now called Istanbul. There the first Christian emperor Constantine established his court in the early fourth century and encouraged the development of a high organized Church, with clergy of distinct ranks and duties. At the end of the fourth century the Empire split in two, a Roman half and a Byzantine half. Ravenna on the Adriatic coast of Italy became for a while the Byzantine Empire's chief city on Italian soil. The Emperor Justinian, and Maxentius after him, lavished attention on it, so that for a time Ravenna was a second artistic capital.

The church of San Vitale, built and decorated in the sixth century, is the most splendid of several churches and other sacred buildings erected at this time. It represents for us here the glories of Byzantine art and also Christianity's first fully-fledged answer to antiquity.

Ceiling painting with *Good Shepherd* late 2nd/early 3rd century
paint on plaster
Catacomb of Priscilla, Rome

The church is a domed octagonal space, surrounded by a secondary space arranged on two storeys. Only above the chancel, where the main altar stands, does the high space continue beyond the octagon. The surfaces of the church are richly bedecked with marbles and mosaics. The mosaic technique used here is of a new sort: not self-coloured cubes of stone, as in Roman mosaic floors, but cubes of glazed ceramic. So the colours are bright, permanent and infinitely variable; and a glazed surface reflects light according to how it is angled. So an interior with Byzantine mosaics is brilliant with colour and also sparkles with light. Mosaic demands some simplification of detail in figurative images, which makes for strength in mural art. It is also perfect for abstract pattern. In San Vitale we find both in great quantity and of the highest quality.

The decorative climax, which is also the climax in meaning, is in the chancel. On the half-dome high above the altar Jesus Christ is enthroned between angels and figures of St Vitalis and the bishop who controlled the building of the church. Above the arches right and left of the altar are Old Testament scenes. Nearby are two mosaics – one of Emperor Maxentius and his retinue, the other of Empress Theodora and hers – mosaic echoes of the processional groups in relief sculpture Augustus had already shown on the Ara Pacis.

The sheer richness of colour and form, the brilliant visual orchestration of the whole, is foreign to Greek and Roman traditions: it owes much to Oriental influences from Persia and elsewhere. And mosaic tends to a flattening of form and a graphic use of line that is quite different from the kind of painting late Antiquity favoured, represented here by the Good Shepherd ceiling.

San Vitale, Ravenna view of the chancel and apse showing mosaics (left) done mostly in the 540s and 560s. The mosaic (bottom left) is located to the right of the windows, and shows the Empress Theodora with her court.

San Vitale (below), from the east showing the main body of the church – a tall, domed octagon in the centre surrounded by a two-storey octagon – and the chancel and apse emerging from it. Begun in 526 and consecrated in 547, San Vitale is an outstanding example of Byzantine architecture.

25

Art of the Dark Ages

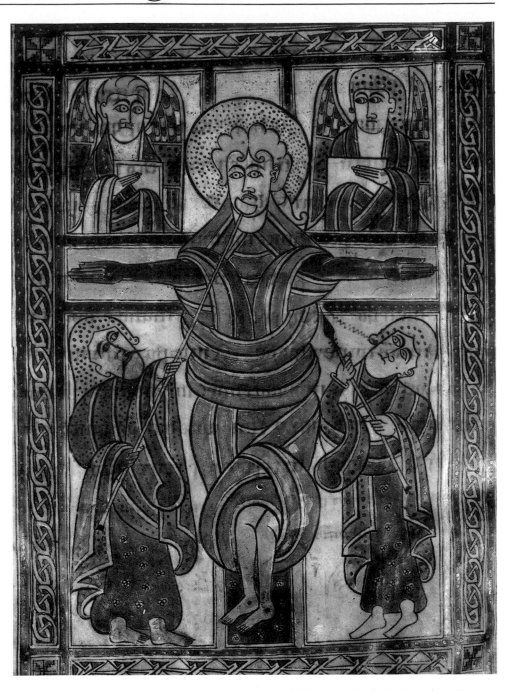

Crucifix page,
St Gall Gospels
(MS 51 folio 266) c. 750
manuscript
29.3 x 22 cm (11½ x 8½ in)
Stiftsbibliothek, St Gallen

The two reproductions shown here are of pages from handwritten texts enriched with pictures. The art-historical term for these is 'illuminated manuscripts', the second term meaning 'handwritten', and the first suggesting 'made bright' or 'given light'. They were the work of monks. These two examples come from the Gospels, the four accounts of the life, acts and sayings of Jesus.

One shows the Crucifixion: Christ on the cross, flanked by soldiers, one offering a sponge dipped in vinegar up to His lips, the other soon to pierce His side with a lance, as told in the Gospels. Two angels, not mentioned in the Gospels, watch over Christ. He is much larger than the other figures. This makes Him not only more prominent in the picture but also more eminent, more heroic, like the figure of Laokoon in the *Laokoon* group (page 21). This is countered to some extent by the way He is shown, beset by the draperies that twist and wind around His body again and again. They have more power and more feeling of mass than the rest of the image. They are almost alive, like Laokoon's serpents.

The great new literature at the time when these illuminations were being made was a literature of heroic epics telling of ceaseless war between man and man and between men and monsters. The Anglo-Saxon epic poem *Beowulf* is the story of how the Scandinavian hero Beowulf slew a terrible monster called Grendel and then the monster's equally fearsome mother. It is dated at about the time of this manuscript – and Scandinavian verse stories of the same kind are dated to around AD 800 and after.

The monks saw themselves as missionaries sustaining the practices of Christianity in a Europe once again without law and order, but also divinely charged with bringing a new law and a new order to the heathen. They knew that there were people, earlier converted to Christianity, who had slipped back into paganism, so they went forth – most of them from Irish monasteries – to found monasteries elsewhere as strongholds of the faith.

The monks may not have been conscious of giving a quality of northern drama to the Christian imagery they put into their books, but it must have added to the persuasiveness of their teaching. It is also possible, since the monasteries were the only centres of study at this time, that some of the men drawn to them were much the same as those who were composing the epic literature of the period. The fusion of Christian and pagan must have been occurring in the monks themselves.

The draperies snaking around Christ are echoed in the patterns filling the border of the picture. Such patterning, sometimes abstract and sometimes formed of long interlaced dragons turning and knotting like ribbons, is essentially northern rather than Mediterranean. It is found on the swords and other ornamented metal objects of the very people to whom the monks were bringing Christ's teaching.

The Crucifixion is evidently a key moment in the story of Christ, and we are used to seeing representations of it almost as the trademark of Christianity. This was not so in the first centuries of the faith. The Greek cross, with arms of equal length, was used as one of several symbols of Christianity, but not the death of Christ. He was shown, rather, as a teacher and a miracle-worker – often looking like a new Apollo. It was chiefly through illuminated Gospels and through doctrinal emphasis on Christ's death as the moment when He brought salvation to mankind, and not – as it well might have been – on His resurrection, that this gruesome image has become the accepted sign. Perhaps we should see this development too as an instance of northern influence.

The representation of the Crucifixion is a narrative scene, still and formal though it is. The other page shows a kind of portrait. The Romans had sometimes included pictures of the author in their manuscripts, usually shown bent over his desk in the act of writing. Here we have St Matthew, who wrote one of the Gospels. Yet he

St Matthew, Book of Kells
(folio 28) late 8th century
manuscript
Trinity College, Dublin

is presented more like a hero, for he was a saint as well as an author. The curving shapes on either side of him represent a seat or throne. They give a hint of space to the image. The rest is primarily pattern, hinting at an arch, a halo, bright-edged draperies, but effective as pattern. The swirling bands and whorls are, again, taken from northern ornament. The main border is filled with spiralling dragons.

The St Gall manuscript was probably made in Ireland and taken to the Continent, to a new and splendid monastery built in what is now the north-east part of Switzerland. The Book of Kells was produced on the island of Iona off the west coast of Scotland at a monastery founded by Irish monks. When the Vikings came from Scandinavia in their dragon-prowed boats to rob and pillage, and to destroy what they could not carry off, the book was taken to Ireland together with other treasures. The time of the Dark Ages, especially the seventh and eighth centuries, but stretching on through the tenth, is associated with the collapse of civilization all over Europe. But what is even more remarkable than the greed and also the bravery that went into this aggressive life-style – the Vikings reached the North American coast six centuries before Columbus – is the persistent drive to tell and to teach through words and pictures.

The Dawn of Medieval Art

Bayeux Tapestry: the death of King Harold c. 1070
tapestry
51 cm x 70 m (20 in x 230 ft)
Musée de la Reine Mathilde, Bayeux

The Bayeux Tapestry is one of the most complex and effective pieces of narrative art ever created. More than 70 metres (230 ft) long and originally somewhat longer, it tells the story of William of Normandy and Harold of England: how Harold came to promise to support William's claim to the English throne but took the throne himself, and how William and his men sailed across to England and killed Harold on the battlefield of Hastings. A final scene, probably of William as king of England, is lost. The narrative method is rather like that of a comic strip.

The tapestry is not a tapestry but an embroidery. More important, it is far from truthful – and this tells us what its function was. Made to hang around the walls of a large room, it was not to be mere decoration but what we today call propaganda. Like the reciting of a poem at a Viking banquet or a Greek festival, it served to tell and retell William's version of how he acquired England, not merely by might but also by right. It justified him and commanded loyalty from others.

The section illustrated here shows a part of the battle of Hastings. Harold is struck down by a knight's sword; an axe falls from his hand. (There is no truth in the story that he was shot in the eye, which stems from a later misreading of the tapestry.) There is no background and no space, and there is very little in the way of supportive detail, which may remind you of the vase painting on page 16. But it all comes across very vividly. A few words accompany the sequence of pictures to make sure we read it correctly, but most of the meaning is carried in the drawing of the men and horses, ships and occasional buildings.

Bands top and bottom accompany the action. Here, in the lower border, there are servants stripping dead knights of their armour; above, along the whole work, there are animals of various kinds, real and unreal, separated by decorative panels. We are witnessing here a prominent return to active, lifelike narrative as formed and developed by the Greeks, yet again there is much to remind us that we are in the north. And no wonder: William's people were themselves Norsemen, who had only recently usurped the land we call Normandy on their account. So there is a tendency to treat everything in terms of lines and bands of colour, and the birds and beasts above come straight out of northern ornament.

The words used are Latin and the telling itself is in a Mediterranean manner, but the accent is markedly Nordic.

The voice of the Beatus Apocalypse is quite different. The text of this manuscript is a commentary on the last book of the New Testament, the Revelation of St John the Divine, often called the Apocalypse. The commentary was written by a monk called Beatus, and it was made into a book with magnificent pictures at a monastery at Saint-Sever in Gascony, in south-west France.

The double-page scene of Christ with the twenty-four Elders is an amazingly powerful evocation of divine power as it might appear at the Last Judgement, and echoes the awesome words of St John. There is Christ as God, with the Elders seated around Him, and the four six-winged beasts – here identified with the symbols of the four authors of the Gospels – crying 'Holy, holy, holy, Lord God Almighty, which was, and is, and is to come'.

The colour is even, but the placing and turning of the elders and the positioning of the angels outside the red circle, all hint at space. This is clinched by the placing of Christ in His blue disk. He could not be in the middle, because of the fold of the page, but it was very effective

Christ and the 24 Elders
Apocalypse of Beatus
11th century
manuscript
Bibliothèque Nationale, Paris

to place Him to the right and higher up. We are made aware of a space in front of and, by implication, around Him: we seem to be looking down upon the *Orchestra* of a classical theatre.

The bright colour and the firm forms of this mighty representation owe much to Arabic influence. From the eighth century until 1212 the Spanish peninsula was in the hands of a great new faith and empire, Islam. On pages 102-103 we shall be looking at some examples of Islamic art. Here we see its action upon European work, a pressure and an enrichment from the south affecting the idiom in which Christian material is presented.

Both works speak of a new confidence and a new assertiveness. The narrative vigour of the tapestry is matched, or perhaps even outshone, by the fierce majesty of the image from the Apocalypse. Both announce the arrival of a great new age of art.

Romanesque Art

The Apocalypse (page 29) also provides the theme and stimulus for much of the finest sculpture made in the twelfth century. It was a time of new and growing cities, of scholarship and the founding of the first universities – public places of learning and study outside the monasteries – at Salerno, Bologna, Paris and, soon after, Oxford. There was a great deal of building and a flowering of the arts that go with building, pre-eminently sculpture. 'Romanesque' means 'Roman-ish'. The builders looked at and derived ideas from the Roman architecture they could see in many parts of Europe, though the way they worked embodied also memories of local traditions, especially in the North. But above all it was a time of internationalism: ideas circulated freely, builders travelled about, church dignitaries and others readily went the length of Europe by horse and carriage or ship, helped by the more secure establishment of Christianity.

The year 1000 had not brought the Last Judgement and the end of the world that many had expected, but the Church went on reminding people of the imminence of Christ's second coming. A new and effective place for large-scale sculpture on that theme was found over the main entrance to the church, in the space above the door or doors and below the arches of the doorway. This semi-circular area is known as the tympanum. An outstanding example of a tympanum carved to represent the Last Judgement is shown here.

The church of St Lazarus stands by the market place of Autun, the busiest place in the city and a focal point for the whole region. Everyone passing the church – remember that this world was not submerged in a daily flood of images – would see this powerful warning of what awaited the many sinners and the few blessed. Christ is the judge; angels collaborate with fearsome demons in dividing the good from the bad and sending the good to a heavenly Jerusalem and the bad down into eternal torment. The message was particularly clear for anyone entering the church, for services and prayer, for confession and for the key ceremonies of life such as baptism and marriage.

Christ is in the centre, enthroned and dominant because of His size as well as His position. The now blank arch around the tympanum once showed the twenty-four Elders. The illumination on page 29 made a splendid and rich scene out of St John's words. The relief carving at Autun is much more shocking, filled with dread and horror. The figures tend to be long and gaunt, expressive in their actions and their faces. Though the whole relief is carefully composed there is a sense of clamour, of shrieking and wailing and the roars of devils claiming another human. It is a tremendously powerful work and,

we for once know who did it. Below the feet of Christ we see, carved into the band of stone in Roman lettering: 'Gislebertus hoc fecit', 'Gilbert made this'. This is rare in medieval art. We often know the names of masons and others responsible for a building and its equipment of sculpture and other things, but a particular item is rarely signed by or credited to one individual.

The great abbey church at Monreale in Sicily belongs to the other Christian camp, the Byzantine region ruled from Constantinople. The apse mosaics show on a very large scale a half-figure of Christ. On the lower bands (not shown in the illustration here) is the Madonna, holding the Christ Child on her lap, flanked by angels and saints, and additional saints below that – the higher the more august. Christ is shown as the 'Pantocrator', the Ruler of All; His gesture shows that He is speaking to us. No scene is represented, no moment from the Old or New Testament, but images to make us more aware of God's power and of the status achieved by some humans through service to God. So if there is no warning here about the fate that awaits the sinner, the worshipper is confronted with an awesome rather than a lovable representation, one that can impress itself lastingly on the memory. Sermons, here as at Autun, no doubt reinforced that impression.

The tympanum at Autun is a descendant of the sculpture-filled pediments of the Greeks (pages 18-19); the Monreale mosaics are a reminder of the gigantic statues set up inside Greek temples to represent the particular god or goddess to whom the temple was dedicated.

When a shift in emphasis came in Christian teaching – from the exhortation to repent and sin no more, to a message about divine goodness and love – the Last Judgement disappeared from the outsides of churches. Inside it was still often shown, but in painted form: Giotto painted such a scene on the inside of the entrance wall of the Arena Chapel. That Michelangelo should have painted the most prominent wall of the Sistine Chapel with it says something for the austere mood of that time (page 64). The Monreale image of Christ – a complex of statements about Christ as teacher, judge and all-powerful ruler, leads on a smaller scale to the icons used by the Eastern Church. They are representations aiming neither at lifelikeness, nor expressiveness but at building a wealth of meaning into a succinct image. The enormous photographs of past heroes and present leaders set up by Communist societies to watch over their parades and sports events belongs to this tradition of the compelling, unquestionable super-image.

Pantocrator and Madonna and Child (apse mosaics) (left)
12th century
mosaic
Monreale Abbey Church, Sicily

Last Judgement: carved tympanum over main entrance c. 1130 (below)
stone
St Lazare, Autun

Giotto

GIOTTO DI BONDONE born in Florence around 1270; died there in 1337

The story goes that Giotto was a shepherd boy. A passing stranger, a painter, discovered him drawing on slabs of stone as he guarded his flock. He took the boy home and taught him painting. The pupil soon outshone his master, becoming the most famous painter of his time and totally changing the nature of art.

We all like exaggerating for dramatic effect. There is something satisfying about stressing a great person's humble origins: it makes for contrast and implies that there is hope for us all. Certainly Giotto became rich and

famous, and we have his paintings to show us how new his art was, and how much it led other painters to learn from him. People often say that the art of modern times (in the widest sense) starts with him. He is in fact the first artist who might be called a revolutionary genius.

The change associated with Giotto is that from the Byzantine tradition to that of Renaissance Italy; from the more or less flat, symbolical and powerfully ornamental images that we saw on page 25 to a sort of painting that is much more lifelike. A painting that is,

GIOTTO
The Lamentation over the Dead Christ
1304–1313 (left)
fresco
200 x 185 cm (79 x 73 in)
Arena Chapel, Padua

MASTER OF ST FRANCIS
St Francis Receiving the Stigmata mid-1290s (below)
fresco
270 x 230 cm (106 x 90 in)
Upper church, San Francesco, Assisi

the narrative focus of the painting. There is little or nothing by way of ornament. It is a plain picture, a simple but convincing stage presentation.

Big changes in art are never the work of one artist and Giotto did not invent this kind of painting singlehanded. Works that used to be thought early Giottos are now considered to be by slightly earlier painters and to have guided him towards this new realism. There are several frescoes that announce the Giotto style in the church of St Francis in Assisi – built in celebration of the great saint who had died in 1226. St Francis abandoned wealth and high society to live in poverty among the poor and to care for them physically as well as spiritually. In their simplicity and directness the frescoes echo the ideals of the saint.

The scene of *St Francis Receiving the Stigmata* has exactly the clarity and the concentration we saw in the Giotto: kneeling in prayer on the mountain, St Francis has a vision of Christ and receives, on his hands and feet, marks (stigmata) like those caused by the nails that pierced Christ's hands and feet. Though the event is supernatural, a miracle, the story of it is told quite plainly. Ordinary people could understand it easily; sermons delivered in the church referred to it and to other similar scenes and encouraged people to think of St Francis and to model their lives on his.

In medieval times religious doctrines were often presented through simply staged 'miracle plays' and it may well be that the new style of painting owes something of its methods to them. Giotto was the outstanding painter in the new idiom. Like a great stage producer putting on a *Hamlet* or an *Oedipus Rex* so that audiences feel that they are seeing the *real* play at long last, and perhaps understanding it fully for the first time, so he 'staged' Biblical stories that were basically familiar to his audiences but had never been made so convincing before.

After he had finished the Padua frescoes he worked mostly in Florence, and Florence became the leading city in Italian art until Rome and Venice took over during the sixteenth century. The fourteenth century Florentine poet Boccaccio, himself most famous as a story-teller, praised Giotto's work because, he said, it pleased people's minds when for centuries painting had only pleased their eyes. How true do you think that is?

Big changes in art always mean a loss as well as a gain. What Western art gained through Giotto's work was a greater sense of reality: his paintings say 'This is how it was' as well as 'This happened' and we believe him, convinced by the space he shows us and the solid figures he places in it and their interaction. What was lost was beauty in the sense of brightness and decorative richness such as Byzantine art valued, and also spirituality. By this I mean the quality of other-worldliness that tells us at once that the subjects represented – on icons for instance – have a special, superhuman significance. Giotto brought them down to earth.

above all else, much more convincing in its story telling, and you may remember that it was the urge to story telling that breathed life into Greek art many centuries earlier (pages 16-21). This is, of course, a tremendously important change: we cannot imagine Western art without it.

Giotto's *The Lamentation over the Dead Christ* is one of 34 scenes painted by him between 1304 and 1313 in a privately built chapel in Padua, the Arena Chapel. These show key moments from the story of the Virgin Mary and of Jesus Christ; to the left of this one is the *Crucifixion,* to the right the *Resurrection*. Bands of pattern separate the scenes but they are linked by the narrative, by scale and especially by common colours (most noticeably the blue of the sky). They are painted in fresco – not as bright as tempera painting, nor as given to rich detail.

Giotto uses a simple pictorial stage, its space defined by a plain landscape that powerfully underlines the meaning of the scene. The slope of the hill and the placing and postures of the figures draw our attention to the head of Christ, again and again. Some of the figures, especially those with their backs to us, seem to be there just for that purpose: to lead our eyes and thus also our emotions to

Duccio

DUCCIO DI BUONINSEGNA born about 1260; died in Siena in 1318 or 1319

While Giotto worked in Padua, Duccio was working in Siena, not many kilometres south of Florence, on a large and particularly splendid altarpiece. It took him and his assistants three years to do, from 1308 until 9 June 1311 when the painting was carried in joyous procession from the workshop to the cathedral. The painting is known as the *Maestà,* a term referring to its main subject: the Madonna and Child enthroned *in majesty* amid a court of saints and angels. It is large and painted on both sides, with additional scenes above and, originally, also below the *Maestà* scene itself, and with 42 scenes from the New Testament on the back. So this altarpiece is as rich in narrative as Giotto's chapel.

There is one key difference: it is painted in tempera on wood, not in fresco on and in plaster. Tempera permits much finer detail and a greater range of colour, and also a decorative and expressive use of lines – outlines as well as, for instance, the edges of garments. One of the greatest delights of this beautiful work is the play of its many colours, delicious in themselves and played off against each other to make strange colour chords.

The composition of the large scene on the front is nearly symmetrical, with heads turned this way or that so as to echo each other but the Madonna and Child group is asymmetrical although neatly contained in the symmetry of the splendid throne. Individual figures seem almost three-dimensional – the Christ Child for instance, and St Agnes on the far right and St Catherine

of Alexandria, far left, who look very much like Gothic statues. The heads are gently modelled in tone to bring out their roundness. But Duccio is not primarily concerned with Giotto's kind of reality: differences of scale make that absolutely clear.

To represent the back of the *Maestà,* I have chosen a double scene: *Christ before Annas* and *The Denial of St Peter.* The painter has merged the two scenes into one, vertically. To do that he breaks the horizontal line that separates the scenes to the left and right, and if you look carefully you will also see that he has made – in terms of realism – a number of intentional mistakes, most obviously in the architecture and the space it suggests. But the result of this is a clear narrative as well as a fine pictorial effect. The assistant who painted this double scene may have been the young Ambrogio Lorenzetti who in 1338-9 painted some very large frescoes in the town hall of Siena. They show towns and areas of countryside with great liveliness but also with this same fine balance of realism and decorative effect. This balance is characteristic of Sienese painting for some time, whereas in Florence, as we shall see, dramatic realism is taken further by great painters of the next two centuries.

DUCCIO
Maestà (front) 1308–1311
(left)
tempera on panel
212 x 425 cm (84 x 143 in)
Museo dell'Opera del
Duomo, Siena

DUCCIO ASSISTANT
(? Ambrogio Lorenzetti)
Christ before Annas and
The Denial of St Peter
1308–1311 (right)
tempera on panel
101 x 54 cm (40 x 21 in)
Museo dell'Opera del
Duomo, Siena

Late Gothic Art

The Ascension from the Breviary of John the Fearless c. 1415 (above) illuminated manuscript 25 x 18 cm (10 x 7 in) British Library, London

The Sense of Hearing (L'Ouïe) from *La Dame à la Licorne* c. 1480 (far right) tapestry 370 x 290 cm (145 x 114 in) Musée de Cluny, Paris

It was produced by scribes and painters associated with the Limbourg brothers who were Flemish by origin and had worked in Paris before coming into the Duke of Burgundy's employment. The page illustrated has unmistakable signs of Italian influence in the scene of *Christ's Ascension into Heaven:* the way the figures are grouped, the bold lines of their draperies and also the forms and placing of the architecture on the right, suggest Italian painting as represented here by Duccio and his assistants (pages 36-37). The filigree pattern of trailing ivy framing the picture is northern and is found on ornamental metal work as well as on manuscripts. The elegant young lady, seated below the scene on an island of grass and flowers, endlessly long-limbed and very fashionably dressed, is northern too and recognizably French. She holds the arms of John and of his wife Margaret of Bavaria: we are clearly informed that this splendid book is a privately commissioned work of art, made for the use of two people and to be for ever associated with them.

Much the same emphasis on ownership occurs in the tapestry. It is one of a set representing the five senses, sight, touch, taste, smell and hearing. This set may or may not have been commissioned. There were centres of tapestry manufacture in northern France and in the Low Countries that produced tapestries for sale to anyone who could pay for them as well as carrying out commissioned work. Where this set was made is uncertain – at Tournai or at Paris perhaps.

If the set was ready-made and then bought, the arms on the banners must have been put in at the last moment. They are the arms of Jean le Viste, not a member of an old aristocratic family but of a rich family from Lyons. He rose to eminence and a title through his work as a lawyer and politician. A set of tapestries such as this one would prove his taste for fine things and his education.

The tapestry illustrated is typical of the whole set and also of the type and style. It is beautifully and carefully worked, with about six chain stitches to the centimetre (or about four million for this tapestry). The design is in some ways routine. The background of flowers and animals on a red ground and the island of grass, flowers and animals on which the symbolical action is placed, recur throughout the set and are found in other tapestries of the period and also, as we have already seen, in manuscripts of the time. The courtly lady playing a small organ with the help of a girl who pumps the bellows is particular to this subject of course, but she appears in similar forms throughout the series and in other tapestries.

The island suggests space but the image as a whole is flat. There is no hint of diminution, of things appearing

The two illustrations on these pages are both from the fifteenth century and from France. They represent a style, or mixture of styles, characteristic of the period and often found in France, but not exclusively French. The style is often called 'International Gothic' to emphasize its non-regional nature.

The prayer-book was written and illustrated for John the Fearless, Duke of Burgundy and of the Low Countries – an international man in a time of fluid frontiers (how fluid is shown by the battle of Agincourt in 1415, which made Henry V of England, descended from William the Norman or Norseman, master of much of northern France and heir presumptive to the French throne).

smaller when they are further from us. There is little or no overlapping to prove that things are behind each other. Instead, a feast of little items is spread out before our eyes, giving the whole work a busy surface. This is re-inforced by the even but clearly visible texture of stitches. The effect of this is not unlike the effect of Seurat's neat dots of colour, and it was Seurat's con-temporary, Gauguin, also working in the 1880s, who insisted once again on the flatness of his images (pages 126 and 128).

The *Ascension* picture is more spatial, but achieves this by means of the unscientific perspective typical of fourteenth-century Italian painting and by this time being superseded by the systematic perspective developed in Florence. We get our sense of space here mainly from the overlapping of the figures and the diminution of the architectural forms from the city gates on the right to the castle on the left. But this is firmly cancelled by the pattern which fills the sky and echoes the surrounding border of pattern. Late Gothic art is an art of the precious surface, not of telling realism.

The Art of Ancient America

Statue of Xipe Totec from
Tepepan, Mexico 1507
volcanic stone
77 cm (30½ in) high
Museum of the American
Indian, New York

The festival of Xipe Totec was one of eighteen, one celebrated in each of the eighteen months into which the Aztecs divided their year. Their calendar and their religion were closely intertwined. They were an agricultural people, very conscious of their dependence on the daily rebirth of the sun and on the action of rain, storms and winds. There were earthquakes and volcanic eruptions to keep their consciousness sharp. Perhaps this should prepare us for the harshness, as it seems to us, of Aztec religious practices. Xipe Totec's names were Our Lord the Flayed One and God of the Seedtime; it was he who watched over spring and, if benignly disposed, made the new crops grow. But it is a long jump from this terrifying image and from the practices it speaks of to the Renaissance image of spring, *Primavera* (page 56). And so one tends to dwell on the Aztec's convention of human sacrifice – of selected members of the society as well as of prisoners taken in wars. But we should also remind ourselves that *Primavera* has very little to do with the labour and the risks of farming.

The Spaniards, who were the first Europeans to set eyes upon the city of Tenochtitlan, the main city of the Aztecs, built on an island in Lake Texcoco and seeming to rise straight out of the water, were staggered by its magnificence. It was a city of about 250,000 inhabitants, far more populous than any European city at the time. Cortes, leading the Spanish expedition, declared it the most beautiful city in the world and in 1521 he destroyed it in the name of civilization and a religion whose conquering image is that of a man-god dying on a cross.

The Aztec state was indeed a hard state. It was run by a powerful military caste and by a civil service of priests. They were supported by hordes of peasants who could also serve as soldiers and had little understanding of the system they served or of the compound of astronomical and other scientific knowledge on which it was based. They laboured to build vast complexes for religious and social rituals, and the pyramid-temples which served for the performing of sacrifices and in some instances also as tombs. But the people standing at the foot of the long flight of steps leading to the top would not have been able to see what the priests were doing – and this seems to be an apt symbol of the structure of Aztec society.

The sculpture combines chilling realism with firm abstraction. This appears to be typical of the whole of Aztec culture. Its carvings could go from extreme abstraction – much simplified representations of beasts and humans – to extreme naturalism, and could also, as here, combine aspects of both. This mixture of realism and abstraction is found in Aztec religion too. The Aztecs were the last in a succession of distinct peoples occupying the area we call Mexico or parts of it: Mayas,

Olmecs, Toltecs, Mixtecs and others. They seem to have inherited a great deal from their predecessors which shows in their own practices and beliefs. They inherited Xipe Totec from the Yopi. And the meaning behind these fragments of doctrine was inherited with them, and confirmed by experience.

The principal pyramid at Tajin, Mexico, built in the 4th century. A pre-Columbian Pyramid of Niches of the Totonac Indians, it is made of stone and adobe, and has 365 recesses on all four sides. The broad flight of steps, interrupted by projecting platforms, rises steeply at an angle of 55 degrees (above).

Pair of ear spools from Coastal Huari (Tiahuanaco) Peru (below)
6th century–
10th century
bone, shell and stone
4.6 cm (1³/₄ in)
Metropolitan Museum of Art, New York
(Michael C. Rockefeller Collection)

The sun seems to have been all-important. He was fire and life. Every day he died, and had to be helped to rebirth, in the face of moon and stars and darkness, in spite of dangers arising from water and wind, by being fed with the 'precious fluid', human blood. That he avidly drank up the blood put out before him, was plain to see. In return, fire could be kindled where the human victim's heart had been. Xipe Totec's service required the skin of a human being in one piece, donned by the priest as it was donned by the deity himself as an image of rebirth.

The cultures of Peru were separate from those of Mexico because of the thick jungle that prevented communication between them. The Inca peoples that arrived there about the time the Normans conquered Britain left behind great temples and palaces built high up in the Andean range, as well as particularly fine, small figures and other objects in gold. The ear spools illustrated here come from Huari and are earlier than the Incas and the Aztecs.

The pair shown is of extraordinary sophistication: a highly developed design derived from dragon-like beasts executed on a very small scale by means of bone and shell inlaid into stone. There are splendid Peruvian textiles that show similar abstraction developed into a repeating pattern. In both cases we are reminded of Chinese work (page 98). The dramatic way in which the forms and colours of the ear spools are organized reminds me of Léger's painting on page 149: like the shell and bone pieces here, his paint areas seem to be inlaid to make one rich, compact surface.

The Tribal Art of North America

The art of the American Indians was an integral part of their daily lives. Their everyday life was in no way separate from what we would call religion and the objects they made served practical and spiritual purposes at the same time. It is difficult for us to feel our way into this, being used to a compartmented life in which art goes with leisure and is far removed from work and mostly also from religious worship. The American Indians lived with the land and with the other creatures on it, and equally with the sun and the sky, and with their awareness of the past in the form of myths and legends, and also with the day and its present needs.

Their art changed. The tribes influenced each other and learned from each other, consciously and unconsciously. Techniques were developed and brought new forms with them. When Japanese fishermen and European sailors first made contact with them, the Indians of west-coast America acquired knives and rapidly developed their wood carving into more elaborate forms. Subsequently they acquired chemical dyes and mass-produced beads, and these too they exploited. But there was no intention of changing art. The whole purpose of art was to guarantee continuity and succession, and also continued effectiveness. Many of the objects we call works of art were for the Indian primarily certificates of family or tribal identity.

The carved and painted screen comes from the house of Chief Shakes at Wrangell, Alaska. He was a chief of the Tlingit people, hunters on land and at sea. It is an unusually large work, most Indian art being portable or wearable. It is part of a house, a screen dividing it into two spaces. It is dated to about 1840 but the date does not tell us much, since this screen is copied from an older one and that one was not unique. Novelty and individuality count for nothing in such works; what matters is potency, and that is assured by the retention of forms found potent in the past.

It represents a bear. Bears, like whales, wolves, ravens and eagles, figure prominently in the myths of the northwest coast – not as dangerous enemies so much as coexistent creatures. The Haida tribes have an elaborate legend about a chief's daughter taken away by bears to live with them and beget bear cubs. Perhaps the many faces on this bear and the hole in his belly through which one passes are evidence of a similar legend honoured by the Tlingit.

The Haida lived on the Queen Charlotte Islands off the coast of what is now Canada. They were relatively isolated and safe there and developed prodigious skills as carvers of wood. The mask illustrated here is typical of their work and illustrates a typical function: it is a dance mask, to be worn by a dancer enacting a part in the performing of a myth, and made so that it can be transformed from one image into another at the right moment. Closed the mask represents, probably, the sun or the moon; when the dancer pulls hidden strings, the triangular pieces which make up the outer mask swing back on leather hinges to reveal a human face. This was probably identifiable as the face of a ruler of the world beneath the sea, the maker of tides.

The mask and the screen share one formal device which is so common to American Indian art that exceptions come as a shock. I mean symmetry – symmetry in the specialized sense of the left half being a mirror image of the right half. In European art total symmetry is often associated with severity and a strict authoritarian spirit. In Indian art it probably indicates balance rather than order at an oppressive level. What it cannot express is mobility or actual movement, but then

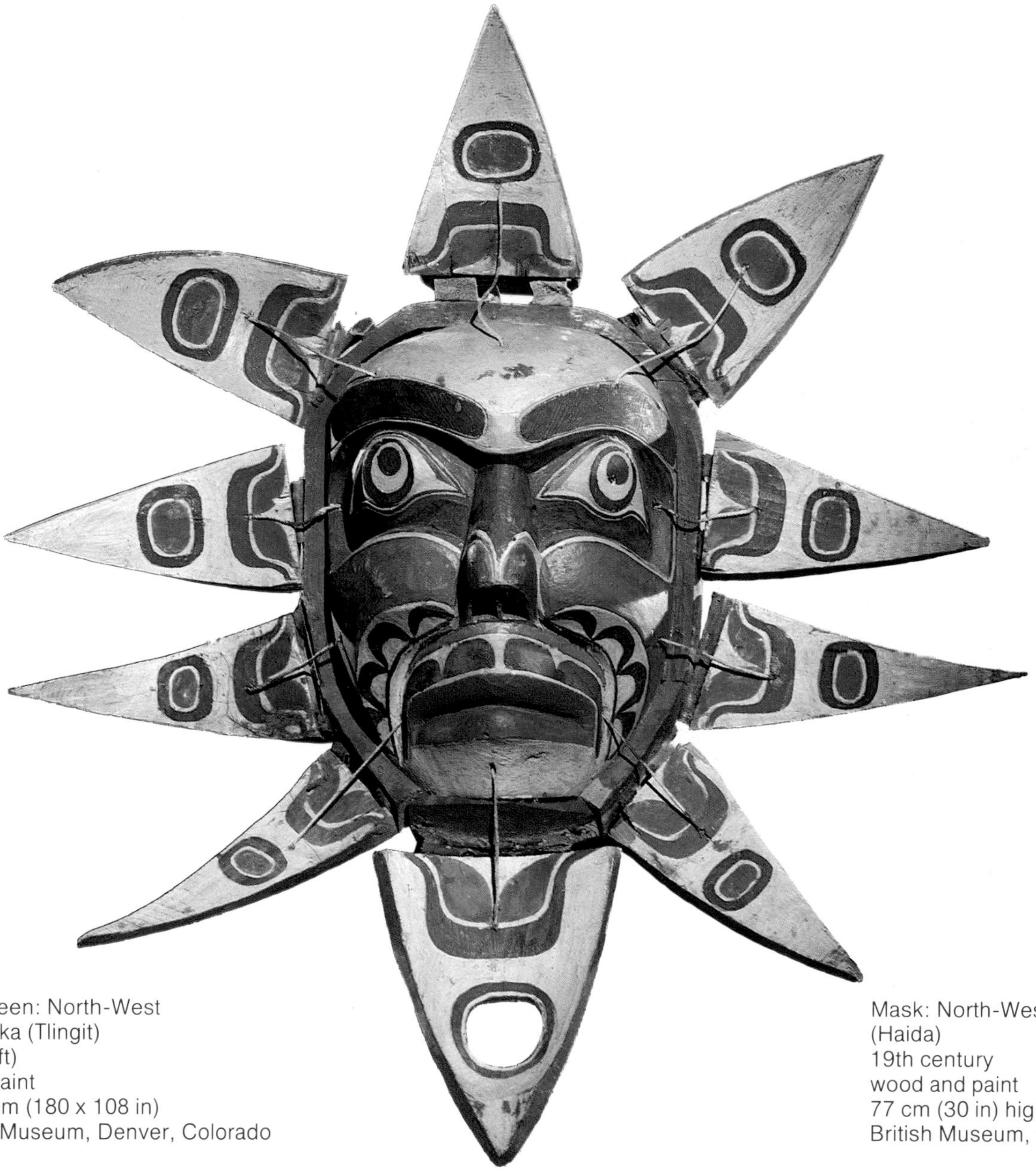

Shakes screen: North-West
Coast, Alaska (Tlingit)
c. 1840 (left)
wood and paint
457 x 274 cm (180 x 108 in)
Denver Art Museum, Denver, Colorado

Mask: North-West Coast
(Haida)
19th century
wood and paint
77 cm (30 in) high
British Museum, London

physical movement is not a necessary part of a house interior and is provided in real terms by the action of a dancer.

In fact, the forms in which the bear screen is painted are strong and swinging forms. They gave a strong suggestion of movement to an artist-scholar copying similar forms on other north-west coast tribal works. The same vocabulary of bold curves is used on the Haida mask and can be found on chests, boxes, coffins and also on blankets made in the area. Where this idiom was first developed is uncertain, though some of the evidence points to the Haida Indians as the originators of it. More important is the fact that it is found over a large area and that it was clearly a shared language of ornamentation, always adhering to the same principles and to more or less identical shapes. It has been shown that templates were used to produce those carefully worked-out shapes, and of course the same templates, one side used first and then turned over, would produce strict symmetry.

The culture of the American Indian now attracts a rather nostalgic and sentimental interest, a consequence perhaps of the greed and cruelty with which his civilization was destroyed by past generations of white men. It may be difficult to avoid that entirely, and I know I risk adding to it in quoting the poem that follows, first published in English in 1902: a night-chant of the Navajo Indians of Arizona. It states a relationship with the world of which whites have little inkling.

In beauty (happily) I walk
with beauty before me I walk
with beauty behind me I walk
with beauty below me I walk
with beauty above me I walk
it is finished (again) in beauty
it is finished in beauty.

Masaccio   Ghiberti

MASACCIO born at Castel Gandolfo near Florence, in 1401; died in Rome in 1428

LORENZO GHIBERTI born in Florence in 1378; died there in 1455

In the fifteenth century Florence was the capital of an independent state. Italy then consisted of several such states, one ruled by the Pope in Rome, another belonging to the kings of Spain, some ruled by dukes, and just two republics ruled by councils formed of their most eminent citizens. Florence was one of these, Venice the other. Both were powerful through commerce, Venice primarily through trade with the Orient, Florence through her international banking operations. Her leading families were rich and took pride in displaying their love of learning and of art. So did the guilds, those protective groups into which the various professions, crafts and businesses joined, and so did the Church, often with the help of private patronage.

Florence was proud of herself. She had extended her territories, and through successful battles had secured them against jealous neighbours. Financially she led Europe. When scholars and artists demonstrated a new and avid interest in the writings and art of antiquity, Florentine patrons backed them eagerly. Florence thus became the centre of what was called the Renaissance, the rebirth of the noble and glorious culture of the ancients. Modern art, meaning contemporary Gothic, began to seem weak, lacking in ideas and formal strength. In a sense the Florentines were trying to turn the clock back. In fact, they had only very limited examples from the distant past to guide them, in art especially, so that they had to invent the new classicism. From this came the vigour and the adventurousness that has made Renaissance art such a rich succession of glorious events.

In 1425 the young Masaccio and an older painter, Masolino, began to paint a cycle of frescoes in the Brancacci Chapel of Sta Maria del Carmine. It was Masaccio's first opportunity for painting large murals. He proved himself the heir of Giotto, a hundred years earlier. The scene known as *The Tribute Money* has all of Giotto's strength and an even greater sense of drama. Its subject is Christ's words about 'rendering unto Caesar the things that are Caesar's' and the circumstances in which those words were spoken: the official demanding payment from St Peter, and Peter finding the coin in a fish's mouth. These ancillary events frame and explain the central group where Christ speaks to his apostles. But speaking itself does not make much of a dramatic scene, and Masaccio had to display all his inventiveness in grouping figures, using gestures as well as serious and significant facial expression to involve us in his theme. Some seventy or so years later, a young man called Michelangelo stood in the chapel to draw Masaccio's figures.

To tell this story Masaccio had to repeat some of the figures within his unified scene. This convention belongs to medieval art; the Renaissance was to turn against it, preferring the one event, one moment, one place concentration of Greek drama. A fine example of a multi-action scene is the relief made by Ghiberti for the doors of Florence Baptistry a few years after Masaccio's fresco, telling the complicated story of Jacob and Esau. This story is told in Genesis and consists of several episodes: Esau returning from the hunt desperate for

MASACCIO
The Tribute Money 1427–8
(left)
fresco
255 x 598 cm (100 x 235 in)
Brancacci Chapel, Sta Maria
del Carmine, Florence

GHIBERTI
Story of Jacob and Esau
1437 (right)
gilt bronze relief
79 x 79 cm (31 x 31 in)
Gate of Paradise, Baptistry,
Florence Cathedral

Perspective view of an ideal
town (below)
tempera on panel
200 x 60 cm (79 x 23½ in)
Ducal Palace, Urbino

food; Rebecca instructing her son, Jacob; Jacob receiving his father's blessing, and so on.

Ghiberti's sculpture is always graceful and we are easily carried along by his elegant, somewhat Gothic forms and entertained by his compelling narrative additions, like the pair of hounds. But we should notice also the technical brilliance of it all. In this square panel – one of ten on the pair of doors – Ghiberti combines very high relief including almost free-standing figures 30 cm (12 in) high on the lower part of the panel which projects forward, with varying degrees of low relief. Combining the two kinds of relief convincingly takes great control,

and so does imposing a perspective system that starts with physical space and turns into an illusion of space. The fine Renaissance building he has invented for his stage gives order as well as grandeur to the panel.

It lacks the concentration of Masaccio's painting, and therefore its drama. On the next page you will see a relief by Donatello which comes closer to Masaccio in its stagecraft and weightiness. But you may feel that Ghiberti's charming, chattier manner has a lot to offer, especially on the doors of a Baptistry in the middle of Florence, where crowds pass by daily. Michelangelo called these doors the Doors of Paradise.

Donatello

DONATELLO born in 1386; died in Florence in 1466

Donatello is one of the greatest sculptors of all time. He began his career as one of Ghiberti's assistants. By the time he carved his life-size figure of *St George* he was a leading sculptor in a city that gave much work and honour to sculptors. He was also a sculptor of a new sort, on top of which his long and busy career showed him varying his work astonishingly, in method and in character.

Two examples will have to suffice here. His *St George* stands half inside a niche on the side of a Gothic guild hall. There are other niches and other life-size marble figures around the building, and the first thing that strikes one about *St George* is that he seems extraordinarily alive. Though he stands there firmly enough, one senses that he is ready to move, to step out and become the active warrior his armour and shield suggest. It is

46

partly his pose that suggests this (notice how his left foot projects), partly the alertness of his face: calm, classical in form and hairstyle, it shows a tension between the eyebrows, almost too slight to be noticeable, that suggests vigilance. His right hand once held a sword.

The figure has none of the elegance that a sculptor like Ghiberti put into work of this kind through flowing outlines and swinging draperies. It seems to be without style, natural; it is not performing for us, the way some of the figures in Ghiberti's relief are (particularly the group of women on the left, who play no part in the story itself; page 45). There is nothing unnecessary about the *St George,* just this vividness of face and pose. Yet the vividness is so controlled, so understated, that he reminds us of the great masterpieces of classical Greek sculpture, like the Apollo on page 18. These were totally unknown in Donatello's time.

centre of the composition he draws our attention to the key action, the head of the Baptist being offered to King Herod on a salver, almost hidden from us by the woman sitting with her back to us. The pressure of that dramatic staircase and of the figures on and next to it also sends us to the group around the table, so that our reading of the whole scene tends to start with the dancing girl in the middle and then turns to the head on the salver and Herod's shocked reaction. Thus Donatello has planned our reading to follow the sequence of the story even though he is presenting one scene, one action, one time as approved by the ancients.

All this says nothing about the character of the scene. Donatello and Masaccio show much the same dramatic seriousness, the same sense of important events and important meanings, and we can assume that they knew each other and spoke about the kind of art they wanted

His marble relief of *The Dance of Salome* is a masterpiece of carving. Using very slight actual depth, Donatello represents for us not only a dramatic action complete with onlookers but also a complicated architectural scene implying a whole town. His use of scale and of different depths of carving contributes to this, and so does the perspective: notice that by focusing the lines of his perspective scheme to the left rather than the

to develop. They were also close to the architect Brunelleschi who is credited with the invention of perspective. Brunelleschi and Donatello visited Rome together for some time between 1431 and 1433. It may well be that the knowledge of classical pediments, columns and arches, as well as the feeling for grandiose architecture that Donatello demonstrates in his relief stems from this visit.

Fra Angelico   Piero della Francesca

FRA ANGELICO born about 1400, probably in Fiesole, near Florence; died in Rome in 1455

PIERO DELLA FRANCESCA born around 1415 in Borgo San Sepolcro, near Florence; died in 1492

FRA ANGELICO
Annunciation 1438–45
fresco
216 x 321 cm (85 x 126 in)
Monastery of S Marco,
Florence

One of the most potent inventions of the Florentine Renaissance was undoubtedly the art of perspective. We have seen Masaccio, Ghiberti and Donatello using it in three rather different ways. Clearly it was a very important element in the new art. Soon it was being imitated in other places, in Italy and beyond the Alps. But what exactly was it, and what for?

I said on page 47 that Brunelleschi, the architect, is credited with inventing perspective. To be more exact, it was probably he who perfected the system used by Renaissance artists and called by them 'true' perspective. The Greek and Roman painters had found ways of representing space but these were much less systematic and convincing. Artists of the Gothic age discovered ways of suggesting space when they wanted to: we noted Giotto's very effective suggestion of a limited space, and the illogical spaces provided by the Sienese painter who worked on the back of the Duccio *Maestà* (pages 34 and 37). Northern painters like Jan van Eyck, for all their naturalism, belong to this Gothic tradition: the perspective they provide is based on observation – of life and of pictures – and is not built into a system (page 54).

But why have a system? It is significant that an architect should have been the one to bring it into being. He has to make exact drawings that incorporate his intentions and make them clear to others. There is evidence that Brunelleschi took into account, by means of perspective studies, how the interiors of the churches he designed would look to people standing in them. Perspective is a branch of geometry and to develop the Brunelleschian system required a command of mathematics that few artists of the time would have had. It also took a particular appetite or desire that seems to have been close to the heart of the early Renaissance.

I can best describe this as a desire for getting things right and for knowing they are right. It is one thing to show a shallow space like Giotto's: he did not want more. Donatello, wanting to show not only one dramatic action but also the circumstances in which it may have happened, in the form of secondary actors and of an architectural setting that contributes to its dramatic power, needs something more than the ability to *suggest* a space: he has to *control* it. He has, for instance, to determine the sizes of his figures according to where they are to stand in the space he is constructing, and also to

Plan of *The Flagellation* (below left), worked out by Marilyn Aronberg Lavin from data in the painting. Piero's perspective is so precise that the position of every element can be calculated back, even the height of Pilate's palace. Imagine your eye at the point of the triangle. Dots in the plan are feet.

PIERO DELLA FRANCESCA
The Flagellation c. 1460
tempera on panel
59 x 81.5 cm (23 x 32 in)
Ducal Palace, Urbino

know exactly how to reduce those parts of his architecture that we are to see receding towards the horizon.

The result is very convincing, but it is not truth. There is no reason, for instance, why the vertical edges of a building should always be shown as running parallel: imagine looking up at a skyscraper. When used correctly, it is a system that gives the artist – and us, the viewers – a sense of clear demonstration, of rightness. It can also be used dramatically, as in the Donatello relief.

The *Annunciation* illustrated here, a fresco at the top of the stairs in a Florentine monastery, establishes a clear space for the Virgin Mary and the angel who has come to speak to her. The effect is calm and harmonious; we enjoy the steady rhythm of the arches. In fact, the space would be much too small. Imagine Mary standing up in it. Fra Angelico, the Dominican monk who painted this and many other frescoes in the same building, must have known this: a more realistically proportioned building would have been more dramatic, more dominant, and

would have worked against the lucid harmony he wanted for his painting.

Piero della Francesca, who studied art in Florence, wanted to use perspective dramatically as well as correctly. We are still not certain of the precise meaning of his *Flagellation*. Perspective permits him to sink the scene of the title into the middle distance and yet keep it absolutely clear, and also to link with it the group of three figures who are in fact quite separate. The diagram shows how exactly Piero has constructed his picture space: he must have made very elaborate calculations and drawings to be able to paint this small panel. Its visual drama becomes more and more powerful as we look at it, yet every part of it is still, perfect, beyond time.

Mantegna

ANDREA MANTEGNA born near Padua about 1431; died in Mantua in 1506 (?)

MANTEGNA
Parnassus 1496–7
canvas
160 x 192 cm (63 x 75½ in)
Louvre, Paris

The notion that artists are interested only in their own work and care only about their uniqueness is false. In the fifteenth century, artists were as avid as they are today to know what others were doing, what techniques they were using, what new stylistic ideas were developing. Today they have photographs, illustrated magazines, galleries and other ways of watching each other. In the fifteenth century they might travel like Van der Weyden; they might go to work in another centre by request as Masaccio did in Rome, Donatello in Padua (working there for ten years, from 1443 to 1453), Leonardo in Milan, and so on. Also works travelled – not to exhibi-

tions as they so often do today, but into collections – and there other artists would be able to study them.

Mantegna was born near Padua and certainly saw Donatello's marvellous sculptures there: bronze figures and reliefs for the high altar of the Church of St Anthony and, outside the church, a magnificent bronze portrait of a general in Roman armour on horseback. He may also have travelled to Florence and Rome. In any case, it is clear that Mantegna developed a strong appetite for classical learning and art. Padua, where he worked until 1460 painting frescoes and panel paintings of religious subjects, was a great centre of learning even if it could not compete with Florence as an art centre. Mantegna then worked in Mantua as court painter to the Duke and Duchess. He painted a room with frescoes representing the Duke's family, not as a row of portraits but in informal groupings as though caught by the artist in their everyday activities. On the vault of the room he painted a circular opening and a balustrade, and figures looking down into the room, and sky above.

Mantegna painted the *Parnassus* illustrated here for the private apartments of the Duchess, Isabella d'Este, a much admired patron of the arts. It is one of a number of pictures, all on mythological themes, that she commissioned from various painters including Mantegna's brother-in-law Giovanni Bellini. They all represent themes from the stories of the ancient gods as told by Ovid and other Greek and Latin authors. These stories were treasured. Their subjects were often rather slight: love affairs, jealousies, the tricks by which one god triumphed over another. But they were rightly interpreted as symbolic statements on important matters.

Parnassus summarizes the love affair of Venus and Mars: they are at the top of the picture, with Cupid who is Venus's son. In the middle distance, on the left, we see Vulcan the blacksmith-god: he is Venus's husband and is cross about their affair. Homer tells in the *Odyssey* how Vulcan trapped the lovers in a net of iron and how the other gods laughed at the scene. Mantegna probably composed his picture guided by a first-century AD commentary on Homer's story, which says that from the union of Mars, god of war, and Venus, goddess of love and beauty, sprang harmony, peace and concord. Thus the painting hints at the union of the Duke and Duchess, at their beneficent reign over the state of Mantua, and their patronage. On the left of the picture Apollo plays on his lute whilst the Muses, representing the arts, dance to his music; on the right stands Mercury, the messenger of the gods, beside his horse Pegasus which symbolizes inspiration.

It is a gentle painting, sweeter in manner than many of Mantegna's works. I have detailed its content because we cannot understand the function of such a painting if we do not know what it meant to those who ordered it and looked at it. We have an ancient theme, represented in what people would have taken to be an antique manner, but bearing meanings that were relevant to the present. The engraving, *Battle of the Sea Gods,* probably depends more directly on an ancient source and has a very strong classical feeling. Many prints can be taken from one engraved plate, and so images of this sort could exercise wide influence. We know that the German artist Dürer, himself a great printmaker, made a drawing from this print (page 66).

Detail of *Parnassus (above)*

MANTEGNA
Battle of the Sea Gods c. 1490
engraving
33 x 19.7 cm (13 x 7³/₈ in)
British Museum, London

A theme from Antiquity, shown in an exceptionally complete antique style, learnt from close study of ancient sculpture and decorated objects. Presumably many copies of this print were available to be admired for their convincing classicism.

Bellini

GIOVANNI BELLINI born about 1430; died in Venice in 1516

GIOVANNI BELLINI
St Francis in Ecstasy
c. 1485
oil on panel
124 x 137 cm (48½ x 51 in)
Frick Collection, New York

Bellini's *St Francis in Ecstasy* was done in oil paint on a wood panel. That alone makes it very different from the fresco in Assisi (page 35), but it is worthwhile comparing these two treatments of the same subject further. In introducing Giotto and the changes in art associated with him, I stressed that in pressing for dramatic force

and clarity and generally for a plainer style with which people at large might feel at home, painters were abandoning the less realistic but rich, ornamental idiom of Byzantine painting. We saw that this idiom was continued and extended in the art of Sienese painters, and you may have felt that something of it survived in the work of Piero – again, not a Florentine – in spite of his firm grasp of Florentine principles of painting (page 49).

Bellini was a Venetian, one of a whole family of painters well known in Venice and the north of Italy. His father had worked for a while in Florence; his brother Gentile was actually in Constantinople during 1479-81 doing paintings for the Sultan there. Mantegna married their sister, and judging by Giovanni Bellini's early paintings he greatly admired Mantegna's severe and markedly classical manner.

Hints of this remain in the firm detail of his *St Francis*, a picture full of things for us to look at. The Assisi fresco is very concentrated: it delivers its subject boldly and without much in the way of secondary information. Bellini seems to want to tell us about the saint's life. In fact he places him in a landscape that one can recognize as North Italian. But notice how this landscape comes in separate sections: the foreground with St Francis and his simple home and belongings and the rocky hillside that seems to enshrine and protect him; the top of the cliff where his friend, Brother Ass, awaits him; the valley beyond that; and then the rising hills, the walled town, the castle and the sky.

The kind of painting we associated with Giotto and also with Masaccio (page 44) does not invite inspection in this way. This makes Bellini seem friendlier, more entertaining. But notice also how firmly the picture is constructed, with vertical and horizontal lines and rising diagonals and generally how our attention is brought back to the saint again and again.

He stands a little to the right of centre. He faces left, a little towards us but more towards . . . what? There is no vision, no supernatural apparition. But there is light. Using the fine control of tone that oil paints permit, Bellini gives us a strong sense of light coming into the picture from the left, flooding it all but illuminating particularly the figure of the saint. His yellowish habit contrasts with the cool blueish grey of the rocks but is partnered by the luminous blue of the sky and by the yellow sunlight trapped up there on the edge of one cloud. Four centuries later, Cézanne was to employ much the same blue/yellow ochre chord to much the same unifying effect in several of his paintings (page 131).

Bellini is the first painter to represent natural light so vividly and so purposefully. We feel we know the time of day, the weather and perhaps even the season from the quality of this light. We also recognize it as indicating, as *being* God's blessing upon St Francis: where Giotto used a symbolic image to make his theme absolutely clear, Bellini uses an aspect of nature that we all associate with goodness and well-being, and to do so is very much in the spirit of St Francis.

It is also very much in the spirit of Venetian painting. The painters that came after Bellini and looked to him as the founder of their school or regional group, are especially remarkable for the use they made of light and colour. Usually they painted in oils; we shall see that they came to use them more freely, more expressively than Bellini. But like him, they used the beauty of nature as the main matter for their pictures and as the material through which to tell their stories.

We can thus see Bellini as a bridge between the Byzantine tradition and the Venetian school of the sixteenth century. Venice had been an important part of the Byzantine Empire and to this day carries many signs of Byzantine culture in its buildings and their decoration.

Detail of *St Francis in Ecstasy*

I am tempted to say that the Byzantine tradition had to some degree survived in that marvellous, semi-Oriental city, through its Gothic and early Renaissance phases, and that the new school of painting Bellini fathered drew some of its warmth from that tradition.

But there is more to Bellini and to his painting than that. If you think away some of the detail, you are left with a strong, almost diagrammatic composition. Do you sense, as I do, a touch of Giotto's firmness in it? Padua is close to Venice. Bellini surely went there, to look at Donatello's sculptures and to visit his brother-in-law, and also perhaps to admire the work of the old master in the Arena Chapel.

Van Eyck   Van der Weyden

JAN VAN EYCK born about 1390; died in Bruges in 1441

ROGIER VAN DER WEYDEN born in 1399 or 1400; died in Brussels in 1464

VAN EYCK
*Giovanni Arnolfini and his
bride* 1434
oil on panel
82 x 60 cm (32¼ x 23½ in)
National Gallery, London

People tend to associate art with being 'lifelike'. We have already seen that some cultures placed great store by making very convincing images of important people. Egyptian sculptures often make us feel that we are standing in front of a living person, for example, but as we walk through the Egyptian galleries of a great museum we realize that either all Egyptians looked very much alike – and very handsome at that – or that the sculptors knew that they had to stick close to an agreed formula or convention of lifelikeness.

54

VAN DER WEYDEN
The Descent from the Cross
c. 1435
oil on panel
200 x 265 cm (79 x 104 in)
Prado, Madrid

You have probably noticed how tricky a business lifelike representation is. Even in photography. We take snapshots of our friends, and when we get them back from the printers we say that this one is a good likeness and that one isn't, even though the camera was doing its job just as fairly in each case. So it seems that we carry a formula for each of our friends' appearance in our heads and want pictures of them to come close to that.

It is not just exact copying that makes a picture persuade us of its truthfulness in this sense. The painting that (probably) shows Giovanni Arnolfini and his Flemish wife Jeanne persuades us that it is telling the truth, but how can we tell? It is painted with oil paint on a wood panel, a technique which Van Eyck perfected and which allows a slow and deliberate touching in of every detail: the fur on the dog and on the robes, the reflected light on the chandelier and in the mirror. It also shows light and shade so as to suggest solid objects and their placing, and a sort of perspective clear enough to make us feel we can read the space in which everything is. In such ways the painter reassures us, so that we trust him to be accurate also about Giovanni and Jeanne.

Perhaps the fact that they are not all that good- or nice-looking helps; the painter was not flattering them, we decide. Yet he gave them very slender, dainty hands, and if they have any bodies under those clothes these must be very long and, in his case at least, thin. So it seems that there was a formula at work here too, a formula perhaps for well-bred people. It is also probable that the chandelier, the mirror and perhaps other objects in the room had symbolic meanings, relating no doubt to

marriage vows. On the wall over the mirror we can read the Latin words for 'Jan van Eyck was here' which were surely not inscribed on the actual wall. But they imply that he was a witness to a significant moment and has here recounted what it was and what it looked like. Above all, he related what the surfaces of things looked like: we peer with satisfaction at the detail.

Gothic art had tended, as we have seen, towards this sort of detailed naturalism, more of the surface than of underlying structure, often for beauty's sake and sometimes to stimulate our pity and sympathy. Rogier van der Weyden's panel of *The Descent from the Cross* illustrates the strengths and the limitations of naturalism. The people represented look very natural; at the same time they look arranged. The event portrayed did not take place in a wooden crate but on top of a hill, Golgotha. We do not know how much space there is inside the box nor where the people are standing. In fact, the more we look the less natural the scene as a whole becomes.

Yet it moves us deeply. The arrangement of the figures, with its built-in echoes right and left and the parallel placing of Christ and his Mother, is both visually satisfying and emotionally effective.

It is thought that Van der Weyden visited Italy, probably in 1450. Certainly his work was known in Florence – where the Medici family owned a fine *Entombment* painting by him – and there are clear signs that his work, and that of other Flemish painters, influenced Florentine painting in the second half of the century, guiding it away from the plain, strong forms of Giotto and Masaccio to a more linear and flat style.

Botticelli

SANDRO BOTTICELLI born in Florence in 1444 or 1445; died there in 1510

BOTTICELLI
Primavera c. 1480
tempera on panel
203 x 314 cm (80 x 124 in)
Uffizi Gallery, Florence

Botticelli was greatly admired in his lifetime, but then forgotten as the art and fame of Raphael and Michelangelo proposed new ideas and models. He was rediscovered in the nineteenth century when he was perhaps loved too readily for the prettiness of his manner and the innocence of his subjects: sweet-faced Madonnas, charming little baby Jesuses, angels with fluttering draperies, gentle colours scarcely touched by shadow. Botticelli was indeed an attractive painter but a much more solid one than the Victorians thought or wanted. He was as much concerned with the meaning of his work as with its visual beauty.

But we are not certain of the specific meaning of his *Primavera.* In the sixteenth century, Vasari, who wrote a famous sequence of *Lives* of the Italian artists since Giotto and may be called the first art historian, said it represented 'Venus whom the Graces deck with flowers,

denoting Spring'. That is probably right. Venus stands in her garden where Spring is an endless season. The Graces dance their seemingly endless round but Cupid's arrow will strike one of them and she will leave her sisters to go and get married. Mercury, to whom the month of May is dedicated, stands on the left; on the right we see the wind Zephyr embracing the nymph Chloris who turns into the goddess of flowers, Flora. Chloris is linked to Flora in the picture by the flowers coming out of her mouth.

In its flatness and with its decorative detail and flowing lines, this painting may remind you of the Gothic tapestry we looked at earlier (page 39). Tapestries of that sort were very much in fashion among rich Florentines in Botticelli's time. They were often hung in reception rooms, above chests or settles placed along the walls. This was the purpose also of Botticelli's painting, and he may consciously have imitated some of the qualities of those Northern works. Yet his picture is full of classical references. The Cupid is actually copied from an ancient sculpture. The other figures follow Florentine tastes of the time with their long elegant figures and dresses

BOTTICELLI
*Lamentation over the Dead
Christ* c. 1500
tempera on panel
110 x 207 cm (43 x 81½ in)
Alte Pinakothek, Munich

fitting closely around the bosom and spreading out below.

It may also be that the painting offers a lesson in virtue and the value of good education. We know that it was produced for the house of a young Medici. Venus represented not only love and beauty but also classical learning as well as the virtues the ancients extolled. The painting may have been intended to remind him daily that happiness comes from a well developed mind capable of understanding the true value of things. The young man's tutors were friends of Botticelli and could have suggested the programme to the painter and explained it to their pupil.

While Botticelli lived in Florence the city experienced a political and spiritual revolution. In 1494 the Medici were usurped from their position as ruling family and for some years the people of Florence ran their city themselves under the guidance of the Church. Botticelli's work at this time shows a deepening religious intensity. His *Lamentation over the Dead Christ* is an outstanding example.

It too is a rather flat picture, but without the decorative attractions of *Primavera*. Everything presses into the foreground; the figures fill the space, fitting together rather sharply, angularly. In this way and others, the *Lamentation* reminds me of Van der Weyden's *Descent* (page 55), and it may well be that Botticelli responded positively to the austere composition of Van der Weyden's paintings. He goes further, excluding anything similar to the other's rich brocades and busy draperies. Gone entirely are the flowers, pretty hairstyles and other charms of his own earlier works.

Instead there is a mixture of styles. St Peter on the right seems to come out of the still partly Gothic world of Ghiberti (page 45). The beardless Christ seems classical, a Greek god. These contradictions add to the stridency of the whole so that we hardly notice its orderly, almost symmetrical arrangement.

Leonardo

LEONARDO DA VINCI born at Vinci, near Florence, in 1452; died at Amboise (France) in 1519

Surely no man ever had a greater appetite for knowledge than Leonardo. The whole of Florentine Renaissance art, we noticed, was driven along by a desire to represent things convincingly – not merely their surface appearances but also as solid objects related to each other in the imaginary space of a picture or relief. Leonardo looked further, and in the process became the leading scientist of his age. He wanted to know how the things he needed to represent worked: bodies, plants, whole landscapes, light, water as river and as deluge, mechanical devices of all sorts. He studied the writings of the ancients but tested book learning and abstract reasoning against personal observation. And being a philosopher as well as an artist and a scientist he looked for the harmony and order behind the diverse facts he found.

I am tempted to say that as an artist he was ruined by science. His pursuits were so varied that too often they took him away from his painting (and from the great sculpture he planned but never made). He began so much and finished so little. What he left behind in the way of art is only a fraction of the body of great and magnificently developing work he had it in him to do.

Yet what Leonardo did leave transformed art. His paintings and drawings, almost from the first, are markedly different from the art he was trained in, and their excellence was recognized at once so that successive generations of artists flocked to learn from them.

One of his most famous works – famous from the day it was done – is the mural he painted in the refectory of Santa Maria delle Grazie in Milan, in northern Italy.

LEONARDO
The Last Supper
1495–8 (left)
mixed media on plaster
420 x 910 cm (166 x 358 in)
Sta Maria delle Grazie, Milan

LEONARDO
Embryo in the Womb
1511 (below)
ink
47 x 33 cm (18½ x 13 in)
Royal Collection, Windsor Castle

LEONARDO
Perspective study for the background of
Adoration of the Magi 1481 (below)
ink with some wash
16.5 x 28.5 cm (6½ x 11¼ in)
Uffizi Gallery, Florence

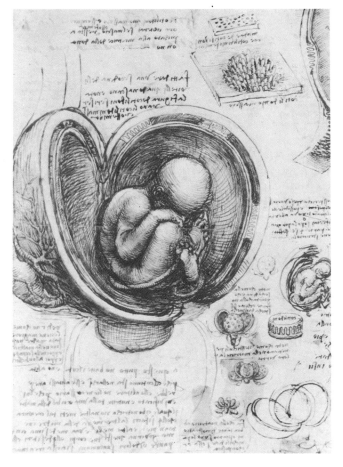

Its theme, *The Last Supper*, had frequently been used as an apt image for a refectory. Leonardo's treatment of it not only changed artists' visual concepts of it but also their, and our, understanding of the implications of the subject. Emphasis had previously been divided between Christ's instituting the sacrament of the Eucharist in breaking bread for His disciples, and Judas's act of treason against Him: the first an important piece of doctrine, the second a dramatic part of the story with relevance for all sinners.

Leonardo focused his treatment on one theme and one moment: the moment when Christ says: 'One of you will betray me'. Each of the twelve apostles reacts in his own way. They sit either side of the central, pyramidal figure of Christ; six on each side, grouped in threes, but asymmetrically placed so that there is something like a wave motion running through them from left to right. As in Masaccio, Donatello and Piero, this process of dramatization is intended to make us aware of the significance of the scene. We attempt to read each person's thoughts and actions, noting surprise here, disbelief there, anger,

declarations of innocence, disputes, and so on. Christ presides over the commotion with calm and resignation. The perspective lines of the imaginary refectory in which this is portrayed meet in His head, in His right eye to be exact: an eye in a triangle is an ancient symbol for God.

You enter the refectory at the other end. Leonardo's painting stretches across the whole of the end wall, leaving the lower part clear so that it is not obscured by people and tables. The painting, especially Christ's head, dominates the whole room. It is emphasized not only by its position in the centre but also, very effectively, by being silhouetted against the window or doorway Leonardo shows at the far end of his room. Apart from that, the light in the painting seems to come from the left, and that is where the windows are in the actual refectory. Leonardo used it very gently on the figures in his painting, modelling their faces very delicately from light to dark and avoiding sharp outlines that might make for clarity but which do not exist in nature and which work against the rich three-dimensionality he wanted. This use of light, quite unlike the clear, high tones favoured by Gothic painting and by most Renaissance painting until now, is called *chiaroscuro,* Italian for 'light-dark'.

Only ten years after Leonardo completed this painting it began to disintegrate. Its history since then has been a sad story of continuing decay, patching, repainting, removing the repainting and so on. It seems unlikely that it can be saved. Instead of using the fresco technique, Leonardo tried a process of his own invention, involving a range of media and fires to speed the drying. But the painting continues to be seen as a milestone in the history of art as well as a work of outstanding beauty. Even in Leonardo's time, people who could not go to see it knew it from painted copies and from engravings.

Michelangelo

MICHELANGELO BUONARROTI born at Caprese, near Florence, in 1475; died in Rome in 1564

MICHELANGELO
Pietà 1498–9
marble
174 x 195 cm (68½ x 77 in)
St Peter's, the Vatican,
Rome

MICHELANGELO
Creation of Adam
1511 (right)
fresco
280 x 570 cm (110 x 225 in)
Sistine Chapel, Vatican
Palace, Rome

Even while he was still alive, Michelangelo was called the divine artist – 'il divino Michelangelo'. Leonardo and Raphael, too, were amazingly famous. We are, clearly, at a climax in the history of art. Historians call it the High Renaissance. It was marked not only by the extraordinary talents and creative intellects of these three artists, but also by great opportunities offered them by appreciative patrons. And, strangely, interested people soon realized that they had witnessed a climax. For all the great achievements of artists in the later sixteenth century and in all the years up to our own time, there has been no doubt that here was a golden moment which might never be equalled. The work of these three masters provided models for others to learn from, but also standards of beauty and grandeur that few thought they would ever attain.

Michelangelo was trained as a painter and a sculptor; he worked also as an architect. But he thought of himself first and foremost as a sculptor, resisting the great painting commissions that were thrust at him. The labour of cutting stone, the creative miracle of removing parts of an inert block to reveal an image that seems to live and can have profound meaning – that seemed to him the true art, an echo of God's creation of man.

In everything he did, through whatever medium, he sought a super-human beauty and energy. Other artists had prepared the way, and we have looked at work by some of them. He studied ancient sculptures. The *Laokoon* group (page 21) was discovered and set up in Rome in 1506 and was to him an image of spiritual as well as physical struggle. It is in these terms that we must try to understand his pursuit of physical beauty, vigour and expressiveness: as a visible form, echoing God's perfection and power, for conveying the hopes and fears, the triumphs as well as the trials, of man's soul.

For four years, from 1508 to 1512, he worked almost single-handed to paint the ceiling of the chapel in the Pope's palace, the Sistine Chapel. The original idea was to paint on the shallow curve of the vault large figures representing prophets from the Old Testament. Almost at once Michelangelo proposed a much more ambitious programme: to show in narrative scenes the early history of God's relationship to man, as told in Genesis, together with symbolical figures (the male nudes) and prophets and sybils (combining the Old Testament and ancient myths), and other figures and scenes foretelling Christ's return to earth as Saviour.

The whole conception is vast, and Michelangelo's style of painting became bolder as he worked. The scene illustrated here belongs to the last phase and was probably done in 1511: The *Creation of Adam*. God has made the physical man. We witness the moment when,

as though by means of a spark leaping between the positive hand of God and the negative one of Adam, God gives life and spirit to mankind. For an instant, God and man look into each other's eyes.

Michelangelo was a profoundly religious man. Everything he touched is supercharged with his quest for great truths in which the human and the divine are brought together. This may be a little difficult to grasp, but that is exactly where his art helps us, in the fresco we have been looking at and also in the earlier *Pietà* he carved in marble. People tend to disregard this work in comparison with his later and more massive achievements, but it shows much the same ambitions in the young artist.

Pietà, meaning both pity and piety, is the name Italians give to images of the dead Christ and His Mother – summary versions, so to speak, of *The Descent from the Cross* and the *Lamentation over the Dead Christ*. A dead god who is also a dead man in the arms of his mother: the poignancy of it is clear.

Michelangelo promised it would be the most beautiful sculpture in Rome. His task was to combine beauty with human and religious expression. It *is* very beautiful, in its parts and as a whole. The tilt of the group, the slightness of the body of Christ, the Madonna's inclined head and simple gesture . . . After we have taken in the beauty, we begin to share the anguish which is both human and, because of the flawless beauty, more than human.

His art seems to come from a world beyond our reach. It owes much to Giotto, Masaccio and Donatello but his insistence on charging everything he touched with the gravest significance goes far beyond any other artist. Contemporaries spoke of his work's awesomeness, and were convinced he was directly guided by God.

Raphael

RAPHAEL born in Urbino in 1483; died in Rome in 1520

RAPHAEL
The School of Athens
1509–11 fresco
550 cm (216 in) wide
Stanza della Segnatura,
Vatican Museum, Rome

Leonardo is associated with a new combination of art and natural science, new monumentality and softly gradated modelling; Michelangelo with monumentality too, charged with enormous energy, uplifting the human towards the divine. We associate Raphael with perfection.

People find perfection hard to take. They don't mind the perfection of a perfect sphere, in geometry or in technology; in art they expect to find signs of struggle, of ambitious aims that the artist wrestles with without ever quite attaining.

Raphael died young and success came to him early. He was successful also in accomplishing the aims he and his time set for him. The perfection in his art is not the perfection of a perfectly turned object but of a perfectly executed leap. You know how a really good gymnast makes his programme of leaps and rolls and sudden stillnesses look easy and natural. That is how it is with Raphael. What went into it was great natural ability, of course, and a deep understanding of the art around him, ancient and modern.

He came to Rome in 1508, having studied art in Perugia and Florence. Almost at once he was commissioned by the Pope to paint frescoes on the walls and ceilings of four rooms in the Vatican Palace. The first of these is the Stanza della Segnatura, the 'room of the signing', a cross between a library and an office in which important documents were issued. On one wall Raphael showed the learned men of Christianity, watched over by Christ and the saints, establishing the basic tenets of the faith. On the opposite wall he painted the fresco illustrated here, known as *The School of Athens*. On one side, then, theology and the new dispensation of Christianity; on the other, philosophy as conceived and refined by the ancients. The two are not in opposition but in harmony.

Raphael may have intended to symbolize this unity in the architectural setting he used. It represents the in-

teror of the new St Peter's in Rome, being built at the time to the designs of Raphael's friend Bramante. (Michelangelo was to revise the design and carry the work forward in the 1540s; see page 65). In this splendid classical setting Raphael presents Plato (probably a portrait of Leonardo) pointing upwards, and Aristotle next to him, and other great thinkers and scholars of pre-Christian times such as Euclid, Pythagoras and Ptolemy. Two statues symbolize their twin ideals: Apollo, representing order and beauty, and Athene, wisdom and social order. As in the Leonardo (page 58), every figure in the painting contributes to its action and its significance. Raphael's stage is much larger. The steps enable him to show a crowd of figures with great clarity. The grouping is complex, the balance precarious, yet it all looks at ease.

While Raphael was working on this fresco, in 1511, more than half of the Sistine ceiling (not including the *Creation of Adam*) was unveiled and could be inspected. Raphael finished his fresco soon after. It looks likely that he added the massive, solemn figure of Heraclitus (in the foreground, left of centre) as an afterthought. A museum in Milan has the enormous, full-size drawing Raphael prepared for all the figures except the Heraclitus. The arrangement in that looks more spacious, a little more elegant; also cooler, more distant from us emotionally. The Heraclitus is a very Michelangelesque

RAPHAEL
Fighting Men (study for *School of Athens*) c. 1510 red chalk over grey pencil Ashmolean Museum, Oxford

Bramante's design for the exterior of St Peter's on a bronze medal, 1506 (below). British Museum, London.

figure, spiritually as well as physically imposing. He adds greatly to the drama and impact of the whole scene, and makes us feel more positively the space between himself and Plato.

Raphael went on to finish the other three rooms, and then on to many other commissions, large and small. To carry them out he built up a team of expert assistants. His invention or design served them as blueprints in the form of drawings; he himself would contribute varying amounts to the actual painting. The drawing shown here is a preparatory rough study for the figures you can glimpse in the form of a relief sculpture below the statue of Apollo. A study of this kind would be developed into a full-size drawing, and the main lines of that would be transferred on to the wet plaster to guide the painter.

Michelangelo

MICHELANGELO
The Last Judgement
1534–41
fresco
1370 x 1220 cm
(540 x 480 in)
Sistine Chapel, Vatican
Palace, Rome

By the time Michelangelo began work on his second great fresco commission for the Sistine Chapel in 1534, the world had changed. Rome, the command module of Christianity and the centre of civilization, had been attacked, occupied and ravaged by the troops of the Emperor Charles V in 1527. There was news too of disruptions within the Christian Church, about to divide into two opposed camps, the Protestant and the Roman Catholic. Rome soon recovered her poise and her artistic life, but there was a feeling that faith would have to be asserted, defined and defended. Much of the religious art produced between the middle of the sixteenth century and the end of the seventeenth has the character of a public celebration designed to confirm believers and dazzle doubters, and the first great example of this is the fresco Michelangelo painted on the altar wall of the Sistine Chapel.

The Last Judgement, the return of Christ at the ending of this world to reward the good and punish the wicked, had often been portrayed on the exit wall of a church or chapel, where worshippers would see it as they left the building. (You will recall that early medieval churches had sometimes shown the subject in sculptural form over the entrance, on the outside; page 31). To show it on the main wall of the Pope's chapel was to give it new prominence, hinting at the Church's role in guiding the world towards Heaven in spite of all its sinful ways. Never, at any rate, had the scene been visualized with such awesome vigour. The heroic figure of Christ the Judge stands in a blaze of light. From his mighty gesture springs a circular motion that sweeps the damned down to Hell and draws up the blessed into Christ's own realm. There is very little use of depth in the painting: everything happens on or near the surface, so that the wall is still sensed as a containing plane, held together by the grey-blue of the background.

Throughout this vast fresco, and generally in Michelangelo's work, his chief unit is the naked figure, especially the male figure. The figure is the object with which he builds his complex images – like the choreographer's use of the figure in creating a ballet, of course, but also like the builder's use of a brick. Michelangelo was not alone in seeing human, physical beauty as a form of spiritual beauty. But no one else had his mastery of the body as an expressive unit. No one had taken such positive command of this unit and made it mean so much. Of course, he had studied anatomy with great care and he was a superb draughtsman. But he also asserted the right of the artist to exaggerate and distort his figures, and to group them in unnatural ways. As human beings we cannot but respond to images of ourselves and identify with their forms and actions. Modern art has included much distortion of the figure and this is one of the things that people find so disconcerting about it, painful even. But Michelangelo distorts too, in pretty extreme ways, and his contemporaries were thrilled and awed by the sight, as we are to this day.

Michelangelo's use of the naked male figure links him to the great age of Greek sculpture. You may like to compare the vehemence of his Christ to the commanding stillness of Apollo (page 18). Of this he will have had little or no direct knowledge; most of the ancient sculptures he knew were Roman or Roman copies of Greek

Michelangelo's design for St Peter's: a late 16th century medal (above) showing his intentions for the exterior. British Museum, London

MICHELANGELO
Pietà c. 1560–4 (right)
marble
195 cm (77 in) high
Castello Sforzesco, Milan

originals. But the *Laokoon* group (page 21) was both expressive in its movement and faces and anti-natural in the relative sizes of the priest and his sons, and it confirmed in Michelangelo an instinct for concentrating all his art on the physical body.

In his last years he came to doubt that he had been right to do so. His drawings became more and more insubstantial and even his sculpture came to deny its own physicality. Compare the *Pietà* in Milan, on which he was working a few days before he died, nearly 89 years old, with that he carved when he was 24. It is difficult to believe that they are the work of one man.

The late work is a private piece, not a commission. As you can see, it is broken and incomplete: Michelangelo has changed his mind. You expect a carver to plan his figure in detail before attacking the stone, but the aged Michelangelo was working, so to speak, free-hand. Having cut the main masses of the two bodies, he demolishes most of Christ's and begins to find parts of it within the mass that had been the Virgin. Christ's head, as we see it now, was part of the shoulder and breast of a larger Virgin. He is shrinking them both, into wraiths rather than bodies.

In its turning away from ideals of perfect form and bodily dignity, this sculpture seems to belong to the medieval world and to the modern. Yet the mind that conceived it belongs to the Renaissance, and it reminds us that the classical beauty of Renaissance art is always a vehicle for meaning.

Dürer

ALBRECHT DÜRER born in Nuremberg in 1471; died there in 1528

DÜRER
*St Michael fighting the
Dragon* (from the
Apocalypse series) 1497
woodcut
39 x 28 cm (15 x 11 in)
British Museum, London

The years around 1500 were years of crisis and brought deep unrest to many people and places north of the Alps. There was much questioning of established faiths and values. Some foretold the Second Coming for 1500 or soon after: Christ would come to judge mankind and the world would end. The sixteenth century saw the Reformation, the Low Countries' struggle against their Spanish rulers, the Emperor's assault on Rome, and many other kinds of strife, on the level of ideas as much as of physical contest.

Albrecht Dürer of Nuremberg was a devout man, troubled by the doubts and dissension around him. He was a goldsmith's son and godson of a printer, and grew up in a world of skilled craftwork and of text and images multiplied on paper. He greatly admired Martin Luther who was working to reform the Church; perhaps he saw himself too as a reformer and a preacher but working through visual, not verbal, statements. He preached through printed images: woodcuts first, and then also engravings. They combine a strong, almost aggressive response to the basic dogmas of Christian belief and a new feeling for worldly facts. Some of Dürer's studies of plants, bodies, landscape and other important components of our visual world approach the scientific sharpness of Leonardo. He developed the art of cutting wood blocks, and of etching lines into copper plates, both for printing on paper, into a much finer, more detailed and also more expressive means than it had been before. And through these graphic means he brought supernatural visions and natural observation into eerie combination.

St Michael fighting the Dragon is an example of this sort. It is one of a series of prints telling of the Second Coming. Whilst the angels battle with the monsters in the sky – and never before had the struggle been portrayed so fiercely – a landscape of mountains, a bay with ships, a scene altogether of space, light and calm, occupies the lower part of the picture. Above, all is crowded and dark and nightmarish; below there is, for the moment, peace. All this is conveyed by means of lines, printed by little ridges of wood: in the upper part lots of them, often close together, parallel or criss-cross, to model the forms and give a general sense of darkness; in the lower part fewer lines and large intervals between them. Dürer's emphasis is clearly on the supernatural scene in the sky. That is what he wants to bring home to us. The stillness of the landscape makes the drama in the heavens all the more emphatic.

Dürer travelled in the German states, visiting artists and printers. He associated with learned men and saw himself as one. Later in his life he wrote a number of treatises on various topics from fortification to proportion and art theory. We know that he copied some of Mantegna's engravings (page 51). In 1494-5 he was in Venice and in northern Italy; in 1505 he returned to Venice for a visit of 18 months, during which he also travelled to other centres and as far south as Bologna. His qualities were recognized by his Italian colleagues and his influence, principally through his prints, spread further south, to Florence and to Rome.

He himself was deeply affected by what he saw and learned, and some of the results of this can be seen in his

DÜRER
Adam and Eve 1504
engraving
25 x 19 cm (9³/₄ x 7¹/₂ in)
British Museum, London

engraving, *Adam and Eve*. Italians favoured the technique of engraving for the finer detail it permits in comparison with woodcuts. Dürer, this print shows, has accepted and understood the tradition of the classical figure. But the forest and the animals in it, and the cliffs behind Eve, show a Northern taste for detailed naturalism and for filling the surface of a picture.

The Renaissance crosses the Alps with Dürer. Craftsman and scholar, printmaker but also renowned painter, he addresses a wide public with his religious prints but works also at times for the Emperor and other notables, a Northerner with his eyes on the old-new art and methods of the South. Soon Italian taste, and later also French taste, cover local tastes and traditions. In the nineteenth and twentieth centuries these are again uncovered, as challenging alternatives to the great tradition that goes back to Greece and Rome.

Bosch   Grünewald

HIERONYMUS BOSCH born at 's Hertogenbosch (Low Countries) about 1450; died there in 1516
MATHÄUS GRÜNEWALD born about 1470-80, probably in Würzburg (Germany); died in Halle in 1528

The tension, the sense of crisis I spoke of in connection with Dürer, is unmistakable in the work of the two painters illustrated here: Bosch who lived and worked in 's Hertogenbosch, in the northern part of the Low Countries which was to become Holland or The Netherlands, and Grünewald who lived and worked in the western states of Germany. We know very little about either artist. Their work was admired in their own time, and then again increasingly in the last hundred years or so; in between it was hardly noticed much. Can you guess why their reputations should have gone up and down so much?

All the work we know by both painters is more or less directly religious in subject and urgent in tone. Priests preached that the devil was everywhere and that mankind was ever and again being enslaved by him, ensnared by promises of pleasure or power. Salvation was at hand for every sinner who truly repented, but the message of the time was that it was almost too late to mend one's ways: the mouth of hell was wide open and humanity at large was rushing towards it, intent only on its own immediate satisfactions. We saw a similar message in the relief carvings over many early medieval church doors (see page 31).

Bosch's *Hell* is part of a triptych: the right panel of three that are hinged together. In the left one we see the Garden of Eden where Adam and Eve dwell at ease with all God's creatures; the centre panel, twice the width of the others, portrays the pursuit of pleasure on earth and the foolishness of that pursuit. *Hell* shows the triumph of the Powers of Darkness over mankind. Mankind is here not being enticed into sin but is now sin's victim, relentlessly persecuted and afflicted. Bosch shows this through countless little scenes of men and women plagued by monsters of every sort. Everything is painted very finely, delicately, and many of the forms are beautiful in themselves, but the whole is intentionally dark, chaotic and frightening.

The Grünewald painting is part of a many-panelled altarpiece painted for the chapel of a hospital in the village of Isenheim, near Colmar. The central subject of this scene is the *Crucifixion:* Christ is dead upon the cross,

BOSCH
Hell (right wing of *Garden of Earthly Delights* triptych)
c. 1500
oil on panel
220 x 97 cm (86½ x 38 in)
Prado, Madrid

Mary Magdalen kneels at the foot of the cross, Christ's Mother stands on the left, supported by the Apostle John; on the right stands St John the Baptist (who was not present at the Crucifixion), pointing to Christ as the Saviour.

Bosch puts before us fantastic images that attract and repel us; some of them seem familiar to us, from our own dreams. Grünewald shocks us with realism, forcing us to recognize the cruelty Christ suffered for the sins of mankind. The scourged body, His hands and feet, the cross bending under His weight: Grünewald makes us see and feel and consider.

In modern times Bosch and Grünewald have become tremendously famous; popular even. Artists led the way. The Expressionist painters of Germany saw in Grünewald a model for the vehemence they wanted in their pictures, and a German model at that. The Surrealists, delving into the world of dreams and subconscious images, saw Bosch as a direct forerunner. Perhaps there are no wrong reasons for admiring admirable art, but we must beware of seeing these sixteenth century artists as moderns. Both of them belonged to the world of Late Gothic imagery and naturalism. The monsters and the realistic horror we see in their work we can find also, less concentrated and often on a more modest scale, in late medieval manuscripts, in gargoyles and other carvings on Gothic churches, in Northern carved crucifixes and groups. These paintings were done for a public that recognized them for the passionate, warning sermons they were.

GRÜNEWALD
Isenheim altarpiece
c. 1512
oil on panel
Unterlinden Museum, Colmar
showing *Crucifixion*
269 x 307 cm (106 x 121 in)
St Anthony (left),
St Sebastian (right) and
Weeping over the Dead Christ
(below) – four out of nine
paintings that make up this
elaborate work

Giorgione

GIORGIONE born about 1477 in Castelfranco, in the state of Venice; died 1510 in Venice

GIORGIONE
The Tempest c. 1505 oil on canvas
78 x 72 cm (30¼ x 28¾ in) Accademia, Venice

Giorgione's *La Tempestà* (the storm or the tempest) remains mysterious. You can see that it represents a man, a sort of soldier, and a woman with a baby in the foreground of a landscape. The landscape of houses and a river includes a pair of broken columns and is dominated by the storm that darkens the sky and leaves some of the buildings gleaming with ominous sunlight. It is a very small picture; private rather than public, and full of feeling. Its mood is quite clear; what is mysterious is its subject. We know that shortly after the painter's death well-informed Venetians could not say what it was about.

Detail of *The Tempest*

The remarkable thing is that this did not seem to worry them. A Florentine would, I think, have demanded an explanation: who are these people? what do they signify? why the storm? Giorgione's fellow-citizens were content to respond to the poetry of light and colour and to the suggestiveness of the scene.

Examination by X-ray has shown that where the soldier stands Giorgione first painted a woman – perhaps the same woman, before changing her position. He may, then, have changed his mind about what figures his picture needed, in which case he presumably did not have a specific story in mind. Or he greatly changed the arrangement of his picture. In either case, he had not preplanned it definitively the way a Florentine would have done. This is partly a matter of technique. You can overpaint with oils in a way that you cannot with tempera. But it is also partly a matter of what he wanted to do. The painting was to embody Giorgione's feelings as much as his thought-out ideas, and for that it needed an element of spontaneity.

People misunderstand the idea of spontaneity in art. Few works of art are dashed off thoughtlessly; those that are are either worthless or the product of long practice and experience. I suggested earlier that the perfect art of Raphael is something like the perfection of a gymnast's performance, endlessly trained for and rehearsed, until it looks easy, natural. Giorgione's desire to paint with a degree of spontaneity can be compared to a footballer's ability, again developed out of experience and practice, to respond to situations on the field as they arise. To leave a painting unplanned is to leave oneself free to respond to it in working on it. The painting is not just executed; it is developed as it is painted. It grows, so to speak, on the canvas.

We are witnessing here the birth of an alternative tradition to that of Florence and Rome, and it is a tradition associated with oil painting. (The Florentine tradition, in comparison, is the same for fresco, tempera and oil painting and also for sculpture: design precedes execution, and execution in most cases follows the design.) It is also, understandably, associated with a more poetic sort of expression and with a less graphic, or designed, style.

There were hints of this pictorial poetry already in the Mantegna and the Bellini we looked at, and Leonardo's example encouraged a taste for softly modelled forms. But Leonardo made less positive use of colour, whereas for Giorgione colour and tone are closely linked. The painting of the Venetian school after Giorgione is famed for its richness of colour and warmth of emotion. And this emphasis on the painting as an arrangement of colours and tones means that less attention goes to correctness of anatomy or perspective. Any Florentine would have seen at once that the woman in *The Tempest* is not well drawn. It is just as well that Giorgione covered her shoulders with a piece of cloth since he seems to have been undecided how to attach her left arm to her body.

It is likely that *The Tempest* is about peace. The soldier carries a staff, not a lance. Broken columns represent fortitude. A woman suckling her child may represent charity; the image, in any case, is a comforting one. The storm will pass. The little stream and the river it serves will run on regardless. Life goes on. Shakespeare's play *The Tempest* was written a hundred years later and has no direct connection with this picture. Yet it is poetry of a similar sort. Specific things are said or done but the meaning of the whole is both bigger and vaguer. Both works stay in the mind because they do not tell us everything.

Titian

TITIAN born about 1487-90 at Pieve di Cadore in the state of Venice; died in Venice in 1576

TITIAN
Pesaro Madonna 1519–26
oil on canvas
485 x 270 cm (192 x 106 in)
Sta Maria dei Frari, Venice

In the sixteenth century the Venetian state stretched eastwards towards Milan and northwards to the Alps, and included the cities of Bergamo, Brescia, Verona and Padua. Venice ruled also over Istria and Dalmatia on the east coast of the Adriatic, and derived great wealth and power from trade with the Orient. Today we think of Venice as part of Italy, of course, but she feels different and separate even now. Byzantine forms and tastes linger there, in the great Byzantine church of St Mark which is Venice's cathedral and in the exotic decorations of many other buildings. Altogether she has a semi-Oriental flavour, more luxurious, more sensual than the West is used to.

You may have sensed some of this in the strange poetry of Giorgione's *The Tempest* (page 70). His friend and pupil became the leader of the Venetian school of painting at a time when the city of Venice was growing and beautifying herself and was undoubtedly a great force in Europe. Titian was born about ten years after Giorgione. Bellini was his principal master and Titian succeeded him as official painter to the Venetian Republic when Bellini died. Soon his work was sought after not only in Italy but all over Europe, by the Emperor Charles V for instance, and by the King of Spain, Philip II.

He was a superlative painter – of formal and informal portraits, of great altarpieces and little devotional pictures, and equally of mythological subjects taken from the ancient poets. Interest in these subjects was relatively new in Venice. (We saw Mantegna's pioneering work on page 50, done for Isabella d'Este; Titian was to paint a group of mythological paintings for her brother, Alfonso.) What strikes one about Titian's way of handling them, and then also that of other Venetian artists, is the new, contemporary feeling they give to these subjects. In Florence and Rome artists liked to show their familiarity with ancient dress and other trappings in portraying mythologies and other subjects, even portraits of their own contemporaries; they called it working *all' antica,* in the ancient manner. The Venetians did the opposite: they made the ancients into citizens of Venice.

This applies almost equally to some of the most splendid religious paintings of the period. Titian's *Pesaro Madonna* (strictly: *Madonna and Child with Saints, the Donor and his Family*) was painted for the Pesaro family who appear so prominently in it and is still in place on an altar on the south side of the Church of the Frari in Venice. Over the high altar we see Titian's splendid *Assumption of the Virgin*. The most striking feature of the *Pesaro Madonna* is its asymmetry, the way it is piled up towards the right. I think this relates to its position in the church: we enter from the south and turn left towards the high altar and see this altarpiece ahead of us and to the left, so the Virgin seems to be facing towards us.

Another point is a more arguable one. I believe that perhaps because we read from left to right, the psychological centre of any picture is a little to the right of its geometrical centre. Also a figure facing the way the Virgin faces, and the whole niche-like group around her, *feels* as though it were facing us. (The same applies to, say, St Francis in the Bellini painting on page 52.) If you

TITIAN
Diana and Actaeon c. 1560
oil on canvas
179 x 189 cm (70½ x 78 in)
National Gallery, London

have a mirror, try seeing the illustration the other way around; if you can get hold of a slide of this painting, or another with the same basic arrangement, try projecting it the wrong way round.

In any case, the grouping, the columns, the steps, the splendid flag and the lively cherubs up there on their clouds – everything adds up to a rich, celebratory scene which to a sixteenth century Venetian would have looked very much of his own time. Decades later, as an old man, Titian painted a series of mythological paintings for the King of Spain. One of them shows Diana the goddess in pursuit of the earthling Actaeon: he turns into a stag and her dogs tear him to pieces. It is a magical picture, far from naturalistic (notice the sharp drop in scale from her to him) and curiously still for all the movement it shows. In Titian's hands the paint itself becomes poetry, replacing other sorts of richness and display.

Correggio

Veronese

CORREGGIO born about 1490 in Correggio; died in Parma in 1534

PAOLO VERONESE born about 1528 in Verona; died in Venice in 1588

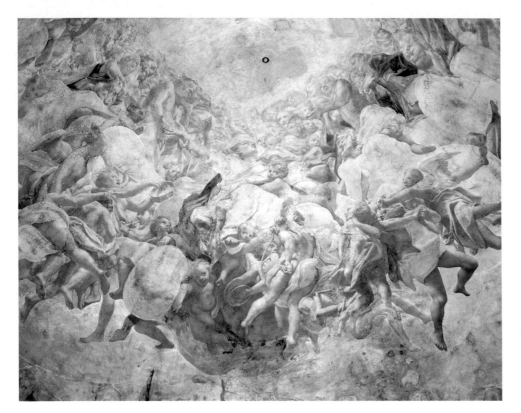

CORREGGIO
Assumption of the Virgin
1526–30 Detail
fresco
diameter of dome about
1100 cm (433 in)
Cathedral of Parma

The great fresco decorations executed by Leonardo, Raphael and Michelangelo, and also by Mantegna and others, encouraged religious and lay patrons to think of commissioning decorative schemes for their churches, town palaces and country houses. The sixteenth century saw many splendid examples, mostly done in fresco. And the tradition has continued, through the seventeenth, eighteenth and nineteenth centuries; only in our own century has the lavish painting of interiors become rare and even frowned upon.

The word 'decorative' has itself fallen on hard times. People are liable to use it disparagingly: 'Oh, but that is just decorative', they say, meaning it may please our eyes but it lacks weight and seriousness. But 'decorate' has associations with 'decorum' which implies aptness and suitability. To enrich the interior of a building with paintings or other decorations that fit the building's purpose, that is, to help the building serve its purpose, makes very good sense. Only in modern times, since we lack any general agreement about what is worthwhile in art, has this tradition faltered. The fact is that the few commissions there are for this kind of work tend to be issued by people who have little understanding of art to

artists who often have little feeling for its special demands. But there are exceptions, and perhaps you know of some.

Also, we tend to react with distaste to the overloaded look and feeling of old interiors. This is a reaction against Victorian taste: nineteenth-century taste tended to be for richly stuffed interiors with lots of bulging furniture, heavily upholstered chairs and sofas, dense curtains and other hangings, and so on. We feel a bit stifled by that, and long for open spaces and blank walls. Renaissance interiors were sparsely furnished, however, churches as well as houses; a painted wall or ceiling dome would have its full effect, and would not be competing with clutter of all sorts. Here we have two examples from the north of Italy, one religious, one domestic. Commissioned to paint the inside of the dome of the cathedral of Parma, Correggio, who certainly knew Mantegna's work and Leonardo's, decided to cover the whole of the semi-sphere with one scene: he would show the *Assumption of the Virgin* – that is, her being carried up into heaven after her death – as rings of countless figures. The Apostles and other bystanders form the lowest ring; the Virgin and the angels carrying and accompanying her form the next ring; beyond them is the ring representing heaven and, floating above that, Christ Himself.

Endless studies went into drawing all these figures convincingly, so that we would seem to see them from below and yet not only see them from below. It is likely

The other example shows the interior of a Venetian villa, one of the several built at that time for the leading families of Venice. These houses, half country residences, half farms, were built *all' antica:* the architect, Palladio had made a thorough study of Roman remains and ancient writings on architecture and had developed from

VERONESE
Interior of the
main hall, Villa
Maser (showing
painted ceiling
plus upper part of
walls)

that Correggio made a lot of little clay or plaster figures and hung them up to study them from different angles and to study the effect of draperies. And then he had to organize them into effective groups, and arrange the groups so that they would be legible from the floor of the church, giving prominence to the figure of the Virgin (she is on that part of the dome that faces us as we look up from the nave). The whole effect is exciting and uplifting. I am tempted to say it is musical: it makes me think of the voices of a choir singing the polyphonic music (with melodic lines weaving through each other) that is one of the glories of the sixteenth century.

these a classical style, serenely beautiful and very adaptable, that was to have wide influence in Europe and, later, in America. Veronese's entertaining decorations in the Villa Maser seem to some people today to be at odds with the calm dignity of Palladio's architecture, but it is a mistake to think of the classical style as cold and straightlaced: that again is a misunderstanding that belongs to the nineteenth century when people tended to reserve the classical style for parliament buildings, gentlemen's clubs and banks.

Portrait Painting in the 16th Century

HANS HOLBEIN (the Younger) born in Augsburg in 1497 or 1498; died in London in 1543

EL GRECO born on the island of Crete in 1541; died in Toledo (Spain) in 1614

LEONARDO DA VINCI see pages 58-59

RAPHAEL see pages 62-63

LEONARDO DA VINCI
Mona Lisa c. 1503–10 (left)
oil on panel
77 x 53 cm
(30¼ x 21 in)
Louvre, Paris

RAPHAEL
Baldassare Castiglione
1519 (above)
oil on canvas
82 x 67 cm (32 x 26 in)
Louvre, Paris

Portrait painting becomes a major art form in the sixteenth century. The Romans gave much importance to making lifelike images of people – not necessarily only the most important leaders of the Roman Empire – and did so primarily in the form of statues and of portrait busts. Portraiture rapidly declined after the first century: portraits were still needed from time to time, not least on coins and seals, but a summary indication of a head might well be thought enough if accompanied by the individual's name. With the coming of the Renaissance (and also in late Gothic manuscripts and sculpture) true portraiture was reborn, and with the High Renaissance it becomes an art fit to stand beside the great narrative paintings which the Renaissance called History (i.e. story) paintings.

The inventor of a formula that would enable the artist to provide both a likeness and an art object equalling in dignity and significance the best busts of the Romans appears to have been Leonardo and the first complete example his *Mona Lisa*. Leonardo painted this portrait in Milan over a period of some years during 1503-10, perhaps adding the landscape some time after he had painted the half-figure. Like the Roman sculptor he has persuaded us to accept part of the figure as representative of the whole (the convention is so familiar to us that we don't question it). He has turned the figure slightly so that the face is almost frontal while the lady's shoulders are placed diagonally in space; the way her arms come together underlines this spatial arrangement and gives a secure visual base to the pyramid of the figure.

HOLBEIN
Georg Gisze of Danzig 1532
(above)
oil and tempera on canvas
96 x 85.7 cm
(37½ x 33¾ in)
Staatliche Museen, Berlin

EL GRECO
Fray Paravicino c. 1610
(below)
oil on canvas
113 x 86 cm (44½ x 34 in)
Museum of Fine Arts,
Boston

The face is modelled with incomparable subtlety. Colour variation is slight, suggesting soft indoor light rather than sunshine. The landscape, misty and unfamiliar, is not to be thought of as a realistic background to the sitting lady: Leonardo was fascinated by the forces of nature, and he must have felt that this scenery added an apt poetic image to his portrait of this particular person.

The *Mona Lisa*'s combination of acute portraiture (this person, at this moment) and a powerful work of art (not a snapshot but a lasting image) was new and drew attention. Raphael soon emulated it with a man's portrait using much the same formula: his *Baldassare Castiglione* is without the mystery of the Leonardo. It offers a plain background instead of a landscape with the result that our attention goes to the man's silhouette and to the light that makes the background glow and bathes the figure in a variety of warm tones. We feel we can know Castiglione from this picture: a humorous and wise man. He was in fact the author of a much-admired book on good behaviour in society, *The Book of the Courtier*, as well as a classical scholar.

Holbein's portrait of *Georg Gisze of Danzig* is of the same type, but he also provides a whole range of secondary information about him. In his hand Gisze holds a letter addressed to himself by his brother; there are more letters to the right, and a piece of paper on the wall telling us who he is and that the date is 1532. Other things show his profession: he is a merchant. The carnations indicate that he is engaged to be married. The Northern love of keenly observed and represented detail is here joined to Southern fullness of form. Character, age, occupation, marital status: the man is there, complete with credentials.

The portrait of the monk *Fray Hortensio Felix Paravicino* has a vivacity that may be the sitter's but comes to us largely through the way it is painted. El Greco learned to paint like this in Venice, under the influence of Titian. In the 1570s he moved on to Spain where he remained until his death, active primarily as a painter of religious pictures. The formula he has used here, of a seated figure cut off not at the waist but below the knees, comes from Raphael, but El Greco has adopted the Northern habit of showing sitters occupied with something other than posing for the portraits. The friar has been studying, comparing the text of two books perhaps. The painter appears to have caught a momentary pose (is Fray Hortensio about to rise?) and also a very particular, intelligent and alert expression in the face. The background glows with light.

In the Raphael and the El Greco light seems to function as part of the personality of the sitter; in Holbein it delivers a wealth of information; Leonardo uses two quite different ways of seeing for his partly informative, partly visionary portrait. Portraits can be much more than an account of someone's appearance.

Bruegel

PIETER BRUEGEL (the Elder) born in the 1520s, probably in Breda; died in Brussels in 1569

At times people have thought of Bruegel's pictures as simple-minded art for simple-minded persons. The painter has often been referred to as 'Peasant Bruegel', indicating his status, subjects and public. This is quite wrong. From about 1550 onwards Bruegel worked in Antwerp, a thriving, rapidly growing city busy with international trade. Antwerp was also a great centre for scholars and artists and for publishing books and prints.

In 1553-4 Bruegel went on a journey south, over the Alps into Italy and as far as Rome. I wish I could tell you where he went and exactly what he saw and did. All we are certain of is that he was fascinated by the scale and forms of Alpine landscape: we have drawings he made as crossed the Alps. In 1555 he was back in Antwerp. In 1563 he moved to Brussels where he married a well-known painter's daughter. Six years later he died there.

We know also that he was a very successful painter, much admired, imitated and collected. Engravings after his work were produced in large quantity; his sons Pieter and Jan became painters too and based their own careers

on carrying on their father's work. Bruegel's paintings were collected and treasured not by peasants but by scholars, by other artists, by aristocrats and especially by the Emperor Rudolf II who had his court in Vienna – which is why Vienna has the most marvellous collection of Bruegel paintings anywhere.

In some ways Bruegel is the successor to Bosch (see page 68): his art too is concerned with human frailty and he gets many of his ideas from Bosch and from Bosch's own sources in illustrated manuscripts. They both probably owed much to sermons and to time-honoured sayings such as proverbs, turning their verbal images into visual ones. Such sayings were often collected and published in the sixteenth century as anthologies of human wisdom; the century also saw many books commenting on human foolishness in worldly and religious terms. Erasmus, the Dutch writer, and Rabelais, the French, provided famous instances.

Bruegel's drawing *The big fish eat the little fish* is in the tradition of Bosch's pictures and was done to be pub-

BRUEGEL (the Elder)
The big fish eat the little fish
1556 (below left)
pen and ink 21.6 x 30.2 cm (8¹/₂ x 12 in)
Graphische Sammlung Albertina, Vienna

BRUEGEL (the Elder)
The Tower of Babel 1563 (below)
oil on panel
114 x 115 cm (45 x 45¹/₄ in)
Kunsthistorisches Museum, Vienna

lished as an engraving. The words of the proverb are the title and focus of the little scene; Bruegel brings their meaning home to us through a variety of little actions that reinforce the main one. For example, he shows us that small creatures oppress even smaller creatures, and also that the big oppressor will meet his end too. As in Bosch, though perhaps in a more relaxed way, fantasy and naturalism go hand in hand and reinforce each other.

If you look carefully you will see that Bruegel's way of drawing varies with what he is drawing and its place in his little picture. His pen makes all sorts of different marks: dots and lines and dashes. Notation is everything; there are no marks for display's sake.

He painted three versions of *The Tower of Babel*. It was a subject well known to his contemporaries from the Bible and sermons and from others' visualizations of it in paintings, prints and book illustrations. This is his largest painting of it. In the foreground we see King Nimrod who, according to a second century AD account,

commanded the whole enterprise. Bruegel offers an amazingly complete picture of what it must have involved. A rocky site gives mankind a good start in its attempt to reach the heavens. Ships bring building materials, workmen, equipment and food. Human activity is ant-like but the architecture that results is astounding, a great engineering feat. And Bruegel shows that he knows how vast masonry arches can be built. In Rome he must have seen the ancient Colosseum, and presumably also the new St Peter's rising under the supervision of Michelangelo.

The tower spirals its way into the clouds. Behind it, the most naturalistic landscape painted by anyone until Rubens and the seventeenth century stretches to the horizon. The contrast between God's work and man's points the lesson of the picture: the Biblical lesson, of human pride coming before a terrible fall (men could no longer understand what they said to each other), and the contemporary lesson also, of the Low Countries' misery under Spanish rule.

Rubens

PETER PAUL RUBENS born at Siegen (Germany) in 1577; died in Antwerp in 1640

Peter Paul Rubens lived an amazingly busy and varied life. His family was Flemish. He grew up in Antwerp and studied painting there until, in 1600, he went to Italy and became court painter to the Duke of Mantua. In 1603 he travelled with a court mission to Philip III in Madrid. There he could steep himself in the royal collection of paintings, especially rich in Raphaels and Titians. He also explored Italy. By the time he returned to Antwerp, in 1608, he knew more of Italian painting than even the

best informed Italians, and it is characteristic of him that he incorporated everything he most admired into his own work.

He was made court painter to the Spanish Regent of the Southern Netherlands (more or less the area we call Belgium), and spent the rest of his fruitful life as courtier-painter, besieged with commissions for large and small paintings but employed also on international diplomacy. To carry out his commissions he had to build up a large and expert team of assistants. Today we idolize conductors who direct a team's performance of music invented by someone else, or film directors working with and through crowds of seen and unseen specialists. Ruben's involvement was a good deal more direct than theirs. Even the largest paintings, even those not to be seen close to (as in the case of ceiling paintings), were likely to have their most important parts painted by him.

The oil sketch he prepared for *The Apotheosis of the Duke of Buckingham* illustrates this and also the role large secular paintings played in the seventeenth century. Buckingham was a particular favourite of the English king. He had risen to high office on the strength of this personal affection and proved to be incompetent and untrustworthy. Rubens was asked to supply a large portrait of him on horseback and also a ceiling painting for the hall of his London house. 'Apotheosis' means being granted god-like status. We see the warrior-Duke, general of the king's fleet and army, lifted by wisdom (the helmeted Minerva) and eloquence (Mercury) towards the Temple of Virtue. Envy clutches at his foot but three voluptuous ladies, the Three Graces, smile on his ascent and promise him eternal fame.

processed naturalism that we tend to accept as innocent truth. Rubens's references are to the symbolic figures used by classical antiquity and his idiom is that of Christian religious art: the sketch carries obvious echoes of the Virgin Mary being carried up into heaven. Rubens certainly knew the work of Correggio (page 74) and added to it something of the energy of a Michelangelo and the colour of a Titian.

Contemporaries could read and understand these references. At a time when it was generally agreed that kings were divinely appointed and protected, favourites could well be shown participating in this supernatural status. Buckingham's eminence made it reasonable to show him as a kind of saint and hero. His friends and enemies would have been surprised, though, at the verve and vividness of Rubens's representation. Imagine it covering the ceiling of a large, high room, and with much the same brightness and life that Rubens put into the sketch. There is an emphasis on movement here that goes beyond even Michelangelo and Correggio, and with it comes a sense of lightness both of rising forms and of their moving into a world of light and joy.

The seventeenth century was very interested in light,

RUBENS
The Apotheosis of the Duke of Buckingham c. 1625 (left)
oil on panel
64 x 64 cm (25 x 25 in)
National Gallery, London

RUBENS
Studies of the head of a black man c. 1614 (right)
oil on canvas
47 x 61 cm (18½ x 24 in)
Royal Museum of Fine Arts, Brussels

This sounds a bit much to modern ears, yet it is only the seventeenth century's equivalent to what tycoons and politicians now call 'image-making' and employ public-relations experts on. A modern Buckingham would perhaps have himself photographed shaking the hands of astronauts or commanding a tank; the references used would imply that he was at home in the world of attack and defence. The idiom used would be that of photographic realism – a piece of carefully selected and

in science as well as in art. Rubens was the master of light used as celebration, as a sort of visual fanfare. He could be darkly dramatic on occasion but many of his paintings convey happiness and affection. This shows especially clearly in his simpler works, in paintings of his family for instance, and in a number of unspectacular studies such as the one reproduced here. It is extraordinary how painting – a process of stroking, after all – can convey touching and love.

17th Century Dutch Painting

JAN VAN DER HEYDEN born in 1637; died in 1712

PHILIPS DE KONINCK born in 1619; died in 1688

JAN VERMEER born in Delft in 1632; died in 1675

VAN DER HEYDEN
View of the Dam at Amsterdam 1660s
oil on panel 68 x 55 cm (26¾ x 21¾ in)
Historisch Museum, Amsterdam

The start of the seventeenth century saw the birth of a new nation and a new kind of country. The people of the Northern provinces of the Low Countries rebelled against their Spanish overlords. It took decades of bitter struggle but by the turn of the century their success seemed certain, and they confirmed it by repelling later Spanish attempts to re-establish their hold on the area.

The new state combined world-wide trade with agriculture and soon became one of the richest parts of Europe under the economic leadership of its most mercantile province: Holland. That is why to this day we tend to call the country Holland rather than the Netherlands, its proper federal name.

Free of their foreign rulers, increasingly confident in their self-rule and international standing, independent also in matters of faith through their adoption of Protestantism, the merchants of Holland created a new sort of culture. This could be described as town-centred and self-centred as well as middle class. It was largely produced for town dwellers and these were not aristocrats

and courtiers but businessmen. It served to support their self-confidence by reflecting their world as an agreeable, entertaining and above all tranquil, orderly one.

That is what their paintings tended to be about – and these paintings were suddenly produced in surprising quantity as well as quality. People commissioned portraits and occasionally narrative paintings of a historical or religious sort, but a great deal of the art produced and bought took the form of landscapes, townscapes and still lifes. These were mostly painted by specialists in each particular type and could be bought from stalls at the market like other native produce.

The ancients had used pictures of landscapes and groups of domestic objects as decorations, and they were known elsewhere too in the seventeenth century, but it was 'history painting' – narrative painting with an elevated theme and carried out in a noble, idealizing style – that was usually considered high art and a proper vehicle for the intellect and talent of a serious painter. Low subjects, such as landscapes, were given little attention in Italy, France or Spain until the nineteenth century.

Today it seems only natural that artists should use their skills to record the world about them, but that is really a misunderstanding: it means we are taking one rather extreme form of art to be the norm. There is no reason why painting should concern itself mainly with realistic accounts of the world as it is any more than writing. We may like plays and novels that show us ordinary life but we also like, and perhaps prefer, writing that draws on the imagination and is not content merely to describe things as they are.

Dutch realism actually was purposeful and very selective, bringing order and significance to the world it seems merely to mirror, and the public of the time knew that. Van der Heyden's picture of the new open square made in Amsterdam by covering part of the river Amstel, and of the new town hall set up next to the old New Church, may look like a snap-shot. In fact it is a very carefully ordered picture, with figures carefully placed to help us to read the space and also to make us feel that this is a calm, friendly world.

Light plays an important role in this townscape, as also in the other two paintings shown here. De Koninck's landscape is vast and spacious and we can almost feel the air moving across it. He has taken a high viewpoint, perhaps the top of a church tower, to be able to show this panorama, but notice how he organized it in patches of light and shadow and also of warm and cool colours, to help us find our way across it.

Vermeer probably used a device called a *camera obscura* to be as accurate as possible in his painting. It was something like a large, basic box camera which could throw a flat image of the scene it was pointed at on a ground glass screen. Thus the image is objective; not adjusted to our expectations or preferences and devoid of the clear outlines our knowing minds are liable to give to things.

The result is calm and beautiful, but only because the painter set up a calm and beautiful scene. Moreover it means something. Think: a woman reading a letter, a large map on the wall. Her form, lit with especial care, suggests that she may be pregnant. Is her man away, a merchant on his travels? Vermeer does not insist on a specific reading. Before we start interpreting the clues we are made aware of a kind of living stillness, of harmony, of contentment.

KONINCK
Extensive landscape with hawking party
1670s
(above left)
oil on canvas
132.5 x 160 cm
(52¹/₂ x 63 in)
National Gallery,
London

VERMEER
Interior with lady reading a letter 1660s
(left)
oil on canvas
46.5 x 39 cm
(18¹/₄ x 15³/₄ in)
Rijksmuseum,
Amsterdam

Rembrandt

REMBRANDT VAN RIJN born in Leiden in 1606; died in Amsterdam in 1669

What makes Rembrandt so special? More than any other artist in the history of art he matters to us all. It is easy to see why, though words can hardly capture the whole of it: whatever he touches, he brings out the ordinary human value of it. He seems to care for us all and this irradiates his pictures like a sort of invisible, spiritual light complementing the rich and sometimes dramatic light he uses in his paintings.

But how does he give us this feeling, and give it so generously, when other painters, even those imitating

him, give us little or no hint of it? There can be no final answer to this, any more than we can say exactly why, in eating, one taste delights us and another doesn't. Or why one person makes us feel warm and fully alive the moment we meet him or her whereas another does not. We can, though, look at his work carefully and look for some of the ways in which he engages our feelings.

His etching, The *Return of the Prodigal Son,* uses a theme full of human meaning as well as Biblical significance. Rembrandt's handling of it brings this out. After a long absence, the young man returns home, weary, almost naked. His old father comes down the stairs to greet him, past worries and anger melting from him as he approaches his son. Others stand by, curious but detached. The space on the left helps us think of absence and returning; the closed right half suggests home and security. This open-and-closedness is echoed

in the heads and arms of father and son, just above the centre of the print. The steps add drama and a diagonal thrust to our reading, which anyway tends to be from left to right. Try to imagine the picture without the young man's staff. What difference would that make?

When he did this print, in 1636, Rembrandt was living in Amsterdam and enjoying considerable success, especially as a portrait painter. He was well off, buying works of art and collecting all sorts of beautiful and exotic things, from Indian robes to musical instruments.

REMBRANDT
Return of the Prodigal Son 1636 (left)
etching
15.6 x 13.6 cm (6 x 5¹/₄ in)
British Museum, London

REMBRANDT
The meeting of Jacob and Laban c. 1652–5 (below)
pen and wash
17 x 21.5 cm (6¹/₂ x 8¹/₂ in)
Kobberstiksamling, Copenhagen

In 1639 he bought a large house for himself, his wife and his children (in fact, only one of them, Titus, survived infancy).

By the time Rembrandt painted his large *Return of the Prodigal Son* he was old, bankrupt and something of an outcast from society. His house and possessions had been auctioned off. His wife had died long ago; Hendrickje, his beloved companion since then, had died in 1663. Titus had remained to look after him and had recently got married: old Rembrandt must have been pleased at the prospect of children and renewed domestic bustle. Then Titus, aged only 27, died too. Perhaps this painting is a kind of farewell.

Try visualizing a kneeling figure embraced by a standing one; you will probably imagine a group in profile, like that in the print. Seen that way, it is clear how the two bodies relate to each other. To show them as

84

REMBRANDT
Return of the Prodigal Son
1669
oil on canvas
264 x 205 cm (104 x 80¾ in)
Hermitage Museum,
Leningrad

Rembrandt does in the painting is both more difficult and less informative, but it has tremendous emotional value. We see the father full-face. Rembrandt has made that head the best lit part of the picture. The old man's eyes are closed; there is pain as well as joy. His position gives the group something close to symmetry, and this is emphasized by the red cloak falling over his shoulders, which also serves as a womb enclosing the young man's delicate head.

It is a large painting; the figures are life-size. Placing father and son slightly to the left and very much in the foreground gives them great immediacy. The other figures may have been merely roughed in by Rembrandt and completed by his pupils after he died; in any case, they are mute bystanders, turning our attention back on to father and son.

This is a painting in the Venetian tradition of rich colour and lighting and of the paint itself and the brush strokes conveying much of the effect: compare it with Titian's late painting on page 73. But there is Michelangelo in it too, a spiritual weight that Titian does not achieve or perhaps want. The greatness of Rembrandt's art is rooted partly in the depth of his knowledge of art – he never left Holland but could there see a great variety of paintings. Human instincts alone do not make a great artist.

The drawing shows another meeting, of uncle and nephew this time and in a landscape. It is a new kind of drawing, pioneered by Rembrandt and one or two other artists of his time. It suggests forms, light, space and movements rather than delineating them directly, and thus it triggers our imaginative collaboration. This too, perhaps, involves us emotionally where a more completely rendered scene might keep us at some distance.

Velázquez

DIEGO VELÁZQUEZ born in Seville in 1599; died in Madrid in 1660

VELÁZQUEZ
The Surrender of Breda
1634
oil on canvas
307 x 367 cm
(121 x 144¹/₂ in)
Prado, Madrid

Rubens visited the Spanish court twice, in 1603 and in 1628-9. He thought nothing of Spanish painting the first time. During his second visit he came to know and admire the young court painter whose studio he shared during his months in Madrid: Diego de Velázquez.

It is an interesting moment in the story of art. Rubens, the Northerner, has come to Madrid as the emissary of his own country and also as a leading figure in international art. In Madrid he gets to know a young painter whom he recognizes as an artist of outstanding promise and whom he befriends and advises. As a result of this advice, Velázquez applied to his king for permission to go to Italy for a while, to study thoroughly the art that even the king's collection could afford him only glimpses of. Off he went, in August 1629, shortly after Rubens's departure. He returned in 1631 having spent most of his time in Venice and Rome and having steeped himself in ancient sculpture, the work of Raphael, of Michelangelo and of more recent Italians, and also, it seems, in the new Dutch painting, examples of which could be seen in Roman collections.

Again, this suggests something of the breadth of interests and appetite that seems to be typical of the century. It is certainly typical of Velázquez himself. Much of his work until this time had been markedly realistic, close to Dutch realism in spirit but rooted in Spanish artistic habits. His eighteen months in Italy added colour and grandeur to his art, and especially a feeling for pictorial drama through composition and lighting.

In 1634 he painted a large canvas for the king. Its subject was a piece of recent history, an episode in the renewed war between Spain and her former subjects, the Dutch. It was to go into a large hall in a royal palace on the outskirts of Madrid, in a series of similar paintings and decorations proving the power of the Spanish crown and the unity of Spain.

The Surrender of Breda commemorates a Spanish victory of 1625. Justin of Nassau, commander of the Dutch troops, hands the key of his city to General Spinola of Spain. We see signs of war in the smoke rising from part of the long-beleaguered city in the background. In the foreground we see victory and defeat welded into one surprisingly gentle action. The victor has dismounted and accepts the offered key more like a visitor than a triumphant foe. On the left stand the Dutch soldiers in their relatively plain clothes. On the right are the Spanish troops, held back by the prominent horse and altogether not especially glorious. Their lances may suggest military power but they are at rest. Velázquez originally painted Spanish banners and flags in their place; I presume these struck him as too ostentatious and so he painted them out and put the lances in instead. The two figures meeting in the middle seem almost like a handshake between the two armies. The whole scene is flooded with calm light.

This picture has sometimes been described as proving Velázquez's kindliness and even sympathy for the Dutch. No doubt he was a kind man: his paintings speak of the dignity of all men and women, children, servants, dwarfs as much as kings and kings as much as dwarfs. But it is wrong to imagine a seventeenth century painter, faced with a commission such as this, following his own inclinations the way a modern painter might. The commission was undoubtedly preceded by discussions and accompanied by instructions.

The Spanish playwright Calderon had commemorated the same event by writing and staging *The Siege of Breda* very soon after it happened. The climax of that play was the moment when Spinola, receiving the key, says 'The valour of the conquered makes the conqueror famous'. Velázquez certainly had this compliment in mind in planning his picture; it is likely that he was told to incorporate it. It has also been suggested that he derived

Detail of
The Surrender of Breda

his group of the two generals from a Flemish sixteenth century print showing the priest Melchisedek bringing bread and wine to Abraham after his victory at Dan, as recounted in the Bible *(Genesis* 14): 'And blessed be the most high God, which hath delivered thine enemies into thy hand', says Melchisedek. Such a reference, with its implications of divine support and human gratitude, would be characteristic of Renaissance and seventeenth century art.

Velázquez's greatness lies not in 'expressing himself', as people today tend to say about artists, but in his skill in bringing together a variety of themes and reference into one convincing as well as beautiful whole. Knowledge as well as special gifts as painter and a subtle, human attitude to the subject come together here. It may well have been his own idea to contrast the simpler clothes and weapons of the Dutch with the splendid, more professional look of the Spanish forces. His brushwork gives sparkle and life to the whole of this unusually large painting.

Poussin

NICOLAS POUSSIN born in 1593 or 1594 near Les Andelys (Normandy); died in Rome in 1665

POUSSIN
The Ashes of Phocion 1648
oil on canvas
114 x 175 cm (46 x 70 in)
Knowsley Hall, Lancashire

When Bernini was in Paris he was shown a collection of Poussin's paintings and was greatly impressed. He called Poussin a great history (i.e. story) painter; 'Monsieur Poussin,' he added significantly, pointing to his brow, 'is a painter who works up here.'

Poussin actually spent most of his life in Rome, but at some distance from the papal court. He was drawn there mainly by his love of classical antiquity. It is said he taught himself Latin in order to read the old texts. Of peasant origins, he turned himself into a man with a very thorough knowledge of the art and theories of the ancients. His chief patron in Rome encouraged him in this by giving him access to a well-stocked library and to a collection of modern drawings of ancient sculptures. But Poussin was also at home in the art of modern Italy, and particularly striking is his love of Venetian painting. I stressed earlier that the Venetians' way of bringing the

myths of the ancients to life was by giving them modern immediacy. Poussin, much more thoroughly steeped in knowledge of the ancients, tried to do something similar by other means.

In *The Ashes of Phocion* we see him striking a new balance between past and present, between a noble theme from history and the world about him. The subject is certainly classical, and rather learned at that. It comes from Plutarch's *Lives* of important and especially honourable individuals: the Greek statesman, Phocion, has been condemned to death unjustly, for refusing to abandon his high principles. His body has been burned outside the city, like a criminal's. We see his wife gathering up his ashes to give them decent burial. It is a story of virtue and fidelity in the face of human fickleness.

Does Poussin play it down? The action of the picture, Phocion's wife bending to her sad task, does not dominate it. More prominent is the temple (copied from a Roman example known to Poussin), the hill behind it and the other buildings near it. They are quiet and solemn. The temple is the only obviously ancient building there but all of them together suggest a past time and a

brooding stillness. Poussin leads us quite deliberately into the space in front of these buildings, past the wife of Phocion and her companion and through the gap in the wall. That middle space is lit with a soft, afternoon light and there are people in it as in a park, doing nothing very particular – a scene of ease and peace, based on the countryside close to Rome. Had Phocion been less honourable, he and his family could still have been part of that world. His wife is spotlit almost harshly amid the shadows cast by the trees. We feel her separateness and the nearly dreamlike enclosedness of the middle ground almost before we start to read and to understand what is shown.

More than that: the whole picture conveys a sense of melancholy, of beauty combined with sadness, of something lost but remembered. We feel this in a general way and it pervades the whole picture. A picture in a minor key? The sensation is like listening to music, and the fact is that Poussin had studied the ancient system of modes, known to Renaissance composers but in Poussin's time being replaced by the system of major and minor keys used by what we call classical music. The modes had distinct emotional qualities and were associated with distinct kinds of and occasions for music: one mode for tragic or very solemn occasions, another for light and entertaining ones, and so on. Poussin consciously gave different subjects a different emotional quality through his use of space, lighting, quantity of movement and colour, and so on.

I have spoken of painters 'staging' their stories and the analogy with a stage production seems particularly apt here. In fact, we know that Poussin built himself a little stage and made clay figures, based on what he knew of ancient sculpture, and arranged and lit them on this toy stage before making compositional drawings from them. Thus he chose a story that seemed to him a particularly telling one and that mattered to him particularly; then he considered long and hard, in his imagination and by means of his stage, how to present it aptly and persuasively so as to make us feel what he felt, and then used his skill as a painter to put it nobly and lastingly on to a canvas.

Head and heart work together. To put it another way: Poussin was so emotional a man and artist that he brought all possible care, all the learning he could muster as well as the artistic judgement, to setting before us an old story with timeless significance.

Claude

CLAUDE LORRAINE born in 1600 at Chamagne near Nancy (France); died in Rome in 1682

CLAUDE
*Landscape with the Nymph
of Egeria* 1669
oil on canvas
155 x 199 cm (61 x 78½ in)
Galeria Nazionale di
Capodimonte, Naples

Claude's family name was Gellée. He has long been known as Claude Lorraine because he came from the Duchy of Lorraine, at that time not part of France. He went to Rome as a young man and studied painting there, but he did not settle in Rome until about 1627.

He and Poussin became good friends. Contemporaries tell us of their going together to sketch in the Roman Campagna, the countryside south of the city; also of their being neighbours in Rome. Partly because of this they are often spoken of together, as though they were allies in art. But how alike was their work?

The first difference is that Claude specialized in landscape painting whereas many of Poussin's paintings have little or nothing to do with landscape. Neither of them ever painted a landscape that did not incorporate a story: they were enlarging the reach and the poetic capacity of history painting, not championing an alternative art form of landscape description as the Dutch did.

The second – and this is an all-embracing one – is that they were very different sorts of people. Their works make this very clear.

We saw with what care Poussin created a landscape, fusing his knowledge of nature with his experience as a builder of coherent pictures, in order to convey the narrative facts and the implications of his solemn theme (page 88). The painting that represents Claude here is sad in theme and mood also. Its story comes from Ovid, the Latin poet who retold the ancient myths in his *Metamorphoses*. Egeria, nymph and wife of King Numa of Rome, has left the city upon the death of her husband to mourn in solitude. Her incessant laments disturb the life of the country dwellers and they try to stem her tears by means of reasoning with her and distracting her from her grief, but to no avail. In the end the goddess Diana, worshipped in those parts, turns Egeria into a cool spring of everlasting waters.

The story is without the sternness of Poussin's. It is bitter-sweet, rather, and Claude does not attempt to make it seem more serious than it is. He is an old man by the time he paints this picture, full of skill and experience and using his poetic gifts ever more freely.

Where Poussin gave us a closed-in space, Claude lets his landscape run to the far-off horizon. He does not paint a continuous and legible terrain through which we can easily pass, yet we sense one unified space. His use of the trees in the left half of the painting and of buildings and hills helps to create this unity, and we know that he has rearranged a particular piece of landscape to make it fit his needs. Also, like Poussin, he has used carefully placed and scaled figures to take us back into the space and help us to feel at home in it.

But what really makes the picture one is the light. From the solid trees silhouetted against the sky, we move back via ever softer forms until light and forms become one on the horizon. Leonardo had shown, long ago, that the atmosphere interferes with the colour and the clarity of distant forms. Claude was the first to make this effect of light plus space into a major element, into the theme almost, of his art.

The patron for whom this picture was painted, Prince Colonna, owned properties in this area of the Campagna. The old round tower, for instance, had been his family's for centuries. The column on the right may be a punning reference to the name Colonna. The buildings emphasize the antiquity of the story and of its setting. The ruins, moreover, tell us that we are looking at the past. They introduce into the painting a flavour of nostalgia that is new to art: not only King Numa is dead, the golden age of which Ovid wrote is dead too.

Hints of this had appeared in Claude's paintings before, and had perhaps helped to make him the successful painter he was, but no painting presents it more openly than this one. Poussin used the past to press upon us grave moral meanings. Claude moves us to melancholy thoughts whilst seducing us with his gentle, often silvery tones. We are witnessing not only the first clear expression of a new spirit in art but also of a new function for art. We shall meet it again in a hundred years time or so, when Claude's paintings, well liked in his own time, are passionately sought after by collectors, especially in England.

Detail of
Landscape with the Nymph of Egeria

Bernini

GIOVANNI LORENZO BERNINI born in Naples in 1598; died in Rome in 1680

Bernini was primarily a sculptor. For six decades he was the dominant artist in Rome, working for a succession of popes not only on a variety of sculpted portraits and monuments but also on major pieces of architecture.

Most famous of these is the great piazza in front of St Peter's, with its sweeping colonnades. It is an effective piece of functional planning: an arena in which the people come together to hear and see the pope; at the same time a noble frame for St Peter's itself, and the most resplendent piece of classical architecture since the days of ancient Rome.

We are no longer used to seeing sculpture playing such a prominent role as it did in Bernini's day. This was partly an echo of ancient practice, though of course in medieval times too sculpture played a more important role than painting. It may be that Renaissance painting, becoming so effective in suggesting three-dimensional forms in space, and also deriving some of its best images from ancient sculpture, stole some of sculpture's reasons for eminence. Painting is cheaper and quicker. But in the seventeenth century, at a time when the popes were especially eager to display the power of the Church, sculpture for a time assumed the dominant role. We may wonder whether it could have happened without such a great artist as Bernini at hand.

His father was a sculptor too but his greatest achievement was undoubtedly the training he gave his son. By the age of 16 young Bernini was receiving commissions from relatives of the pope. In his early twenties he became president of the Roman art academy. Eight popes employed and honoured him and the kings of England and France were proud to have him carve their busts. The latter even persuaded him to come to France, travelling like a prince, in order to advise on the rebuilding of the royal palace in Paris. His team of assistants, paid for out of papal funds, was large and included all the best younger sculptors of the time.

His *David* may remind you of Michelangelo – especially of Michelangelo the painter. This sculpture has all the vehemence that Michelangelo had given to some of the figures on the Sistine ceiling and also to his Christ in the *Last Judgement* (page 64). To achieve this in carving required enormous technical boldness and skill. The whole figure, every part of it, is shown in a moment of extreme physical and psychological tension, just before unleashing the deadly stone at Goliath in an

BERNINI
David slaying Goliath 1623
marble
lifesize
Galeria Borghese, Rome

BERNINI
Costanza Buonarelli (bust)
c. 1635
marble
lifesize
Museo Nazionale, Florence

explosion of heroic vigour. David had usually been shown after the act, with the head of the giant at his feet. Here we see the most dramatic moment, and we can almost sense Goliath standing some way behind us as David looks past us at the approaching enemy.

How could Bernini study that pose? Today one could take photographs of athletes in action or get information from film records, selecting the moment of greatness from a succession of frames. Bernini must have got his model to go through the action again and again – it is not a pose one can hold – and caught its main features by means of quick sketches. His knowledge of human anatomy was already remarkable. He also made a special study of the face, and its expression of concentration, resolution and fear. David's features are like his own as we know them from drawn and painted self-portraits. Bernini may well have spent time before a mirror, identifying with the Biblical hero and willing his face into the right intensity in order to study it, draw it and turn it into marble.

But his sculpture is not merely naturalistic. David owes as much to the classical tradition as to observation, to the same ancient examples as guided Michelangelo. If we find it difficult to draw the line between this tradition and natural appearances it is because the Greeks had studied nature deeply in developing their artistic forms from it. It is rare, though, that artistic inheritance and the urge to be realistic are brought together so effectively. Rubens and Bernini are similar in this combining of the living world with the world of art they had studied.

Like Rubens, Bernini too distinguished between public and private art and he could be as informal and intimate in his private works as he could be grandiose in works addressed to the world at large. The portrait bust he carved of a young woman he loved, for instance, is a magnificent piece of realism. We forget it is without colour, not to mention life.

Art in the Service of the Church

GIOVANNI BATTISTA GAULLI born in 1639; died in Rome in 1709

GIOVANNI LORENZO BERNINI See pages 92-93

BERNINI
The Chair of St Peter 1657–66
marble, bronze, stucco, glass
about 20 m (65 ft) high
St Peter's ('East' end),
Vatican, Rome

Bernini's sculpture greatly enriched the inside of St Peter's. Statues of saints, and monumental tombs of popes, some of them rich in colour (when he used a variety of materials) as well as in form, invite our attention as well as draw from us an emotional response. Over the high altar, which stands above the tomb of St Peter, Bernini erected a tremendous canopy or *baldacchino* of bronze with gilding. And beyond that, at the far end of the church, we see a very complex work that rises the full height of the interior and is known as *The Chair of St Peter*.

The throne that we can see has inside it a wooden chair believed to have been used by the saint. Its display symbolizes the unbroken succession of the popes of Rome from the apostle charged by Christ with leading the Christian community. On the back of the throne is shown Christ's command to St Peter, 'Feed my sheep'. Just above the throne we see the keys Christ handed to him and the papal tiara supported by *putti*. The throne itself is supported or steadied by four Fathers of the Church, early saints whose writings provided the bases of Catholic dogma. The main support of the throne, and by implication of the Church, is supernatural: the cloud beneath the throne is part of a vision of divine power and glory, represented by the clouds and crowds of angels that seem to spring from the dove of the Holy Ghost, shown in the stained glass.

Thus the whole work amounts to a demonstration of faith and confidence, a confirming statement at a time when Catholicism was battling against the spread of Protestantism in Northern Europe. It brings together heaven and earth, the divine and the historical. Physically it uses a variety of elements and materials: the wooden relic inside the bronze throne, the bronze putti and Fathers – all fully three-dimensional – and then the painted stucco clouds and angels, the stained glass, and of course actual light, apparently coming from the dove and glinting along rays of gilded plaster. We must imagine it at its vast scale and in its architectural setting, also as we would see it through the *baldacchino* and past the service given at the high altar to which *The Chair of St Peter* provides a backdrop, and accompanied by the music of the period.

The church of Jesus in Rome, the Gesù, is the main church of the Jesuit Order which was at the forefront of the Catholic campaign to overcome militant Protestantism. Wherever the Jesuits were able to establish themselves they built churches which echoed the form and character of the mother church in Rome, especially in the seventeenth and early eighteenth centuries. (The Brompton Oratory in London, built in the 1870s, is a particularly late example and a very complete one.) Like the Protestants, the Jesuits placed great value upon preaching as a means of spreading and strengthening faith. They trained themselves to be public speakers, and the form and decoration of their churches were developed as part of a programme of persuasion.

On the vault of the Gesù is a work in fresco painting and plaster sculpture that in several ways echoes Bernini's *Chair*. As we stand in the church, looking up, it is difficult for us to tell the painting from the sculpture and both from the architectural setting; they combine to

The *baldacchino* by Bernini, built 1624–33, towers over the high altar, above the tomb of St Peter. It is one of the masterpieces of baroque art.

GAULLI
The Triumph of the Name of Jesus 1674–79
(left)
fresco
Church of the Gesù, Rome

make one impact and to deliver one message: *The Triumph of the Name of Jesus*. This victory implies also the forthcoming victory of the Church and of the Jesuits over the heretics, but the mood of the work is more one of celebration than a call to arms.

The sculpture is by Raggi, Bernini's best pupil and assistant. The painting is by Gaulli, a friend of Bernini's and a particular admirer of Correggio and of Rubens. Again, we must see this decoration as part of a whole – the church itself with its other decorative paintings and sculptures, the music and also, here especially, the spoken word. The building and decorating of the Gesù

coincides very closely with the birth of opera – or rebirth, as it was thought to be, of the ancient drama of the Greeks. As in the Rubens, we see religious and secular celebration using the same idioms and resources. It is only in very recent times that people have come to think it necessary to oppose the two and to demand different styles for them, but by then styles themselves had become rather prim and artificial things, to be put on and taken off like Sunday-best clothes. The seventeenth century was troubled by religious wars and political revolution but it was not short of faith. That faith gave warmth to artistic display.

Art in the Service of the Court

CHARLES LE BRUN born in 1619; died in 1690   CHARLES JOSEPH NATOIRE born in 1700; died in 1770

ANTOINE COYSEVOX born in 1640; died in 1720

Two outstanding decorative schemes are illustrated here, both secular and both French. One was done for that king of kings, Louis XIV, as part of the lavish enlarging and remodelling of the palace of Versailles and belongs to the end of the seventeenth century. The other was executed in the 1730s as part of improvements made at the Hôtel de Soubise in Paris for a nobleman.

The Versailles example forms part of a sequence of rooms developed in the 1680s and 1690s. The square Salon de la Guerre leads into the Galerie des Glaces at the other end of which is the Salon de la Paix. War Room, Gallery of Mirrors, Peace Room: together they form the main reception area of the palace. Here foreign rulers and their ambassadors were received and here was displayed the power and glory of the French crown. All the power and glory that architecture and art could offer were mobilized to give weight and memorability to that message.

The architecture is grandiose but simple and communicates through scale rather than complex forms.

Together the three rooms span about 120 metres (394 ft); the archway, the mirrors in the Gallery and the arched windows opposite them are about 8 metres (26 ft) high. The floor was originally of marble and patterned throughout. Upon it rises an internal composition of painted and sculpted information unequalled outside churches for its fullness and also its quality.

A lot of people were involved in carrying it out. At their head stood the painter Le Brun (1619-1690) who had studied in Rome, was an admirer of the art of Poussin and was by now head of the French Royal Academy of Fine Art as well as First Painter to the king. The all-over design and programme was his. Outstanding among the contributing specialists was the sculptor Coysevox (1640-1720) who also carved a number of monuments and fountains for the park outside. His finest piece is the oval relief we see here. It shows a victorious Louis crowned by fame as he rides over his enemies. The pale marble makes it seem a cool and restrained work; in fact it is a relief unusually rich in

Salon de la Guerre
(left)
Palais de Versailles

Salon de la Princesse
(right)
Hôtel de Soubise-Rohan
Paris

movement and space, going from the shallowest carving to fully three-dimensional carving in the horse's leg. This and other sculpture is partnered on the walls by marble panels and mirrors. The ceiling is given to sculpture and painting in collaborative celebration of the king.

The contrast this makes with the Salon de la Princesse in the Paris house can only partly be explained in terms of scale and purpose. Times and tastes have changed. Even before Louis' death in 1715 his courtiers had grown tired of the grandiose routines of court life at Versailles and had begun to move back to Paris, in search of a more personal, more informal way of life. The Salon de la Princesse is a particularly fine example of the kind of interior they favoured.

In altering the house the architect, Boffrand, had introduced the oval plan into a sequence of rooms the rest of which are rectangular. This oval space is shaped internally by arched and otherwise curved panels, mirrors, windows, paintings and decorative cartouches (small framed panels) containing groups of musical instruments or other objects in low relief. White dominates; gold is the only other colour outside the paintings. The only sculpture is the delicate mouldings, reliefs and ceiling ornament. Nothing is weighty. There are no firm architectural divisions. Notice particularly that you cannot quite tell where the curving wall stops and the gently domed ceiling starts. Everything is light, fluent.

The contrast with Versailles is marked, yet both schemes are founded on Renaissance tradition. They speak as well as enrich: there they spoke of royal might; here they speak of grace and wit. The paintings, by Natoire (1700-1770), tell the story of Cupid's love for the nymph Psyche, a light-hearted tale that also served as a compliment to the charms and character of the princess. The difference between the two interiors shows the adaptability of that tradition and its classical roots to different demands. The architecture of the two buildings, scale apart, is more or less identical: simple but elegant through its good proportions and workmanship.

Chinese Art

The art of China goes back in time to the earliest days of Egyptian art and architecture, and continues in an unbroken succession to this day. Cultural influences and political upheavals have pushed it this way and that, but the artistic stream has flowed on without the major breaks that divide up the history of western art.

Our awareness of this art goes back to the earliest days of trade with the East. It was in the late thirteenth century that the Venetian merchant, Marco Polo, travelled to China and to other parts of the Far East and then sat in a Genoese jail dictating the story of what he saw. By that time China had already developed the skills and the chief categories of her production, not least pottery and porcelain ware of such variety and delicacy that it imprinted its excellence on our language: to this day we speak of 'china'. An awareness of Chinese painting did not come till much later, in the eighteenth century. To the Chinese, painting was *the* art form, associated with the highest flights of poetry and valued as a private possession of particular spiritual value as well as taste. Everything else, even the finest porcelain cup, was classed as craft production.

The bronze vessel illustrated here represents the earliest stages of Chinese civilization. It is a very fine piece of bronze casting. The mould for it was made out of pieces of fired clay, carved to yield the forms and patterns we can see. The culture for which it was made reminds one of ancient Egypt and ancient Mexico: the king was a god-on-earth, a total dictator in spiritual as in worldly matters. Vessels such as this one were made for rituals, and also to be buried with the important dead. It is a *yu* (awkwardly translated as 'bucket'), made to contain wine. Its form is that of a monster and a man; on the monster's back is a small deer, serving as a handle by which to lift the lid. The surface of the vessel is covered with dragons and other beasts in low relief, more or less geometrical in design; any space left between them is patterned with little 'thunder spirals'.

It may strike you as a fearsome piece, comparable to the grim productions of the Aztecs and of Romanesque France. But you could well be wrong. Look carefully and

CH'IU YING
The Emperor Kuang-Wu fording a river
(detail of scroll: riders and landscape) 2nd quarter 16th century
colours and ink on silk
111 x 65.5 cm (43½ x 26 in)
National Gallery of Canada, Ottawa, Ontario

you will see that the man is clinging to the monster, not being devoured by it. Perhaps it is his protector, and its grisly expression only meant for those who might think of doing him harm. To this day Chinese festivals require a parade led by a very fierce-looking but thoroughly benign dragon.

Chinese painting is one with Chinese writing or calligraphy. The masters of each are often the same people, scholars, poets, philosophers, never craftsmen. We would call them amateurs. Anyone who becomes adept in the art of Chinese writing is also a potential painter. But more important than the matter of skill is the attitude these masters showed to their work. It is best expressed in their own words:

Calligraphy is letting go. A person wishing to write must first release what is in his heart . . . If he sits first in silence with quiet thoughts, he will be able to catch ideas as they come. Words then do not come from his mouth; his mind then does not think. Profound and mysterious, spiritual and beautiful; nothing could be more perfect. (2nd century)

I am most afraid of producing a painting that will be too competent . . . Less is more, which is the advanced stage of the painter . . . To be clever is not as good as being simple. Too skilfull a rendering can be read at a glance. Simplicity incorporates dark mystery. (17th century)

Our illustration shows a part of a narrative scroll painted in the sixteenth century – at a time when, some experts would say, Chinese painting was already past its best. Maybe so, yet this is exquisite on the levels both of execution and imagination.

It is a vertical scroll, painted on silk and mounted on a backing of silk and paper so that it can be hung on a wall or rolled up and stored. Other Chinese paintings are in the form of long rolls to be unrolled and read, usually from right to left, section by section, and never displayed as a whole composition. In either case, the Chinese used their paintings the way we use our records and tapes, selectively according to mood, not for permanent decoration. The master paints – as he writes – squatting on the floor. The colour of the silk itself stands for water, mist, sand and sky; he adds white, blues and greens and here and there other tints to pick out rocks and foliage and the figures and horses going through his invented landscape. It all seems real and vivid yet it is far from naturalistic. There is no modelling on the figures or horses; space is hinted at by intervals rather like silences

in music, not described or measured. Little calligraphic strokes make the forms of rocks and trees and other details. Emptiness in one part is countered by busy-ness in another.

A sixteenth-century Chinese wrote of the work of a good painter that 'a whole day spent by a window studying even a small span of his landscape painting will by no means reveal all its significance and its savour'. I am not certain whether he wants the window for the good light or the view; it would be marvellous to be able to compare this painting with the actual landscape within which it was imagined and set down.

Chinese calligraphy (right):
signature of the artist
Chia Ching, a contemporary
of Ch'iu Ying
1522–1566

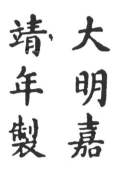
大明嘉
靖年製

Sacred vessel (yu),
Shang dynasty
c. 1500–1027 BC
cast bronze
35 cm (13½ in) high
Musée Cernuschi, Paris

Japanese Art

Portuguese arriving in Japan
(screen) early Edo period
17th century Musée Guimet, Paris

The Japanese received their culture from the Chinese much as the Romans got theirs from the Greeks. Unlike the Romans, though, the Japanese were an island people. For long periods they kept themselves apart from the rest of the world, repelling would-be invaders and keeping tight controls even on useful contacts with the outside world such as through trade and learning.

Having adopted Chinese methods of writing and painting, and also the Chinese view of a painting as an object for private contemplation, the Japanese also adopted Chinese forms of scroll painting and went on to add new ones. The hanging scroll was taken over and turned into the chief object of decoration and significance in the traditionally very bare Japanese interior. One such painting, hanging in an alcove as in a shrine and accompanied perhaps by one flower or a fine piece of pottery, would be the entire equipment of that room, to be exchanged from time to time with another scroll painting from the owner's collection. For the rest, the lines and proportions of the room were allowed to speak without the clutter the West finds normal and necessary, and also without the decorative surfaces so lovingly bestowed by the Near East. To enhance the effect of this simplicity even further, the Japanese invented the sliding partition, a doorway that becomes part of the wall when it is closed rather than interrupt the surface and its proportions or advertise mobility. For larger rooms they also invented the painted folding screen, two or six panels hinged together, and often made and used in pairs. Two screens set up in relation to each other can create a sublime visual enclosure within the economical setting of Japanese architecture.

The seventeenth-century screen illustrated here is unusual in its theme, but shows well the Oriental love of flatness as a very positive element in its design. Again it is interval rather than anything like western perspective, let alone modelling with light and shade, that yields a convincing sense of space, so that the many figures and their boats and the buildings among which they move, stand and sit are easily accommodated. Everything is

Again we have this close kinship of painting and calligraphy, image and word-images, so strange to a westerner. The reader is invited to read both with similar attention, the text for its visual grace or emphases, the image for its play of pattern and flat space against telling brushstrokes. The example illustrated, showing pilgrims on their way through a rather bleak landscape, was selected partly for its particular interest and partly because of its pre-echoing of the diagonal tree device used by Gauguin and Van Gogh in the 1880s when Japanese prints of this sort were all the rage with go-ahead artists in Paris (pages 128-129).

Traditional Japanese interior of the 16th century (above) showing a raised corner of the room with two large mats, set aside for the contemplation of a landscape painting and a flower in a vase

KUNIYOSHI
View of the post-stations of Hodogaya (second of set of twelve prints) c. 1835
coloured wood cut
22.9 x 35.6 cm (9 x 14 in)
Victoria and Albert Museum, London

clear and crisp, not least the barbarian visitors in their laughable pantaloons, contrasted here with the elegant slimness of the Japanese figures. Everything is firm as well as delicate; nothing is obscure or vague. Yet our reading of all this interesting detail is preceded by our encountering a large and powerful design of gold areas against dark paint areas: gold standing for earth and also, when patterned, for mist and clouds; dark green areas of paint standing for sea, foliage and roofs.

Such screen paintings were done for palaces and the houses of the wealthy. The materials themselves must have been expensive. For something more like a mass market of businessmen and professionals of various sorts living in towns, the Japanese developed the art of wood-block printing in black and white or in colour. The prints were sometimes made as independent objects, more often as illustrations for books, the writing in them being printed by the same method. Specialist artists produced the original images with brushes and inks on paper; specialist craftsmen carefully cut their design into hard, finely grained wood such as that of the cherry tree, and similarly engraved the calligraphic forms of the writing.

You can see why. What the artist has done seems very simple but is extraordinarily effective. Without any of the time-honoured techniques so important in the West – close study of anatomy, modelling, perspective, accurate rendering of the surfaces of things and of light and shadow – he has constructed an amazingly lifelike image. In other words, the skills that the western art student struggled so long to achieve could be done without: Kuniyoshi's skills included capturing the likeness of his fellow man but not in any great detail nor in order to bring out each man's individual looks, and his observation of landscape seems to have taught him to suggest general characteristics rather than capture a particular bit of nature. He does not even feel the need to tell us where exactly the pilgrims in his print are standing or what they are standing on. Yet the whole image is alive with visual drama, and also with humour. He too, like his contemporaries, the Romantic painters of Europe (pages 118-119), puts man in opposition to nature: the grandeur and the permanence of nature and nature's space is made to comment on man's self-importance, littleness and agitation.

Islamic Art

The tile shown here probably comes from the Royal Mosque in Isfahan, one of the great centres of the Islamic empire. It is, in a sense, a piece of architecture rather than art, and typical of Islamic architecture which was often made lustrous inside and out with ceramic ornament of this sort. The architectural forms tended to be simple and the interiors of the mosques almost devoid of equipment and furnishings. Tiles covered many of the vertical surfaces and rugs clothed the floor; apart from this the architecture was exceptionally silent, without symbolical elements.

The tile is a pattern of lines in white and turquoise. Technically, the lines of turquoise and dark blue slip are laid on a white ground, but here we read the dark blue as background. The pattern they make is worth studying carefully. Clear enough at first glance, it turns out to be quite complicated. The forms repeat but there is no symmetry: the repeats rotate rather than mirror each other, and they meet and knot in the centre of the tile. This rotation gives the pattern a shifting, dancing quality.

The lines were not invented by the designer, but the pattern was, or rather it was developed from previous use of the same elements. These are letters: Arabic script. What they say, four times, is the key statement of the holy book of Islam, the Koran: 'Allah, there is no god but he'.

The artists of Islam were the greatest pattern makers the world has seen. Sometimes they used purely geometrical elements and sometimes they used geometricized forms of animals and plants; often they used script.

There is no place in Islamic public art for figures, and this meant that the artists could bring into their art all the energies, the inventiveness and cunning that in Western art went into such matters as anatomy, modelling, lighting, perspective and the representation of movement.

The religion called Islam was founded by Mohammed in the seventh century. Within a century it had spread from Arabia along north Africa and through Spain to the Pyrenees. It also spread to India and from the end of the fourteenth century until the early twentieth it dominated the Balkan States of south-eastern Europe. In 1529 and again in 1683 the forces of Islam besieged Vienna.

All this speaks of Islam's military might but little of the culture of which that was but a part. To summarize it sharply, Islam was the chief beneficiary of Greek civilization after the collapse of the Roman empire. While barbarians brought chaos to much of Europe, the Arabs preserved and in some respects developed the scientific and philosophical heritage of Greece. Western astronomy, medicine and mathematics are directly indebted to Islam (the fact that we use Arabic numerals is a telling symbol of this), but to Islam we also owe our knowledge of the key texts of Antiquity. The instinct to preserve and develop rather than to destroy guided Islam in its empire-building. No religion is stricter than that of Islam, but culturally it was ready to mingle its traditions with local ones. The result is that there was Spanish-Islamic culture in Spain, Persian-Islamic in Persia, Byzantine-Islamic in Turkey and Istanbul (the former

perspective nor recession in the picture. It holds to the flat page; the incursion of written text and the extrusion of the onion-topped dome knit the image into the sheet.

Chinese example certainly influenced miniature painting of this kind, and it also shows in Islamic textiles, mingling there with Near-Eastern traditions that existed before Islam was born. One small example serves here to represent a rich and important part of Islamic art production in the form of knotted carpets and woven and embroidered textiles. The design of this embroidery is typical of carpet design of the Caucasus area: a geometrical pattern, again a rotating device, derived from a dragon motif that may remind you of motifs on the Chinese *yu* on page 99.

Tile, probably from Isfahan (far left)
early 17th century
ceramic
35.5 cm (14 in) square
The Art Institute of Chicago

Figures in a mosque:
Khamsa 'Five Poems of Nizami' (left)
late 15th century
illuminated manuscript
19 x 12 cm (7½ x 4½ in)
British Museum, London

Embroidered cover from the Caucasus (right)
18th century
silk on canvas
111.5 x 132 cm (44 x 52 in)
Victoria and Albert Museum, London

Constantinople), as well as other varieties, all linked by the Koran.

The centre of all Islamic thought is that book, but books in general were greatly valued as transmitters of knowledge as well as of stories and poems. They might be illustrated and sumptuously bound. The miniature illustrated here is one out of nineteen in a book of poems. It represents the interior of a mosque, with scholars and other men, and, on the left, one of the rare pieces of equipment needed in a mosque, the 'mimbar' or pulpit. Pattern abounds, both as architectural ornament and as script on the mosque; panels of writing at the top left are parts of the poems. All the forms are elegant, clear and flat, and disposed rhythmically over the surface rather than according to any evident rule. Our high viewpoint makes the floor look spacious, but there is no

Islamic carpets and other objects were known in Europe from at least the fifteenth century on. You can see one on Georg Gisze's table, on page 77. But there is reason to think that Islamic influence was at work earlier too, on the Beatus manuscript (page 29) and generally on elements of Gothic architecture and Late Gothic art (pages 32-33 and 38-39). The tapestries of France suggest connections with Persian miniatures.

The flowery islands in illuminated manuscripts as in tapestries may echo the Persian taste for enclosed gardens and parks, called by a word from which we derive 'paradise'. Around 1900 Islamic carpets began to be studied seriously as major works of art, and a vast exhibition of Islamic art shown in Munich in 1910 is very much part of the history of modern art. It gave positive encouragement to abstracted and fully abstract painting.

Watteau

Hogarth

JEAN ANTOINE WATTEAU born in Valenciennes in northern France in 1684; died at Nogent in 1721

WILLIAM HOGARTH born in London in 1697; died there in 1764

Watteau's career falls between the decorations at Versailles and those in the Hôtel de Soubise and seems to lead us from one to the other. His family was Flemish, like that of Rubens, and Watteau brought into French art interests and qualities that belonged to Flemish painting. In Paris, where he settled in 1702, he was able to make a close study of Rubenses in the royal collection.

He learnt vivacity and deftness from them, but also got from some of them the idea of a new sort of genre painting. Genre painting (*genre* means kind or sort) refers to representations of ordinary, anonymous people doing ordinary things, as opposed to history painting which refers to important actions by famous people. So genre painting is not story telling but description, and this type of art was often used to poke fun at people in general. Following Rubens, Watteau developed a new

sort of genre painting, known in France as the *fête galante,* an elegant entertainment.

The Pleasures of a Ball is a fine example. Nicely dressed men and women have come together for a very informal party. They dance, talk, flirt. Beyond their splendid but also airy setting we see a fountain and trees, all melting into the distance like a Claude landscape.

Watteau had a remarkable success with paintings of this kind. People saw in them the informality they wanted to achieve. They found this art natural after the high-minded themes and noble style of Raphael or Poussin and the rhetorical displays demanded by the court of Louis XIV. They said it was natural because it aimed to please rather than emulate the ancients, and because it was based on close study of human behaviour rather than on classical models.

The English painter and printmaker, Hogarth, had a similar interest in human behaviour. His pictures, single works and also sets telling a story in sequential scenes, portray the urban life of his time. He was aware of the high traditions of art. He was aware also of Watteau and new tendencies in French art. But he was aware, above all, of the rise to public favour of a new literary form, the novel. Like the novelists, particularly his friend Henry Fielding, he wanted to entertain spectators whilst also delivering instruction. He called his narrative pictures 'moral histories'.

His art is represented here by a plate from his book, *The Analysis of Beauty* (1753). In that book he tried to explain beauty, as it relates to art and design, without calling on the authority of the classical tradition. Beauty was to be understood through studying things and effects that please, and he decided that the form that was common to all the things that please our eyes best was the S-curve, the serpentine line, in two or three dimensions. His print shows this principle at work. The pair of dancers on the left are beautiful: two echoing S-curves. The other dancers make clumsier shapes and obviously please our eyes less – but I am sure he meant us to find them amusing. Around this scene he has placed a variety of other instructive examples. Top left, for example, he shows the motions involved in country dancing and (below) in the minuet: he implies that the dance is the serpentine line in motion.

In his desire to instruct, Hogarth was feeding into genre pictures one of the functions of history painting. This Watteau does not seem to have done or wanted to do. He and Hogarth share a keen awareness of what we call body language today, of people's motions and poses relative to each other and how these reveal our motives and hopes, but Watteau does not comment on the scenes he shows us.

Yet his contemporaries were perhaps wrong to call his pictures natural. They are fantasies. The clothes, the architecture and the garden are totally unreal, the whole *fête galante* is a vision, a dream, an unending light opera quite unlike the real world. Watteau implies that happiness can only be a dream. In the nineteenth century the poet Baudelaire recognized the unreality of Watteau's art and called it *surnaturel*, supernatural.

WATTEAU
The Pleasures of a Ball 1719
(left) oil on canvas
50 x 61 cm (19¾ x 24 in)
Dulwich Picture Gallery,
London

HOGARTH
Plate 2 from *The Analysis of Beauty* 1753 (below)
engraving
37 x 50 cm (14½ x 19½ in)
British Museum, London

JOSHUA REYNOLDS born near Plymouth in 1723; died in London in 1792

JEAN ANTOINE HOUDON born in Paris in 1741; died there in 1828

REYNOLDS
Nelly O'Brien c. 1763
oil on canvas
126 x 100 cm (49½ x 39 in)
Wallace Collection, London

Not long after he painted the portrait shown here, Reynolds became Sir Joshua Reynolds and first president of the Royal Academy of Art in London. He was an apt choice for this important role: one of the best painters in England, he was also a learned man who knew the high art of Rome at first hand and he associated with eminent writers, actors and musicians as well as with lords and ladies.

Academies had been set up in Italy and then also in France and elsewhere as professional associations that combined the practical function of enabling artists to meet and to exhibit their work to the public with the uplifting one of teaching, explaining and defending the standards and traditions of classicism. But the high art we associate with Raphael and Michelangelo and their followers, and more recently with Poussin, had not made much impression in Britain, neither on painters nor on their patrons most of whom were content to commission portraits of themselves, their horses and their houses, and to leave high-minded ideas to foreigners.

Establishing the academy, it was hoped, would change all that. Reynolds delivered annual discourses on art in which he summarized the principles of the high art he wished to see thriving in England: how art was to be learned through the best examples of art and how painters should learn to read nature in their terms, selecting from nature those parts and proportions that the ancients and the most eminent moderns had shown to produce the most elevated beauty. He warned his students against the uncouth ways of Dutch realism and against the easy charms of modern French painting. He spoke with warmth and conviction, and with all the eloquence that the excellent English prose of that time permitted.

Yet his own best paintings come close to realism and echo something of that French charm. Rarely do they display the classicism he was recommending to his colleagues and pupils. This was partly because English patrons still did not seem eager to commission the history paintings that were classicism's chief vehicle. Reynolds did develop a form of portraiture that involved showing his sitters in the guise of a Roman priestess or echoing some other obviously ancient role and pose. But his best paintings, those to hold our admiration over the years, tend to be his more informal, naturalistic portraits.

Nelly O'Brien shows a well-known actress of the time, but off-stage, seated in a garden with her dog on her lap. The light falls down on her from the left but her face is lit by light reflected up into it from her magnificently painted dress. Thus it lacks sharp lines and shadows, and our attention fixes on the lady's eyes. The result is so charming, so natural, that we tend not to notice what a strong symmetrical, geometrical shape she forms in the picture. Reynold's admiration for Raphael, it turns out, is not at all at odds with his gift for the informal and the vivid.

So we notice both a conflict between his high ideals and his best practice, and then also an underlying unity between classicism and informality. Perhaps, considering the charm of Raphael's portrait on page 76, we are wrong ever to see these as contradictory. But the academies and their teaching had tended to put them in opposition, and this is a problem that we shall have to refer to again.

It is relevant to the career of Houdon, the French sculptor. He had spent three years in Rome, sent there by the French academy as a reward for his abilities. Back in France, he devoted almost all his time and certainly his major talent to making portrait busts of important men – not kings and ministers but writers, philosophers and other 'men of genius' as the century called them – creative men of intellect and spirit.

HOUDON
Gluck (bust)
terracotta
67 cm (26 in) high
Royal College of Music,
London

Houdon excelled in capturing their likeness and also some sense of their activity. The composer Gluck, for instance, we feel we would recognize from that extraordinarily living representation, but we also sense the mental energy of the composer of *Orfeo* and other profoundly beautiful operas and the profound thinker about the role of opera in society.

107

Chardin

Stubbs

JEAN BAPTISTE CHARDIN born in Paris in 1699; died there in 1779
GEORGE STUBBS born in Liverpool in 1724; died in London in 1806

Chardin in France and Stubbs in England were both successful painters. They were praised by critics and kept busy by patrons wanting to have their work. They were accepted in their national art academies. Both worked for royalty on occasion, and frequently for the nobility. Yet each knew that he could never count himself an artist of the first rank.

Chardin was known as a painter of still life. Stubbs painted horses; occasionally he also painted scenes of country folk at work in the fields, and also narrative pictures using animals as heroes – trying to turn animal pictures into history paintings – but it was as a portraitist of horses that he was admired and supported. He was, in fact, a proven expert in the anatomy of the horse; his book, *The Anatomy of the Horse* (published 1766), was the product of years of grim work dissecting and drawing cadavers. Towards the end of his life he embarked on a treatise comparing human anatomy to that of tigers and fowls.

Both were considered outstanding artists but in minor categories of art. We know that the authority of the academies was to be challenged in the nineteenth century: in the eighteenth century it was being undermined. The categories in which painting made its most dramatic advances in the nineteenth century were precisely those that academic theory kept out of the limelight, landscape and still life most of all. The eighteenth century encouraged these without honouring them. A gap opened between theory and practice, and this was widened by propositions like those of Hogarth who put all his emphasis on visual qualities and implied that beauty in art had nothing to do with the example of the ancients and with academic principles at all.

Chardin was seen as a painter of the Flemish type, good at copying the appearances of things, especially of food and household objects, and not concerned with intellectual matters. People admired his skill with paints, and his way of bringing tones and colours into visual harmony. Above all, they praised the naturalness of his work and seemed relieved not to have to react to it with sophistication. 'To look at the work of Chardin,' wrote Diderot, the famous philosopher-critic, 'I have only to keep the eyes nature gave me and to use them well.'

Cézanne's response, a hundred years later, was: 'This painter was as cunning as a fox'. He understood Chardin's subtle ways of building a group of simple things into grand compositions on a small scale. The group of very ordinary objects in the *Kitchen Table* do not look particularly arranged, but notice how the slice

of melon meets the upward curve of the cloth, and how the lit strip of wall, together with the pastry cutters, gives the painting a firm ending on the right. There is lots of space, but the objects sit fairly close together to make an informal group.

No one looking at Stubbs' work noticed its extraordinary qualities. Racing had become 'the sport of kings'; the training and breeding of high quality race horses involved great investments and profits as well as prestige. Their owners wanted visual as well as verbal records of their star performers. Stubbs was known to be good at supplying clear and persuasive portraits of them, still or in action. A hundred years later the camera was to prove that horses do not gallop the way he and everyone else showed them, with all four legs off the ground, but then that kind of accuracy was not demanded and would have been thought to produce clumsy representations.

No one noticed that Stubbs was both a pictorial architect and a pictorial poet. The example shown here is a double picture: a portrait of the horse with attendant humans on the left and, on the right, an action shot of Gimcrack winning his race. Stubbs uses a low, clear horizon and floods his curiously empty picture with light that unifies the two scenes. Everything is placed precisely and rhythmically; at the same time he makes sure that our eyes go from Gimcrack on the left via the standing jockey to their joint triumph in the distance.

It is the art of the nineteenth century, most particularly of Cézanne and Seurat, that has taught us to respond to these qualities and to care much less about subject matter. To some extent we have turned against the idea of serious, discussable themes in art. Have we lost something in the process?

STUBBS
Gimcrack on Newmarket Heath, with trainer, jockey and stable lad 1765
(above right)
oil on canvas
102 x 193 cm (40 x 76 in)
Private collection

CHARDIN
Kitchen Table c. 1729
(right)
oil on canvas
28 x 34 cm (11 x 13 in)
Glasgow Art Gallery and Museum (Burrell Collection)

David

JACQUES LOUIS DAVID born in Paris in 1748; died in Brussels in 1825

DAVID
The Oath of the Horatii 1784–5
oil on canvas
330 x 427 cm (129 x 168 in)
Louvre, Paris

David's *The Oath of the Horatii* is, I think, the first painting to have been praised as 'revolutionary'. People flocked to see it in Rome, where he completed it in 1784, and again in Paris where it was exhibited in 1785. They were shocked by its novelty but also exhilarated by it. They agreed that it marked a turning point, and so we still see it today.

What was new about it? It is, clearly, a history painting. Its success reasserted the primacy of this category of art: an art of instruction as well as delight. It is also an extraordinarily spartan, austere picture. To eighteenth century eyes it must have looked amazingly devoid of

grace. In a boxlike space provided by classical architecture of unusual bareness, we see a dramatic action performed by three men, grouped as one on the left, confronting one man standing in the exact centre of the composition; on the right a cluster of women react with dismay and only the little boy watches the action. There is a lot of empty space and a lot of bare picture. The position of everything is absolutely precise; everything is kept distinct, separate. The light serves mainly to help with this clarity, but it also adds its touch of drama to the arms and the swords.

Thus, as in Poussin particularly, we have some of the sense of what is going on before we know the story. It is a famous and complex one, dating from the earliest days of ancient Rome and told by Livy and other Roman historians. There is a dispute between the kingdoms of Rome and adjoining Alba. Rather than engage in war, the two states decide on a contest to the death between three Roman brothers, the Horatii, and three Alban brothers, the Curatii. David shows the Horatii swearing to give their lives for their country, if necessary. Their father lifts up their swords and looks towards heaven. The two women on the right are Camilla (in white), sister to the Horatii, and Sabina, the wife of one of them. She is also sister to the Curatii, and Camilla is betrothed to one of them. Whoever wins there will be pain and loss. The resolution of the young men and the father takes on an added dimension; we find ourselves imagining a similar scene, more or less duplicating this one, in the household of the Curatii.

So the story is not one of valour and victory but of self-sacrifice for a higher good, and that is precisely what the eighteenth century read in this picture. In 1789 the French Revolution broke out. David became a Deputy to the National Convention, voted for the execution of the king and generally showed himself to be revolutionary in his political actions as well as in his art. But this does not mean that his picture was a call to revolution. For one thing, the Horatii were offering their lives in defence of a kingdom; for another, the painting was bought by the French king. It was a call to morality and seriousness, in art as much as in human affairs.

It implied a rejection of the light-hearted manner and matter of so much eighteenth century painting, and restated what academic theory had long maintained, that it was art's prime duty to teach moral precepts through noble and persuasive examples. David was not alone in wanting to lead art back into this role, but his painting was the most telling manifesto and the most influential model of the campaign. Instead of movement and flowing curves, firm, almost geometrical forms. Instead of delicious brushwork and colours, a plain and legible organization of tone and colour.

In this David was not only the son of Poussin and champion of the history painting tradition. He was also the father of propaganda art. Once the Revolution started he used his art in direct support of its principles and its leaders, organizing public festivities and ceremonies as well as doing his paintings. He became something very like a cultural dictator, reorganizing the Academy of Fine Arts, opening the royal collections in the Louvre Palace to the public as a museum, and generally using his political power as a means of reforming art and its role in the state. His influence affected all aspects of design, including fashion (the 'Empire line' in dress was derived from his picture). Many of the next generation of French painters studied under him and worked for him on his large projects.

The movement or tendency of which *The Oath of the Horatii* was the first masterpiece has become known as Neoclassicism. The word means 'renewed classicism' but the movement sought more than that. Knowledge of antiquity had greatly increased during the eighteenth

century through the accurate recording of ancient remains, in Greece and the Near East as well as in Italy, and Neoclassicism wanted the accuracy made possible by this. Also there was a new taste for classicism, a regard for strikingly different qualities in it. The Neo-

Detail of *The Oath of the Horatii*

classicists spoke of the 'noble simplicity and quiet grandeur' of the best works of antiquity, and they came to realize that these were usually Greek works.

The Oath of the Horatii owes little or nothing to Greek examples, although this was probably not clear to people at the time. What David did do was something even more original than turn to Greek models: he looked for the earliest and least sophisticated examples he could find of Roman art and architecture (probably thinking them the work of Greeks on Italian soil) – the most *primitive* examples, we would say. Through his work and teaching, Neoclassicism became associated with primitivism whereas traditional classicism had been more concerned with splendour and magnificence. His picture showed how this preference for 'noble simplicity and quiet grandeur' could be met by a simplified art.

Flaxman

Canova

JOHN FLAXMAN born in York in 1755; died in London in 1826

ANTONIO CANOVA born in Passagno near Venice in 1757; died in Venice in 1822

Classicism had always been associated with clear delineation (as opposed to rich colouring and the kind of brushwork that leaves forms without clear edges). It had also been associated with sculpture since ancient sculptures were available as models. So it should not be surprising that sculptors play leading roles in the development of Neoclassicism. Today the two sculptors discussed on these pages are little known outside the professional world of art history, yet they were enormously influential in their day.

Flaxman probably taught Neoclassicism even more effectively than David, because he taught it through sets of prints that were published and republished in several European cities from the 1790s to the 1840s. These prints, mostly illustrating the writings of ancient authors, could easily be adapted by painters and sculptors for their purposes. They were the result of very close study and of a gradual refining of Flaxman's sole means: line. The example given here, from the set illustrating Homer's *Iliad,* shows how succinct the results could be. The

figures are displayed as in a relief or an ancient vase painting (page 16), spread out and more or less in profile. One line gives them somewhere to stand; there is no further description of their setting. There is hardly any shadow and absolutely no modelling: in so far as we read these images as being of figures in the round, our imagination makes them so, working on Flaxman's carefully controlled line and composition.

It was in Rome that Flaxman worked to achieve this simplicity. The Venetian sculptor Canova had also come to Rome and distanced himself from the naturalism and charm of Venetian eighteenth century art to achieve his grand and powerful style. If Flaxman's prints pervaded every part of civilized Europe, Canova achieved international fame on the scale of Bernini's, supplying Napoleon and the Emperor of Austria with major sculptures as well as the whole of Italy, and teaching and employing a team of assistants who were to become master sculptors themselves. Through the work of Flaxman and Canova, Neoclassicism became an international and all-embracing style, used from Edinburgh and Leningrad (then the capital of Russia and called St Petersburg) to America, and by emperors and kings as much as by republics, for public and private buildings, for parliaments, churches, banks, railway stations and museums, for two- and three-dimensional art and for all aspects of design.

FLAXMAN
The Fight for the Body of Patroclus (engravings for the *Iliad,* plate 22) 1793
engraving
18 x 34 cm (7 x 13¼ in)
British Library, London

Hyde Park Screen, London, built in 1825. Designed by Decimus Burton, it is a fine example of Neoclassical architecture.

But by 1800 there were other styles to challenge this one, and more were added in the nineteenth century. The period from, roughly, the 1790s to the 1840s is called the Romantic movement to indicate a widespread turning away from traditional principles in all the arts towards that emphasis on personal expression that we nowadays take for granted, rightly or wrongly. Turner and Delacroix are two well-known representatives of Romanticism in painting (pages 116 and 118), but Neoclassicism was also part of the Romantic movement.

Style became a matter for dispute and specialization. In architecture this is most obvious as we can see buildings put up next to each other in totally different styles, each with its implied meanings (Gothic could be used to emphasize Christian beliefs and national traditions, Neoclassical to invoke the democratic image of ancient Athens, and so on). In sculpture, Neoclassicism was to dominate for a hundred years, so strong was the influence of Greek and Roman models. In painting, Romanticism represents something like a stylistic explosion, as artists seek idioms that will represent their individual standpoints as well as persuade others of their genius.

Canova must be seen as the inspiration behind some of the more pretentious classical pieces of nineteenth century sculpture. For example, he made very fine, large statues of Napoleon about 1808, one in marble and one in bronze. The Corsican, by then Emperor of the French and lord of much of Europe by force of arms, was tubby as well as short; Canova of course showed him as an antique hero, marvellously proportioned and stark naked. To modern eyes, used to the 'facts' of photography and film, this sort of idealization looks odd, yet similar works were produced long after Canova's time.

Canova's monument for Maria Christina, the deceased empress of Austria, is also in its way a piece of idealization and symbolism. But like *The Oath of the Horatii* it is also a remarkably effective piece of theatre. We see a pyramidal monument such as the Romans sometimes had built. A procession of figures, led by Piety, carries an urn of ashes into the tomb, watched by the lion of Fortitude and a figure representing Mourning. A relief figure of Happiness holds up a portrait of the dead woman, an oval relief surrounded by a serpent biting its

tail, an ancient sign for Immortality. Notice the absence of specifically religious symbols, and the combination of happiness and sadness. Canova's generation took a dignified view of death, seeing it as sleep and associating after-life with the dead person's continued existence in the minds of the living.

CANOVA
Monument to the Archduchess Maria Christina 1799–1805
marble
574 cm (226 in) high
Augustinerkirche, Vienna

113

Goya

Francisco de GOYA born in Saragossa in 1746; died in Bordeaux in 1828

GOYA
They will all fall
(Los Caprichos, plate 19)
c. 1798
etching
18 x 12 cm (7 x 4¼ in)
British Museum, London

'When reason sleeps, monsters are born.' These words appear on one of the plates on Goya's suite of etchings *Los Caprichos* (caprices, fanciful inventions). They imply that, like most thinking people of the eighteenth century, Goya believed that reason was the light by which human affairs including art must be conducted. But he also showed, in his practice, that art could proclaim the need for reason and humanity's general failure to behave rationally by portraying the opposite.

He was a tremendously skilled painter and graphic artist, and familiar with the great art of his predecessors through examples in the Spanish royal collection and from travelling in Italy. He also had behind him the Spanish tradition of realism, on which Velázquez also

had drawn (page 86). In addition he lived in violent times. He was employed by the Spanish king, but the monarchy and the country were morally and economically weak and easily fell prey to interference and then also to invasion from France. Goya used his art both to portray and to protest against the evils of his day, and in so doing he dedicated art to a new range of expression and content.

He was not merely a realist. *Los Caprichos* (fantasies, moods) are images reflecting the vices and follies of humanity through unreality. But that unreality is – as it was in the case of Watteau (page 104) – founded on acute observation of actual people. There had of course been satirical prints before, both of the sort we would call political cartoons and the more general kind, mocking people at large by exaggerating their defects. Goya's should be seen as at least partly humorous in intention – later he did prints about war that were certainly without any hint of humour – yet there is no denying their sharpness and their urgency. Like Bosch's and Bruegel's pictures (the Spanish royal collection had several examples; pages 68 and 78), these prints referred to situations and also to proverbs and sayings that the public could easily respond to.

If there were traditions supporting Goya's admonishing of the world through satirical prints, there were none relevant to his masterpiece, the painting known as *The Third of May*. Napoleon had sent his troops into Spain, first in support of the Spanish king and then to remove him. On 2 May 1808 there was a popular uprising against the occupying army in Madrid. French soldiers were attacked and killed by the ordinary people of the city. During the night and the day that followed there were savage reprisals. Citizens were taken away and shot in their hundreds, whether or not they had been involved in the attacks. *The Third of May* is Goya's memorial to the event, painted six years later. Is it an eye-witness account?

The important thing is that it seems to be one, and also that he has turned it into a painting that enlarges the particular event into a universal statement. We see Madrid in the distance. Historians tell us exactly where this shooting took place, but Goya has not given us a portrait of the place: he has simplified it and organized the shapes of the landscape to serve as an effective stage for his action. I often think that he must have seen Giotto's frescoes, perhaps the one illustrated on page 34. In any case, like Giotto, he knew the virtue of a strong, bare statement.

Giotto may also have taught him to use the backs of figures. We sympathize with the men being shot, whose

GOYA
The Third of May 1808 1814–5
oil on canvas
266 x 345 cm (105 x 136 in)
Prado, Madrid

expressive faces and gestures we see clearly. If we look closely, we see a wound in the open palm of the man with the white shirt, a mark identical to that left by the nail in the hand of the crucified Christ and to the *stigmata* said to have been bestowed on St Francis. So there is symbolism as well as stage craft at work here, and of course Goya's dramatic use of light – the sudden light given by the lantern and the general glow in the painting that announced the dawn. And the soldiers are almost symbolic too. They are turned away from us, faceless, dehumanized and machinelike executors of someone's orders.

If we saw their faces we would perhaps feel that they, too, were caught in a web of power and greed not of their making. Goya does not want us to think of them in this way but rather to feel in our bones the fear, the fury and the sheer puzzlement that fills the faces of their victims.

Yet the painting refers us to more than the event: Goya is telling us about two aspects of mankind, the weakness of what we normally refer to as humanity and the strength, in humans, of what we call bestiality.

Its size, its visual character and above all its serious content make us read this as a history painting. But these are ordinary, unnamed people, and the event is an unspecific one: a scene of execution to represent several such actions. Like Reynolds with his more formal portraits, Goya was pioneering a shifting and fusing of the traditional academic categories. And the implications are, of course, democratic: the fate of anonymous citizens is put on a level with historical heroes, mythical deities and even the story of Jesus Christ. But the aim here was also nationalistic: the pair of paintings was commissioned by the Spanish government.

115

Ingres

Delacroix

JEAN AUGUSTE INGRES born at Montauban in 1780; died in Paris in 1867

EUGÈNE DELACROIX born at Charenton-Saint-Maurice in 1798; died in Paris in 1863

The first half of the nineteenth century saw in French art a tug-of-war between classicism in its new stricter guise of Neoclassicism and Romanticism. Ingres was the willing champion of Neoclassicism; Delacroix was seen as leader of Romantic painting but never accepted the role.

Neoclassicism represented a fairly specific set of views on art: the need to adhere to the best, the purest ancient models; the superiority of line and design over colour and tonal contrasts; the value of clear disposition as against effects of space and movement; the moral superiority of appealing to the mind by these means as against stimulating us through our visual sense.

Romanticism seemed to uphold the opposite in every case. More important, though, was its apparent opposition to the logic and the sense of order that had always been the stated basis of classicism. Romanticism stood for a stress on individualism, on the impossibility of knowing anything other than through one's own perception; also on the unconscious, or what people generally call instinct, rather than reason and conscious thought as the true impulse behind our actions. These were recognitions about human nature and about the bases of creativity that still operate for us today. Neoclassicism, even while it argued against them, shared them.

Ingres had been a pupil of David and a passionate student of classical models in Rome. He was there from 1806 to 1822. Soon after his return to Paris he was accorded his role in the cultural battle, and he preached the exclusive virtues of classicism until his death. When we look at his art we see many other influences at work. He had a liking for the painters of the early Italian Renaissance, then often referred to as 'the primitives', and also for their contemporaries in the North with their smooth and painstaking rendering of every detail. He had a taste for Oriental themes and for subjects from medieval history and literature. In all these he was at one with the Romantics he disdained.

The painting illustrated here takes its theme from the revered father of Greek poetry, Homer, and from the plays of Sophocles; it was used also by Greek vase painters. We can sense their example, and also Flaxman's, behind the ways Ingres has arranged the figure of Oedipus – flatly, on a plane parallel to the picture surface and in strict profile, and kept what action there is between the man and woman-monster on that same plane. He has combined linearity with delicate tonal modelling to give his forms three-dimensionality.

His colour is functional – it helps us to understand what the forms are – rather than decorative or stirring.

He had painted a large picture of the subject in 1808. This small one is very like it, size apart, and it seems that he painted it when considering alterations to the large one in the 1820s. This suggests more than a passing enthusiasm for its subject, though it is without the intellectual beauty for which the ancient world was admired. The sphinx is a mythical being of obscure meaning; the riddle she posed had brought instant death to everyone who attempted to solve it. Perhaps it is not surprising that Ingres also portrayed subjects from the myths of the barbaric North (on which Wagner was to base his cycle of operas in the 1850s, 1860s and 1870s).

Delacroix's large mural seems straightforward in comparison. The subject comes from the Bible, of course, though it is likely that any artist would read into it some of his personal struggles with self-doubt, with tradition and with the limited understanding the world brings to such work.

Delacroix is clearly a painter in the Venetian tradition. There is space in his painting, and movement into space;

there is an attractive fullness of forms and richness of colour. We can see his strong brushwork in the original painting (not in the reproduction), and it is there not to hint at personal emotions but to keep the colours alive. He contrasts colours so that they brighten each other; he also puts touches in different hues of the same colour side by side to keep a one-colour area lively: a lot of different greens, for example, for grass and foliage.

Both painters, though their means are different, aim at intensity so that their vision of their chosen subject should strike deeply into us. If Ingres put all his conscious effort into drawing and modelling, Delacroix put his into what he called 'the musical part of painting': lively colour and colour contrasts, contrasts of light and dark, open and closed spaces, with the action disposed in them to bring out its poetry as well as its facts.

INGRES
Oedipus and the Sphinx
c. 1827 (left)
oil on canvas
17.8 x 13.7 cm (7 x 5¼ in)
National Gallery, London

DELACROIX
Jacob wrestling with the Angel 1853–63 (right)
fresco
715 x 485 cm (281 x 191 in)
Saint-Sulpice, Paris

Turner

Friedrich

JOSEPH MALLORD WILLIAM TURNER born in London in 1775; died there in 1851

CASPAR DAVID FRIEDRICH born in Greifswald on the Baltic coast of Germany in 1774; died in Dresden in 1840

The eighteenth century discovered a new way of considering our relationship to the world, one close to the heart of Romanticism: the concept of the sublime. When we confront extreme forms of nature – great mountains, dark chasms, thundering waterfalls, raging storms and seas, the vast night sky and the endlessness of oceans – we are moved by a sense of fear and awe that is deeply pleasurable as well as disturbing. The same happens when we read of ghosts, murders and monsters. The general effect of such things is to make us feel small and helpless; we become like children or like prehistoric man attempting to understand his harsh environment in order to survive it, yet remain protected by civilization and modern knowledge. This intrusion of an element of fear into our cushioned life, and the images that produce it, are called the sublime.

It gave rise to new excitements in literature and art: to horror stories about gaunt knights and helpless damsels in crumbling castles, crime and the detection of crime, and man-made monsters such as Frankenstein. It also helps us to understand why landscape painting should have come to play such an important part in the development of art in the nineteenth century. There were no substantial ancient prototypes to guide and constrain the landscapist; instead there was growing scientific knowledge about geology, botany, meteorology and so on. Nature could take infinite forms and these could be chosen or even invented to mirror all sorts of moods. And since nature could now be felt to carry such powerful meanings – most obviously of man's weakness and his brief existence before the vast and recurring forces of nature – landscape painting could be valued for its poetic content and thus brought up to the status of history painting.

In the painting shown here, Turner combined history with landscape to make sure of that. The picture originated, in one sense, in a storm he witnessed in Yorkshire and in the mountains he had seen and drawn in England, Wales, France and Switzerland. In another sense, it sprang from his feeling for ancient times, especially for the struggle between Rome and Carthage – a pre-echo of the wars between England and Napoleon's France. It

TURNER
Snowstorm; Hannibal and his army crossing the Alps
1812 (left)
oil on canvas
145 x 236 cm (57 x 93 in)
Tate Gallery, London

FRIEDRICH
Two Men contemplating the Moon 1819 (right)
oil on canvas
35 x 44 cm (14 x 17 in)
Staatliche
Kunstsammlungen, Dresden

also embodies a new compositional device: the visual and thence the emotional effect of a spiralling composition, a pictorial vortex.

Turner used this many times. Here it draws us into the landscape whilst also convincing us of nature's terrible power. The picture was a great success when it was exhibited. 'All that is terrible and grand is personified in the mysterious effect of this picture', wrote one critic, lining up words which together define the sublime. Turner was to go on to stronger visual effects and fewer narrative elements. Soon people found his pictures quite incomprehensible, but a later world, accustomed to Impressionism and to abstract art, has learned to value them as among the most powerful works of the century.

If nature could be used to convey sensations of awe and fear, it could also serve to express ideas about the supernatural, the divine. For many Romantic painters, landscape became a form of religious art – again, therefore, taking on the status of history painting. Friedrich painted a number of landscapes with Gothic ruins and crucifixes that clearly indicate his religious

message. In others, the symbolism is less obvious, yet there too he was working to create a new sort of religious art for modern times. The leafless oak tree in *Two Men contemplating the Moon* may suggest suffering, and the stone slab beside it, the top of an ancient dolmen, may suggest the passing of time. But the whole picture's meaning is much more specific once we know how to read it. The two men, Friedrich himself and a pupil, have walked along the stony path of life. The tree and the stone speak of the false, now dead cults of ancient times; the waxing crescent moon is a symbol of Christ.

Both paintings depend on a deep familiarity with nature and are factual in this sense. Yet both are also visionary: facts provide the raw material, but the artist sees himself as a visual poet expressing something beyond the facts. When people failed to understand the later art of Turner it was because they mistook his facts for fantasy: his knowledge of nature went that far beyond theirs. Just as science could become too specialized to be followed by the averagely educated citizen, so also painting could go beyond common knowledge.

Courbet

Manet

GUSTAVE COURBET born at Ornans (France) in 1819; died in La Tour de Peilz (France) in 1877

EDOUARD MANET born in Paris in 1832; died there in 1883

COURBET
Apples in Landscape
1871–2
oil on canvas
59 x 73.5 cm (23 x 29 in)
Mauritshuis, The Hague

'Realism' has many meanings. People who use the word bend it to their purpose. Courbet's admirers called him a Realist; he himself sometimes called his art Realism. He meant to indicate something more than that his paintings portrayed the real world: they portrayed (most of them) especially real aspects of the world, and in especially real terms. Thus he did not paint dreams or visions, but neither did he paint people or events he had not personally witnessed, and then they were preferably ordinary people and ordinary events. The people of Ornans where he grew up, the people of Paris where he worked most of his life, and his family and friends.

The still life shown here was painted in prison or in the hospital Courbet was sent to on parole from prison. He had been involved in the Paris Commune of 1871, a popular uprising against the Emperor Napoleon III and his armies after their disastrous defeat at the hands of the Prussians. After days of bloody fighting, the national government regained Paris, and Courbet was one of those tried and imprisoned for their share in the revolution. It was then that he painted still lifes of fruit and flowers brought him by his sister and his friends.

It shows, even in reproduction, another aspect of his Realism: the paint is rich and thick as though Courbet was trying to match in paint the physicality of the fruit, its density and weight. This has the effect of reminding us also that the picture in front of us is an object made of canvas and oil paints, a man-made thing like a chair or a shoe. Like Delacroix, Courbet is in the tradition of Venetian oil painting; he adds to that something of the Northerner's factuality though not in Northern terms of smoothness and fine detail.

Manet's picture of people in a Paris park looks at first sight like another form of Realism. The word he and his supporters preferred was Naturalism, implying an objective, impersonal recording of the world, without much in the way of preference or message. The picture does rather suggest a snapshot of a crowd of people, but we soon see that Manet has arranged his more important elements so that we can find our way across his crowded canvas; that there are few of the shadows – cast by tree-trunks, for instance – that we would expect to find even in subdued sunlight falling across those cream and white clothes; that, altogether, his picture must be a studio

MANET
Concert in the Tuileries
Gardens 1862
oil on canvas
76 x 117 cm (30 x 46 in)
National Gallery, London

production assembled from separate studies of figures and groups.

In fact, it includes portraits of several of Manet's friends. One of them, not easily seen directly behind the woman looking straight at us, is the poet and art critic Baudelaire, eleven years older than the painter and a powerful influence on his thinking. In his reviews, Baudelaire had for some time been asking for a modern art for modern times, one that would show Parisians in their Paris clothes and setting, and find in them a heroism like that the ancients found in their world.

Manet's painting goes some way towards meeting this call. If we ask ourselves why, in spite of the artifice by which it was achieved, the picture does seem so like an outdoor scene, we will find the answer partly in Manet's way of detailing some parts and leaving others indistinct. This is very like the way we see: our eyes focus on one face or object and we see that clearly while other things appear less and less clear the further away they are from the point of focus. It is partly in the way he used paint and colour. The paint itself is light and fresh, especially compared with Courbet's, and Manet's liking for setting

black or dark grey against whites and creams, with here and there a touch of brighter colour, gives his picture an airy freshness rarely found in more solid oil painting. Many of his contemporaries did not like this: they found it harsh and flat and quite lacking in the grace and dexterity they looked for in serious painting.

Today we greatly admire this freshness, this insistence on suggesting the way a scene actually *looked* as opposed to what it consisted of, item by item. Perhaps you can understand people's reaction to Manet in the 1860s better if you consider that, first, he seemed to paint living persons with less care than Courbet, say, gave to his apples, and that, secondly, his picture really is not about anything definite – just men and women and children, chairs and trees, in the park. They expected serious painting to say something serious.

WILLIAM HOLMAN HUNT born in London in 1827; died there in 1910
WINSLOW HOMER born in Boston, Massachusetts, in 1836; died in Prout's Neck, Maine, in 1910

Hunt was one of the original members of the group of young painters who called themselves the Pre-Raphaelite Brotherhood. They exhibited for the first time in 1849, marking their paintings 'PRB' to indicate their membership of a group. This was at the Royal Academy in London, and it attracted a lot of notice. They claimed to be cleansing art of the artificiality and darkness that had come into it with Leonardo and Raphael, and to be reasserting both visual honesty and the value of moral subjects.

In a way, their campaign was not unlike David's two generations earlier, and there was in them something of Friedrich's honest piety (pages 110 and 119). Hunt's painting *The Scapegoat* illustrates the lengths to which they were willing to go in the pursuit of truth. Its subject

was suggested by the Bible, though it was not one that promises an interesting pictorial result. By studying the Talmud, the Jewish book of law, he found out more about the ritual of loading an animal with human sin and sending it out into the wilds to wander and die. He also spent two years in the Near East, collecting data for a number of paintings, and went especially to the shores of the Dead Sea for this one, taking with him a white goat and waiting patiently for the specific effects of evening light, day after day.

This light, the goat stuck in the salty mud of the dried marsh, and the awesome landscape as a whole, all suggest punishment and sacrifice. The title, an inscription from the Bible on the frame and a full account of how and where the picture was painted – given in the catalogue – Hunt did everything to make the point of his carefully wrought picture clear. He had painted a Biblical subject with all the correctness and truth that scholarship, patient recording and the right objects in the right place could give it. Yet the critic of *The Times* found it 'difficult to divine the nature of the subject', and most other people seem to have had the same problem.

HUNT
The Scapegoat 1854
oil on canvas
85.7 x 138.5 cm
(33³/₄ x 54¹/₂ in)
The Walker Art Gallery,
Liverpool

Had they lost the skill of reading pictures? More or less factual illustrations were beginning to appear in the swelling tide of newspapers that brought them their facts, new every morning. Photography had been developed and was becoming a standard by which one judged visual truth and collected visual information; photographs of distant lands, and of the Holy Land especially, were being taken and being well received.

In America, Hunt's contemporary, Homer, met with a revealing response from some people but was generally rather more successful. Homer had not had an academic art training but had come to painting through doing illustrations for magazines like *Harper's*. He spent some months in Paris in 1867 and was in England during 1881-2 where he seems to have absorbed some influence from the Pre-Raphaelites as well as from ancient art, so that his art became rather more monumental and grand.

The Nooning was done before that change. He was working in New York but painting New England scenes of marked local character and vividness. Everyone felt that here was a painter whose themes and manner were unmistakably American. Plain, familiar subjects, described without comment beyond the implied one: this is worth painting, truthfully and vividly. In 1875 the novelist Henry James wrote of Homer: 'he is a genuine painter; that is, to see, and to reproduce what he sees, is his only care'. James went on to complain – in a way that surprises us today – that Homer lacked imagination, that his subjects were detestable and his work altogether

'horribly ugly' and not at all 'pictorial'. Mark Twain's *Tom Sawyer* was published the year after.

The problem was much the same in Paris, New York and London: men of taste and education looked for themes and qualities that go-ahead painters no longer wanted to provide. They looked for rich painting, suave lighting, handsome forms, and found instead a pictorial prose that seemed bleak and unintelligent. They always underrated the art that went into it, and also the serious implications of giving ordinary people and ordinary scenes the respect that art had normally given only to the great and the dramatic.

Like the others we have been discussing, Homer took his art as seriously as his subjects. For example, he studied colour theory in the best books, and said that a painter could not 'get along without a knowledge of the principles and rules governing the influence of one colour on another'. And his use of clear, rather flat forms probably shows the influence of Manet and of Japanese prints (page 100) as well as of his practice as an illustrator.

HOMER
The Nooning, probably 1872
oil on canvas
33.3 x 49.6 cm (13 x 19 in)
Wadsworth Atheneum,
Hartford, Connecticut
(The Ella Gallup Sumner and
Mary Catlin Sumner Collection)

Monet

CLAUDE MONET born in Paris in 1840; died at Giverny in 1926

MONET
Impression: Sunrise 1872
oil on canvas
50 x 62 cm (20 x 24¹/₂ in)
Musée Marmottan, Paris

The doubts that critics and the wider public felt before the Realism of Courbet and the Naturalism of Manet turned into a torrent of abuse before the pictures they labelled Impressionism. The name was taken derisively from one of Monet's exhibits in the first group show of 1874 he and his friends put on in a rented space in Paris, *Impression: Sunrise.*

Today it represents the most widely loved kind of painting, the most avidly competed for in the sale rooms and the most patiently queued for when it is exhibited. In fact, so completely has the world been won over by its charms that Impressionism's aims and methods are often taken to be norms. Many art lovers now equate normal painting with taking a small canvas out of doors in order to note on it, rapidly and without attention to detail, the ever-changing face of nature in terms of light and colour. Some wish this process to remain innocent of any personal emphasis: 'This is how it looked and made me feel'. Zola, the novelist who wrote in the Impressionists' defence, called their art 'a corner of nature seen through a temperament'. That would do for what many people now expect a painting to be.

Yet Impressionism is obviously a very exceptional, very extreme form of art. It is true that Turner, Courbet, Manet and others had prepared the ground. The Impressionists were certainly aware of these painters and even wanted Manet to be seen as their leader – but Manet was not keen to be associated publicly with a group of artists so loudly mocked by the press. They were also aware of Delacroix's methods, especially the value he placed on leaving brushstrokes distinct and unfused: 'the colour thus gains in energy and freshness', he had written. There was also behind them a long tradition of small oil sketches made out of doors, sometimes as preparation for paintings to be put together in the studio more slowly and with more detail.

But the most important support came from Dutch seventeenth century painting (pages 82-83). The methods employed then were different but the response to the world embodied in those paintings was much the same: a positive, optimistic and above all uncomplicated response. Painting of this sort confirms man's hold on the world, and this was as apt for the citizens of the new Dutch republic as it was for a broad middle-class public becoming prominent in French society and economic life. It is as though landscapes had to be cleared of religious references and of ancient heroes for the new public to be able to say, 'This is our world'.

Why, then, did the Impressionists meet with such abuse? Newspaper art critics of course led the way, using the Impressionist exhibitions for repeated denunciations. Here are some phrases from a review written in 1876: the exhibition is the work of 'five or six lunatics' who 'take up canvas, paint and brush, throw on a few colours haphazardly and sign the whole thing', displaying 'human vanity running amuck to the point of madness' and presenting as art 'the negation of all that constitutes art'.

In that last phrase is our clue to the misunderstanding. Art was associated with subject matter, with conventions of representation, and with specific skills of drawing and painting as well as of staging a scene to make an effective image of it – none of which Impressionism was concerned with. The implied message of Monet's picture is 'This is what it really looks like, once you stop reading nature in terms of paintings', but people had learned to see works of art in terms of art and did not think it the painters' business to bring in wholly new notions of pictorial truth. They knew this was not art because it was not like Michelangelo or Poussin, or even like the carefully delineated Dutch landscapes which were beginning to be popular.

Should the Impressionists perhaps have presented themselves as scientific artists, pursuing optical research through the medium of paint? This was a time when science and the arts were coming together in a variety of ways: Zola's novels, for instance, gave detailed accounts of the lives of the working classes that came close to being documentary, and the naturalistic theatre, with its sets accurately recreating people's sitting-rooms, re-enacted dramas about ordinary people. In the 1880s and after, Monet went on to paint long series of pictures of the same subject or motif at different times of day and under varying effects of light, and the results look like a

scientific investigation when seen together. The cathedral at Rouen, haystacks in a field, the pools and water-lilies in his own garden at Giverny – he looked and recorded, and again looked and recorded, and the process developed its own intensity and poetry.

And here is the deepest mystery. We don't look at *Impression: Sunrise* for its accurate statement of what sunrise looked like over the harbour of Le Havre one morning in 1872. We look at it because it is poetic. We accept that it shows a particular place at a particular time, but what we enjoy is the incompleteness of the way the scene is painted, because that involves us in the painting, makes us collaborate with it. Above all we feel that the picture is joyous, lyrical – a small, light but poignant poem of praise. We enjoy the broadly brushed on greys and oranges, and the sharper strokes of blue-grey and green-grey that give us the objects in the landscape, and the orange disc and its echoing strokes of orange that we read as reflections of light on the water. We enjoy them as information but we enjoy them even more as pictorial pleasures just as in reading a lyrical poem we can enjoy the rhyme and rhythm and internal echoes, and the vividness of individual words, even while our main attention goes to the meaning of the work. Impressionism has taught us to enjoy the act and process of painting.

So well do we like Impressionism that it is difficult for us to find any sympathy for those who denounced it. Critics, we tell ourselves, are always wrong: when they don't hate good new things, they fall over themselves to praise anything new. Where Impressionism was concerned they were confronted by a manner of painting that made it impossible for them to exercise their judgement in the way they were used to, and by a language of painting they found truly difficult to read. Impressionism won: we have all learnt to read it.

But in 1895 an intelligent and art-loving man stood in a gallery before a picture that glowed with colour and struck him as amazingly beautiful yet totally unreadable. The catalogue told him that it was by the Frenchman Monet, and that its subject was haystacks. The man was Kandinsky, the place Moscow. A year later he left Russia for Germany, turning down the professorship in law he had been offered. He had decided to become a painter (page 146).

Seurat

Degas

GEORGES SEURAT born in Paris in 1859; died there in 1891
EDGAR DEGAS born in Paris in 1834; died there in 1917

Impressionism continues as a way of painting to this day but its life as a vanguard group in France was short. By the 1880s the group around Monet was dispersing. Pure Impressionism was too limited. The Impressionists themselves began to bring other elements into their work; other painters, having tried Impressionism's concentration on the purely visual value of a subject, rejected the transient appearance of nature as a sufficient theme and looked for solid pictorial modes capable of carrying more complex meaning.

Seurat's training had been in the tradition of Ingres and classicism. Impressionism led him to attempt a classical form of naturalism. He admired the Impressionists' way of capturing effects of light through distinct marks in contrasting colours. But he decided that he would have to turn that into a controllable system whilst also constructing his compositions so as to be able to predetermine and control the effect they would have on the viewer.

This sounds very elaborate, and perhaps his little landscape, *The Bridge at Courbevoie,* is a simple thing that does not warrant this talk of control and system.

But look at it analytically. Horizontals: bridge, landing stages, boats, far shore. Verticals: masts, figures, fence, reflections, chimney. These echo the edges of the picture and thus stabilize it. Diagonals: the powerful slope of the near bank, paralleled in the fence and picked up elsewhere. Other formal accents: the soft foliage top left, which gives the picture space (try covering it up with your fingers), the tree on the right and the sail. The last two are rising forms, moving swiftly amid all the straight lines and echoed in the smoke from the chimney. The diagonals go down, left to right, but these lines soar and our spirits soar with them.

Seurat knew they would: there was scientific research into the way we are affected by shapes and colours just as there was scientific information about the structure of light and the interaction of colours. By basing himself on this impersonal knowledge and combining it with a simple, recognizable scene – here an industrial suburb of Paris – he sought to create a democratic art, accessible to everyone and without burdensome rhetoric but full of harmony. A form of visual music, perhaps. Music had long been conscious of its effect on the listeners' feelings.

126

SEURAT
The Bridge at Courbevoie
1886–7 (left)
oil on canvas
45.8 x 54.6 cm (18 x 21½ in)
Courtauld Institute Galleries,
London

DEGAS
Woman washing herself
1892 (right)
pastel on paper·
63 x 48 cm (24¾ x 18¾ in)
Lefèvre Gallery,
London

By using rhythm and movement and by colouring sound with harmonies and discords and also through the different qualities heard from different instruments, music had developed a highly elaborate system for unspecific but very direct communication. In the nineteenth century music had become the most democratic, the most widely consumed of the arts. You will recall that Delacroix placed great value on what he called 'the musical part of painting' (page 116). Se rat and others of his generation wanted to achieve the same sort of directness and the same controlled communication.

Degas came from the same classical training as Seurat. He was thought something of a misanthrope by those who knew him, amusing as he could be in company. And there were some who pointed to his many pictures of women – ballet dancers, washerwomen and the many anonymous women he showed at their toilet as in the picture shown here – as evidence that he was a misogynist. Today we often think that those who liked to paint and sell pictures of delicious damsels were perhaps more truly the woman-haters. Degas was certainly fascinated by women and the way they move. Whether he loved them or not becomes unimportant once we realize that what he was doing, in his ungallant pursuit of the female animal, was to reinvent the language of figuration itself.

Seurat used toy-like simplifications for his figures; in fact, he simplified all the forms in his paintings towards, and perhaps beyond, a Neoclassical stillness and universality. Degas was not much concerned with individual character but he was intent on catching a particular motion, especially those that reveal even a beautiful body as something quite different from what the classical tradition relied upon. He was reinventing classicism.

Impressionism pushed him into adapting his innate classicism to accommodate the facts of natural appearance; both the non-European formulae he found in Japanese art and the unclassical 'facts' revealed by photography supported this direction. Degas became an ultra-realist where the human image was concerned. He spoke of himself observing women as though through a keyhole (and note the sense of isolation, not intimacy,

implied in that). It was as though in order to avoid the old time-honoured beauty he had to stalk reality, catch it in its most unguarded moments. A friend has recorded him saying, 'Beauty is a mystery; no one knows it any more. The recipes, the secrets are forgotten. A young man is placed in the middle of a field and told, "Paint". And paints a sincere farm. It's idiotic'. The keyhole approach precluded false sentiment as well as offering new formal possibilities.

But there is much more to a Degas picture than that. He was a great poet where colour was concerned, bringing rich and strange hues into sonorous harmony. But he was also a great pictorial architect. Notice in the picture here, his use of verticals and diagonals (no horizontals) as its framework and, in that framework, the eloquent play of curves, hard against soft, fast against slow. The same friend tells us how Degas at one point spoke angrily of those who thought that painting was a matter of observing and copying closely; 'what I mean', he added quickly after a moment, 'is that everything in a picture is the inter-relationships'.

Gauguin

Van Gogh

PAUL GAUGUIN born in Paris in 1848; died in Atuana in the Marquesas Islands in 1903

VINCENT VAN GOGH born at Groot-Zundert (Netherlands) in 1853; died at Auvers-sur-Oise in 1890

GAUGUIN
*The Vision after the Sermon:
Jacob wrestling with the
Angel* 1888 (left)
oil on canvas
73 x 92 cm (28³/₄ x 36¹/₄ in)
National Gallery of Scotland,
Edinburgh

VAN GOGH
The Sower 1888 (right)
oil on canvas
73 x 92 cm (28³/₄ x 36¹/₄ in)
Rijksmuseum Vincent van
Gogh, Amsterdam
(E. G. Bürhle Collection)

In a letter of July 1888 Gauguin described a painting he had just finished as 'wholly Japanese by a savage from Peru'. The following month, writing to the same friend, a painter, he offered this advice: 'Don't paint too much directly from nature. Art is an abstraction! Study nature, then brood on it and think more of the creation which will result'. In between writing those letters he painted *The Vision after the Sermon*.

His words are as extraordinary as the painting. Do not paint from nature but from your imagination; I, Gauguin, make pictures that are very Japanese and I am a savage. He had spent part of his childhood in Peru. In his youth he had worked on merchant ships and served in the French navy. But then he had settled down, become a stockbroker and made a good marriage. He also began to be a Sunday painter. He met some of the Impressionists and bought Impressionist pictures, and then, in 1882, he threw up his job and, in effect, his marriage, in order to be a painter. To get to the point at which he could overcome the Impressionist principle of working directly from nature took time and confidence and a variety of other influences.

The Vision after the Sermon marks the turning point. He painted it in Brittany where it was cheap to live and

where there were other painters he could learn from and also dominate. There were also the Bretons in their traditional clothes, and their folk art and the simple piety which it expressed. That is the theme of the painting. The Breton women have come out of the church, and with them their priest (on the right). He has told them of Jacob's strange contest with the angel and, as they leave the church, they have a vision of this Biblical event.

Gauguin has arranged the women to form a frame for this vision and to suggest a space for it, but the painting is almost entirely flat. The crimson ground makes it flat and so does the tree trunk slanting surprisingly across the composition. The colour and the tree both suggest Japanese prints (page 100); the wrestlers too come from there.

That October he went down to Arles in the south of France, accepting Van Gogh's invitation to live and work together. The Dutchman, a failed preacher and missionary, had recently moved down there after two years in Paris. He knew the Impressionists and had spent time in Seurat's studio. For all his impetuousness he was a very thoughtful and learned painter who had looked hard at old and new art and had studied, especially, the

theory and practice of colour. In the bright sunshine he found not only a Japanese world known previously only from the Japanese prints he owned but also a Delacroix world. In that searing light he could understand the methods Delacroix had evolved after experiencing the light of North Africa. This too meant going beyond Impressionism to something more consciously constructed.

But close contact with nature continued to be essential for Van Gogh. Gauguin felt he knew better and tried to persuade him that 'art is an abstraction'. *The Sower,* painted that autumn, was Van Gogh's response. It is partly visionary: the dark silhouette of the man sowing and that slanting tree must have pleased Gauguin with their flatness. Behind them Van Gogh painted his mightiest sun, a sulphurous evening sun that seems to promise both life to the seed and death to the sower. But most of all it gives light to the ground, in the form of several strong, contrasting colours, in firm touches that at the same time shape the ground and give it direction.

Both painters were natural expressionists, in that they used art to convey feelings both through the images they used, which tended to have symbolic meaning whilst also relating to the world around them, and through their use, above all, of colour. Gauguin often made his unnatural; Van Gogh heightened it until it acquired hypnotic force. Gauguin was not religious by temperament; his use of religious themes was a linking of his art into the tradition of art as part of human existence, not art as a sophisticated object for collectors and museums. Van Gogh, profoundly religious, stands in the Romantic tradition of charging landscape with profound meaning, and sowing and the sun are ancient symbols, instinctively understood by everyone, for procreation and life.

That December, partly because of Gauguin's pressure upon him, Van Gogh had a breakdown. Gauguin fled to Paris. Van Gogh was soon back at work but he suffered further attacks of madness. In July 1890 he shot himself and died two days later. He had sold only one or two paintings all his life.

Later Gauguin went off to live in the South Seas, more or less like a native. He rejected Europe geographically as well as culturally. This made him the hero of all those eager to show their impatience with the polite conventions of art. Gauguin's example taught not only the virtues of turning inwards, away from nature, to one's imagination, but also the virtue of feeding that imagination on barbaric images.

Cézanne

PAUL CÉZANNE born in Aix-en-Provence in 1839; died there in 1906

Many modern artists have looked to Cézanne as their master and father, as the essential turning point between the old art and the new. He in his last years came to believe this too. 'I am the primitive of a new art', he wrote to a young painter; 'I feel that I shall have followers'. But like all great artists he was a complex person and his work did not propose one outcome. His followers took this or that as his main contribution to art; we must try to understand him without reducing him to a formula.

For a while he worked like an Impressionist though he was never satisfied with the slightness of the typical Impressionist picture. Earlier he had worked like Courbet, using paint thickly and emphatically for portraits and still lifes, and then also, like a Delacroix gone wild, he produced clumsy scenes of murder and violence. In the 1880s and '90s he produced a long series of portraits, landscapes and still lifes in which he tried to turn Impressionism into a method for capturing not the passing appearance but the more permanent, living character of the subject or motif in front of him.

He worked very slowly, needing many sittings for the sort of picture an Impressionist might do at one go, or two or three. He learned to reduce the multitude of colours he saw to simple colour chords: a landscape might demand a range of blue-greens and a range of yellow ochres. In putting down his patches of these colours Cézanne would be at once locating a specific object on the canvas and also establishing a constructive relationship between each patch and the patches already on the canvas. The accuracy he was after was only indirectly related to the motif: it was the presence on the canvas of each touch and of the object each touch was there to establish that mattered most. And these had to balance the effectiveness of the picture as a composition with his experiencing of the motif. That is what took the time.

He did not want a markedly three-dimensional effect as in, say, Courbet: 'It has taken me forty years to discover that painting is not sculpture', he said. Neither did he want Manet's flimsiness or Impressionism's looseness. What he wanted to do, he said, was this – bringing his two hands slowly together, interlacing the fingers and tightening their grasp. There was nature, large, wonderful and alive, and there was his living apprehension of it: these had to be brought together in a painting that would have the strength of an old master.

Our bodily positions reveal our attitudes to ourselves and to others. Pictures similarly convey a sense of conviviality or conflict, of harmony and tensions. We cannot help sensing them in human terms. Cézanne was inordinately sensitive to such relationships in art as in life. So he constructed firm pictures that yet allowed things in them an unprecedented mobility. He gave his painted objects a quality of flatness so that they would not break the picture surface by asserting their volume, but he also gave them enough modelling to suggest something of their mass. He stressed the intervals between things whilst also showing us their interdependence,

CÉZANNE
After Chardin: Still Life with Pitcher about 1890
pencil on paper
12.2 x 20.8 cm (4³/₄ x 8¹/₄ in)
Kunstmuseum, Basle

breaking their isolating and identifying silhouettes here and there and running his paint across from one object to the next. Others had learned from Delacroix and from colour theory that colours affect and distort each other; Cézanne, in his slow observing, noticed that shapes do something similar, distorting and dislocating each other through a sort of visual magnetism.

The little drawing illustrated here may make all this clearer. It happens to be a drawing after part of a picture by Chardin and serves to remind us of his admiration for him (page 108). Notice how he repeats the outline of the pitcher to find its true relationship to other curves, even though it has to be made asymmetrical and therefore 'wrong' to this end. He changes its height in the same way and tilts the oval line that defines its top to make it look more open, more round than in the painting. Its modelling is left uncertain lest it assert itself too much as a distinct object in contrast to the other forms. We need to refer to the painting to know that the round object on the right is a ladle-strainer, its long handle rising to the left of the pitcher and resting against a large cooking pot lying on its side. The other rising diagonal, echoing the ladle's, turns out to be the edge of a large fish, a skate. Everything is made to link up, co-exist. The climax of Cézanne's work comes at the end, in three large figure paintings. One is shown here. He spoke of 'doing Poussin again from nature'. But his *Bathers* has so diagrammatic a character that we think also of a David redone from nature (page 110). Cézanne was not here working from nature: he had not got a lot of naked women to arrange themselves in front of a landscape. He had studied individual models, and also sculptures and photographs, to develop his own sort of figuration. They are, obviously, much simplified: look what he does with the faces, hands and feet. Also, he packs them together in pictorial units, echoing the main lines of the trees which are similarly abstracted. He made his figures serve in the same way that he expected from his long-suffering wife. Once, when she got uncomfortable during yet another long sitting, he yelled at her, 'Be an apple!'

But his figures are human beings, not apples, and they are part of a serene landscape whose harmoniousness triumphs over its diagrammatic firmness. Compare their union with the trees with Courbet's failure to bring apples and landscape together. Cézanne's women are not bathers, of course, but naked women existing calmly in a radiant world. He offers us a vision of happiness, of the Golden Age of which poets wrote in ancient times, before pain and strife came into the world. This was Cézanne's main legacy to those who came after him; it was at this time that he called himself 'the primitive of a new art'. The world is no nearer peace, but we have learned not to mistake his delicate management of paint as incompetence and are rewarded by a new sort of masterpiece, a history painting without pomp or learned reference.

CÉZANNE
Bathers 1898–1905
oil on canvas
208 x 249 cm (82 x 98 in)
Philadelphia Museum of Art
(W. P. Wilstach Collection)

Rodin

AUGUSTE RODIN born in Paris in 1840; died there in 1917

RODIN
The Prodigal Son c. 1885–7
bronze
138 cm (54¾ in) high
Victoria and Albert Museum,
London

The nineteenth century produced a great deal of sculpture: statues for churches, government buildings and public spaces; elaborate tombs and fountains; large and small figures of ancient gods and goddesses and evergreen damsels for museums and the mantelpieces of the well-to-do, portrait busts for public and domestic purposes, and so on. Much of it was poor stuff, routine work by more or less proficient craftsmen. Some of it was excellent by any standards. But it is clear the century's sculpture could not match its painting for innovation and achievement.

We have already noted that developments in nineteenth century painting occurred mostly in landscape. Only towards the end of the century do we find painters – notably Degas and Cézanne (pages 126, 130-131) – bringing into figure painting the innovatory spirit previously employed in landscape. The implication is that the human image was so charged with traditional ideas of form and meaning that new ideas had to be explored through other means. If this is so, it must have been a particular burden to sculptors whose art was essentially and, it must have seemed, inescapably an art of figuration.

Rodin, single-handedly, reactivated sculpture. He broke the almost unchallenged hold of classicism, first by mingling influences from medieval sculpture with a sense of monumentality he derived from Michelangelo, the painter as much as the sculptor (pages 60–61, 64-65). Secondly, he seized hungrily on all the unconventional and thus the more expressive movements and poses he could discover in living people. Again and again he drew models as they moved about his studio, catching the positions of a moment in almost instant sketches.

He was primarily a modeller. He worked in clay, manipulating the material until it attained the form he was seeking, and then having it cast in plaster and in due course in bronze. The original material is squashy and moist; the final object is hard but light-reflecting or lightless according to how it is treated. *The Prodigal Son* shows clearly its origin in clay. Form flows into form, legs into torso into arms, chest into neck into head. There is little firm detail. There is no certainty of a skeleton inside the flesh. The question of accuracy scarcely arises: we don't ask whether Rodin has got every part of the anatomy right because what engages our attention is the expression of the figure as a whole.

Remember, this is a life-size figure. That rippling surface would not surprise in a small work. But here forms determined by the shaping figures and by the reluctance of clay to take on fine detail are put before us on a much larger scale and confront us with a new body image: elusive, intangible, an apparition more than a factual presence. The title helps us to confirm its meaning, but then we find the same figure appearing in other Rodin sculptures. It is back to back with a female figure in *Fugit Amor* (Love Flies). And in 1887 it was exhibited as *The Child of the Age*. Its meaning must be unspecific; nonetheless it is certainly an image of yearning, perhaps of despair. For this we do not need a title. We sense it by identifying with the position of the figure.

If *The Prodigal Son* is like a flame, *Balzac* is like a mountain. Rodin had sought the commission for a statue of the great French novelist, but struggled for a long time for a way of showing both his likeness and his creative energy. In the end he concentrated these in the face, which is almost a caricature in its exaggeration of some features – especially the eyes and the shapes around them – and its generalization of others. This gives the face an amazing vitality, and also makes it legible in daylight and from a distance. Instead of distracting us with an account of the man's clothes and shape, he found a monumental and at the same time truthful formula for that: Balzac is shown in the act of writing, wearing the dressing gown he wore in his study and striding up and down the room in his effort to form his ideas into art.

'It is the first time', wrote one critic, 'anyone has had the idea of extracting the brains of a man and putting them on his face!' Rodin had gone too far, he added, and others agreed. The statue was refused by the society that had commissioned it, and it was not set up until 1939. They had expected an impressive portrait; Rodin had incorporated elements of portraiture into a powerful symbol for human creativity, going from the particular to the general in meaning as in form.

By the turn of the century Rodin enjoyed great international fame, often for sweeter, more easily acceptable works. His influence on other sculptors was very powerful, so much so that some of the more strong-minded of them had to turn against him. 'Nothing can grow in the shadow of great trees', as Brancusi said (pages 140-141). Through his large and widely varying output Rodin proved the possibility of a figure sculpture independent of classical models and ideals of beauty. He showed that meaning could come through the sympathy we instinctively feel for posture. It is interesting, but not all that surprising, to find that he was very excited by what he saw of the beginnings of modern dance. He made sculptures of Nijinsky and other dancers. They fit well into his exploration of expressive movement.

RODIN
Balzac monument 1898
bronze
280 cm (110 in) high
Boulevard Raspail, Paris

Munch   Picasso

EDVARD MUNCH born at Loten (Norway) in 1863; died in 1944 at Ekely near Oslo

PABLO PICASSO born at Malaga in southern Spain in 1881; died in Mougins in southern France in 1973

The two paintings shown here have a lot in common. Even before we read their titles or attempt to read their meaning from the images we can tell that they are sad and troubled pictures. Their colours and their languid, hanging forms suggest this, and so does the hollow space in them.

Death in the Sickroom gets much of its effect from the spaces between the figures in it. Some of them are clustered together, some are solitary; no one addresses anyone else and the only faces we can see are blank. From front to back of the picture space is a long way.

The boy in the corner seems remote from the group in the centre and from the group on the right. Though there is all this space the figures feel slight, silhouettes more than weighty bodies. Notice how the three figures in the foreground are fused into one silhouette though they remain separate in spirit.

There is something stage-like about the composition, and again we are reminded of the plays that Munch's generation went to see and the novels they read, in both cases often about what we call real life: the dramas we all witness in our lives or close at hand. Ibsen, for example,

134

was the great playwright of the time and he was a Norwegian; later on Munch was to do sets for plays by Ibsen. So Munch's subject matter was not unique to him. What was unique was his personal involvement with it. He grew up in a house of sickness and death. His mother died when he was four, his sister Sophie when he was 13. The second event is probably recalled in the painting. It is his other sister, Inger, who stares at us from it, blank with misery. The boy in the corner probably is an echo of Munch himself, 16 years earlier.

There is a personal element in Picasso's painting too, though it is less easy to grasp. We know from his drawings that the young Spanish painter changed the persons shown in the picture several times before finishing it. In one of them the man on the left has Picasso's own features; in another Picasso stands on the right, next to an easel on which there is a picture similar to the upper

one of the two shown here. The man on the left now has the features of his friend Casagemas. Casagemas had been in Paris with Picasso in 1900, had fallen in love with a girl there, had found himself incapable of consummating his love and had committed suicide some weeks later.

So *La Vie* (Life) is not a narrative scene but uses a reference to a specific tragedy in its generalized statement about life and love. It is the largest and probably for Picasso the most important painting of what is called his Blue Period, and it is by no means the most miserable. Its message is a gloomy one, whatever it is, yet it leaves us possibilities of hope. The figures in the pictures within the picture are full of sorrow, but the couple on the left express love and the woman on the right, though rather forbidding in her expression, is handsome and holds a healthy baby. It is the funereal colour that insists on a pessimistic reading of the scene.

Munch the Norwegian and Picasso the Spaniard came to Paris from two ends of Europe. That they should go to Paris to complete their art training was by now almost to be expected. Paris had replaced Rome as the art centre of the western world; Munich was probably the second centre after Paris, and Berlin was beginning to be important. Munch was in Paris in 1889-90 on a scholarship and was influenced by what he saw of the work of Gauguin and Van Gogh; he was there again in 1896. In 1892 he was in Berlin where he had been invited to exhibit paintings at the Berlin Society of Artists. His works caused a tremendous scandal and the exhibition had to be closed a few days after it opened. From then on Berlin, and soon also the rest of the German art world, was divided into Munch's fierce supporters and his equally fierce enemies, and Munch spent much of his time from then on in Germany. The writers and artists associated with the broad tendency called Expressionism looked to him as their guide whilst also sharing his admiration for Gauguin and Van Gogh.

Picasso made a number of trips from Barcelona to Paris during 1900-03, and settled in Paris in the spring of 1904. We shall see more of his work on the pages that follow and that will show him in a more obviously revolutionary role as well as in a lighter, intellectually more playful vein. But it must be emphasized that the Picasso we see here, expressing a joyless view of life but also very much concerned to use his art to convey his personal awareness of his immediate world, is as real as the cool innovator he was to appear to be in the years around 1910 (pages 139).

Braque   Picasso

GEORGES BRAQUE born in 1882 at Argenteuil, Paris; died in Paris in 1963

PABLO PICASSO see pages 134-135

PICASSO
Guitar 1912 (above)
sheetmetal and wire
78 cm (30¹/₂ in) high
Museum of Modern Art, New
York (gift of the artist)

PICASSO
*Bottle of Vieux Marc, glass, guitar
and newspaper* 1913 (right)
collage with charcoal
62.5 x 47 cm (24³/₄ x 18¹/₂ in)
Tate Gallery, London

BRAQUE
The Portuguese 1911 (left)
oil on canvas
117 x 82 cm (46 x 32 in)
Kunstmuseum, Basle

In 1908 Picasso and Braque, the Spaniard and the Frenchman, embarked on a joint adventure that has remained a climax in the story of modern art. They worked closely together, 'like two mountaineers roped together', said Braque later. They went step by step without knowing exactly where they were going. It looks as though Braque led the way at first, and that Picasso was the initiator of the new direction taken in 1912. That year Picasso moved to a studio across the other side of Paris, but there remained an element of collaboration and interaction in their work until war came, in 1914, and Braque went into the army.

What they did was soon labelled Cubism. But it has nothing to do with cubes, though the label tempted observers to see geometry in their pictures. In Braque's *The Portuguese* we get hints of rising triangles, suggesting transparent planes as though we were looking at it through rather neatly shattered glass. We can also see soft brushstrokes, often horizontal touches, and lines – lines as lines and lines that seem to be describing objects but leave them incomplete, suggested rather than stated. We see tone rather than colour. There seems to be some

light because there are some shadowy areas, and there is some sense of space, but it is all rather uncertain. The feeling we get is that of a shallow relief structure made of edgy but impermanent material.

What is it a picture of? It is so difficult to read that the difficulty we have in reading it seems to be what the picture is about. A puzzle? A tease? I believe that there is an element of playfulness in this Cubism (absent in other painters' versions of Cubism). Picasso and Braque were doing a highwire act, teetering between the pulls of abstraction on one side and legibility on the other and having us teeter along behind them. In this picture we get hints of various sorts. The title suggests (especially in French) a man. With that clue tightly grasped we set off. With luck we soon find a top hat, a hint of a face; bottom centre a slanting shape with a circle, curves and some horizontal lines, all of which turn out to 'be' a guitar. The lettering could suggest a poster on a wall, a dance poster perhaps: GRAND BAL it could be. In the top left quarter are linear symbols that indicate a bottle and a glass. So: a man playing a guitar in a bar?

Does it matter? Is it the finding that counts or the searching? You may think that Picasso and Braque planted those clues merely to engage our attention, to keep us looking while the spatial and formal character of the picture as a whole makes its impression on us. Perhaps they themselves needed the man and his trappings to control their building up of this strange new picture language.

If we ask ourselves how new it is, we come to a curious conclusion. First: that in many respects Cubism is rooted in pictorial traditions especially honoured in France. The symmetrical pose and the emphasis on line at the

expense of colour are both decently classical; the careful organization of the image as a structure of planes suggests Chardin (page 109) as well as Seurat and Cézanne. The fusing of figures and setting and the interrupted paint surface both again suggest Cézanne. Second: that it subverts tradition in a particularly radical way. The whole Renaissance tradition had been founded on certain assumptions derived from Greek tragedy and obviously central to any art dealing with significant actions. We can summarize them as the unities of space, time and language. One moment, shown in one coherent space, and with one style or method of representation. Cubism goes against each of them.

Cubism does not merely hide its motifs: it breaks them apart, fuses them with the space around them and with the background, makes them seem so unstable that they seem mobile, and then uses quite dissimilar kinds of representation in one painting. Compare, in this instance, the lettering, the top hat and the glass.

Cubism can do this because it is not delivering an important narrative or message. The man and his guitar seem to be the occasion of a pictorial debate, not its true subject. Many Cubist paintings are of still lifes; here we can say that the man is less important than his hat and other stage props. The picture is about seeing and reading and making pictures.

It is also beautiful, in a light way. Getting to the Cubist pictures in a well-stocked art gallery, after the Post-Impressionists, is rather like reaching Watteau after Poussin and Le Brun.

Picasso made Cubism go one step further in its undoing of tradition when he introduced non-art materials into his pictures. Braque's lettering may have given him the hint. At any rate, in 1912 Picasso began to stick pieces of paper and oilcloth and then also whole objects on to his canvas or paper grounds, and Braque followed him at once to develop his own version of it. The process is called collage. Both as a process and as visual evidence of a mental process – a process of building or assembling rather than delineating or de-scribing – it is central to much modern art.

In that same year, Picasso also constructed – assembled and fixed together – a sculpture that resembles a guitar. He made a cardboard version, and then the sheet metal and wire object we see here. We call it a sculpture; we could also call it an alternative, unplayable form of a guitar. It has no base or other indication of where it belongs. Picasso used to hang it on the wall like a picture or an African mask, but he also liked to get it down and seat it in an armchair, like a person. It is not modelled or carved, and its making did not call for any of the skills traditionally associated with sculpture. It has no mass, only planes and actual space. Similarly, his collage picture, though it hints at shadows here and there, has no space in it, but in effect it actually comes forward from its ground plane of blue.

Brancusi

CONSTANTIN BRANCUSI born in Hobitza (Romania) in 1876; died in Paris in 1957

BRANCUSI
The Kiss (side view) 1907
stone
28 cm (11 in) high
Muzeul de Arta, Craiova,
Romania

Brancusi was of peasant origin and grew up in a world of hand-carved wooden utensils, furniture, posts holding gates and porches, and also commemorative monuments in cemeteries and elsewhere. He imbibed primitivism as his native idiom. He also had an academic training in sculpture, mostly in modelling naturalistic figures and heads. In 1902 he got his diploma. In 1903 he set off for Paris, going on foot via Munich and Basel. In Paris he attended more art classes and worked as Rodin's assistant for a while in 1907. That same year he made his first characteristic sculpture. In many ways it is the opposite of Rodin's.

The Kiss is very obviously carved. We see the stony-ness of the object even before we recognize it as two half-length figures in a tight embrace. The sculptor seems to have removed as little as possible of the original block, implying that he is not interested in technique and a more detailed and naturalistic representation. He has cut out inessential details – noses, ears – and deprived us of the sweetness of pose and form and also the seductions of nakedness that the theme might seem to promise.

The image that results is that of a primordial kiss, of total and timeless union between man and woman in the fusion we call love but which is also our basic biological necessity. That said, we can begin to notice the subtleties. The man's proportion of head and arms are slightly different from the woman's; their hair is different; the placing of the arms, which seems quite natural and contributes greatly to the emotional pull of the work, cleverly obscures necks and chins and thus permits the block-ness of the total form. The arms bend at ambiguous points which one writer has called the 'elbowrist'. Her hands hold gently the back of the man's head; his meet horizontally behind her neck and long hair. The sculptural lump turns out to be a delicate, enchanting poem that implants itself in our imaginations with unusual clarity.

Brancusi's reputation as sculptor is associated with this emphasis on carving as a collaboration between man and material, not the traditional victory of one over the other. But much of his work was modelled and cast. Often he did sculptures in series, developing a theme in carved and in modelled form, adapting its shape and detail as his ideas about it changed and also to go with different processes and materials. But he did not, after his earliest works, use the broken and flickering surfaces of bronze exploited so dramatically by Rodin: instead he used bronze for its smoothness and brightness, often polishing its surfaces with endless patience until it seems to dissolve under light.

In about 1910 he started making bird sculptures, stimulated probably by a bird fabled in Romanian folk lore. The first two were carved in white marble; the next three, probably of 1912, are in bronze; the sixth is in grey marble; the seventh in yellow marble, and so on. Illustrated here, in polished bronze, is (probably) the twenty-first out of twenty-seven.

It is a swift, soaring form, light and streamlined. It differs from those just before it in the series by swelling more slowly from the 'neck' where the tail becomes the body and by a different angle for the sliced-off plane at the top. One barely misses the beak, head, wings, feathers and colour that say 'bird'. Brancusi gives us an image of birdness. It incorporates and expresses the

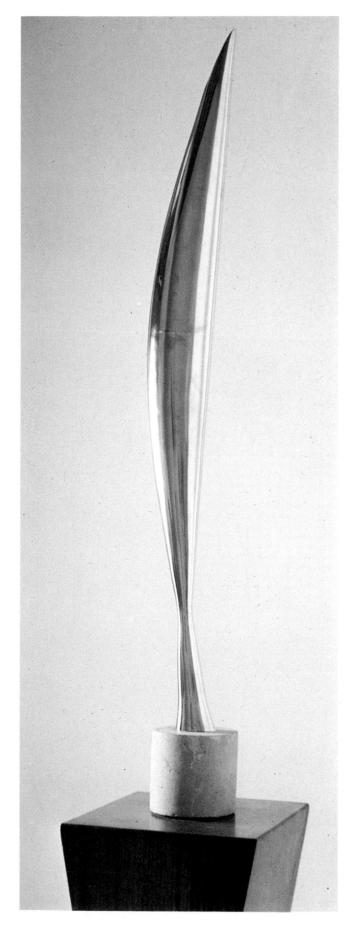

BRANCUSI
Bird in Space 1928
polished bronze
137 cm (54 in) high
Museum of Modern Art,
New York

associations we put upon the thought of a bird rising up into the sky – freedom, joy, oneness with endless space, Shelley's 'Blithe spirit'.

We could also say that this sculpture stands for modern technology, that the peasant Brancusi here counterbalances his innate primitivism with an excited response to the miraculous world of technological energy and speed. This is quite possible: certainly his generation was stirred by the extraordinary enlargement of man's powers by electricity, aeroplane and motor car, X-rays and radio. Designers had hardly begun to think about streamlining when Brancusi made this elegant form and he had already used a similar form in his bird sculptures of 1918-19.

What is certain is this: that Brancusi and other artists of his time saw no conflict between the new world of technology and the ancient world of mysticism and spiritualism. Brancusi's mind was filled with the old legends of Eastern Europe. Like many other thinking men and women of his time, he was deeply interested in Oriental mysticism. And we find that the Oriental mind responded to his. In 1933 the Maharajah of Indore in India bought three of Brancusi's birds and commissioned him to design a temple of meditation to be built at Indore and to house the birds. In 1935 Brancusi visited India for some weeks. He was enchanted by what he saw of Indian culture. He returned to Paris via Egypt and his native Romania. The project, sadly, came to nothing.

Brancusi was culturally a multi-national, combining in himself the Romanian folk heritage and European academic traditions, feeding them into the productive vortex of Parisian modernism and reaching out towards universal meaning through simple, distilled sculptural form. Why did people ever find this kind of art ugly and aggressive? Most of Brancusi's sculptures use themes other than the human figures. Some are totally abstract. None, from *The Kiss* on, deals with painful or tragic ideas. He saw no conflict between wholly abstract forms and forms derived from objects or living creatures. It was the message embodied in the form that counted for him, not the form's origin. Like Mondrian and Matisse, he was an artist of affirmation. Brancusi said, 'It is pure joy that I am giving to you.'

141

Delaunay

Kirchner

ROBERT DELAUNAY born in Paris in 1885; died in Montpellier in 1941

ERNST LUDWIG KIRCHNER born in Aschaffenburg (Germany) in 1880; died in Davos (Switzerland) in 1938

DELAUNAY
The Cardiff Team 1913
oil on canvas
196 x 132 cm (77 x 52 in)
Stedelijk Van Abbemuseum,
Eindhoven

Behind both Delaunay's art and Kirchner's stands the example of Gauguin and Delacroix and the idea of colour as a means of stirring us emotionally. But Delaunay was linked through friendship with the group of Cubists who formed around Picasso and Braque and developed Cubism in various directions. You can see in Delaunay's painting an underlying geometrical structure that may remind you of the half-hidden structure in

KIRCHNER
Artist and Model c. 1910
oil on canvas
150 x 100 cm (59 x 39³/₈ in)
Kunsthalle, Hamburg

event and image, and that of a very ordinary sort that everybody could connect with. But to the football match he added even more popular images: the Eiffel Tower, the large ferris wheel that used to stand in southern Paris and was much loved, an aeroplane referring to a great French achievement, Blériot's flight across the English Channel in 1909. And, even more general, Delaunay introduced hoardings with words on them: *astra* is Latin for stars, 'magic' means what it says.

Kirchner was the leading member of a small group of painters who worked together from 1905 on in Dresden and from 1911 on separately in Berlin. They are now seen as part of the wider German movement, Expressionism, to which all the arts, especially poetry, drama and film were to contribute. The label implies strong, often intensely personal statements and at the same time the opposite to Impressionism as an art of description. A lot of Expressionist work is vehement in its denunciation of the modern world, of the harshness and anonymity of city life and the physical and mental sicknesses one can associate with industrialization and the loss of our roots in nature. The coming of World War I in 1914 added further justification and point to such protest.

The best paintings of Kirchner and his friends came rather earlier than Expressionist poetry, drama and film, and were not markedly angry. Many were full of high animal spirits, notably their pictures of sunlit lakes and bathers. Some are cooler in their view, as when they painted cabaret scenes and circus acts. What their work had in common at this stage was that it opposed vividness and energy to the dreary exercises in pictorial politeness Kirchner and his friends claimed to see every year in the exhibitions put on by artists' societies in Munich and Dresden. They wanted to fill art with life. Like Van Gogh, whose work they saw and admired in Germany, they wanted to address themselves to ordinary people and to rescue art from its enslavement to middle-class conventions.

Kirchner's painting of himself and his model has a lot of visual strength. The colours bounce off each other, blue off orange, pink off green, and the brushwork itself suggests attack. Ragged shapes on the floor and on the wall add to the visual noise. If we imagine the picture without this vividness it becomes a relatively straightforward thing. The subject is more or less conventional, and there is space of a traditional sort to accommodate the painter and the model seated behind him. It is the manner that makes this an Expressionist work.

Delaunay's painting, less aggressive in manner, is the more revolutionary in its conception since it brings together different kinds of imagery from a variety of sources and welds them, as though by collage, into a celebration of life. Kirchner uses the energy of colour and the challenge issued by his brusque manner to give new life to an inherited form and theme, but his meaning remains unclear.

Braque's painting (page 138). But here it is the colour that strikes us first – the blue sky contrasting with reds, oranges and yellows, and the large shapes of colour seem to represent posters – and this links him with the German tendency called Expressionism.

Delaunay's subject was, in one sense, a very specific one. The Cardiff rugby football team came to Paris to play against a French team, and the visit occasioned a lot of excitement. Delaunay saw a photograph of one moment from the match in a newspaper, a sooty image without any background but showing men leaping for the ball. He had been painting very colourful pictures, full of curved forms in contrasting colours that seemed to press and move against each other; otherwise they lacked recognizable forms though Delaunay gave them titles like *Sun and Moon* to indicate their cosmic, universal meaning. In *The Cardiff Team* he anchored his idea of art as a reflection of broad, general feelings in a specific

143

Duchamp

MARCEL DUCHAMP born in 1887 at Blainville near Rouen; died at Neuilly, Paris, in 1968

Old art and new art, primitivism and sophistication, the fragmentations of Cubism and the stridencies of Expressionism – into the midst of all this contradictory evidence of what art should look like and be about, Duchamp dropped a very substantial philosophical spanner.

If art is not the business of making beautiful things, as Goya and others had shown; if it is not a matter of exact and skilful imitation of the world and especially of ourselves, as many artists had implied since Impressionism and as Cubism now asserted so tellingly; if it is not the stating and restating of important beliefs or the retelling of important stories, and not even the clear representing of things like still lifes and landscapes into which we can feed meaning – then what is it?

In 1913 Duchamp, a painter and brother to a painter and to a sculptor, mounted a bicycle wheel on a kitchen stool. 'It was just a distraction', he said about this later. 'To see the wheel turning was very soothing, very comforting'. In 1914 he purchased a bottle rack in a Paris department store and gave it an inscription. In 1915, in New York, he bought a snow shovel and named it *In Advance of the Broken Arm*. For this he invented the term 'ready-made': he did not make the object nor alter it; he chose it and took it from the world of purchasable and specifically functional things into the world of less specifically functional things we call art. He chose it, he said, with total 'visual indifference'. He was not saying that everything was beautiful and deserved to be art.

He was saying that what determines the art-ness of a work of art is the artist's intention – not skill, not originality, not strong feeling, but the artist's will and act. What counts is not the object but the idea, the conception.

It seems arrogant – because it does not start by justifying the artist's right to be an artist. But Duchamp's attitude is only an inversion of our attitude to the idea of the great artist. It is an extension, perhaps to nonsensical lengths, of the Romantic notion of the artist as a super-human genius, required to be very new and very lawless and yet terribly profound.

There is a satirical element in all Duchamp's actions, but that does not mean that his work is just a leg-pull. His ready-mades may be more important as evidence of an attitude than as art objects, but much of his work combined such philosophical fingering of the roots of art with brilliantly inventive processes and visual results.

In 1913 he wrote a note to himself: 'A straight horizontal thread one metre long falls from a height of one metre on to a horizontal plane whilst twisting freely, and gives a new form to the unit of length'. The establishment

of the metre – one ten-millionth part of one-quarter of the Earth's circumference – was one of the most permanent achievements of the French Assembly after the revolution of 1789. To undermine, even playfully, the absoluteness of that unit of measurement, a masterpiece of rational collective action, was a brilliant idea. In the months that followed Duchamp made the prescribed action happen three times, fixed the three threads as they had fallen and, following them, cut three unstraight rulers, and then made a box to house the whole kit in. One metre + chance = a new sort of metre and a set of unruly rulers.

Similar but vaster care plus chance went into his most famous work, familiarly known as *The Large Glass*. It is one of the most elaborate works of art ever produced and it was made by Duchamp alone, slowly over years, incorporating themes that had long occupied his art and notebook.

Between four sheets of glass, using paint, lead wire and metal foil, dust and human hair and varnish, he constructed a semi-abstract image that is both a symbol of all our lives and a glimpse into his own. The nine metallic shapes in the lower panel, left, symbolize the bachelors of the title. Their positions have been plotted using the three un-rulers three times each and setting the lines

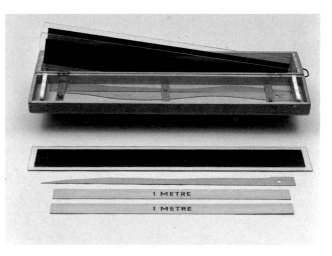

produced by them into strict perspective. The mechanical devices in the same panel, symbolizing the bachelors' longing for the bride, are also shown in perspective, and so are the three circular devices taken from opticians' charts whom Duchamp referred to as witnesses in the non-drama his work almost enacts. Alas, the perfect perspective has no visual force because it is on glass.

DUCHAMP
a drawing of his
Bicycle Wheel 1913 (above)
Duchamp fixed the wheel to
a kitchen stool as 'just a
distraction'. The original
no longer exists.

DUCHAMP
Three Standard Stoppages
1913–4 (left)
assemblage
28 x 128 x 23 cm
(11$\frac{1}{8}$ x 50$\frac{7}{8}$ x 9 in)
Museum of Modern Art,
New York (Katherine S.
Dreier Bequest)

DUCHAMP
*The Bride Stripped Bare by
her Bachelors, Even (The
Large Glass)* 1915–23 (right)
oil and lead wire on glass
277 x 175 cm (109$\frac{1}{4}$ x 69 in)
Philadelphia Museum of Art
(Katherine S. Dreier
Bequest)

The upper panel presents the bride on the left, a strange configuration of movable and partly hollow semi-anatomical elements investigated by Duchamp in paintings and drawings of 1912-3. And so on. The work refers outwards to art and science and also to the early stage of scientific speculation and experiment we call alchemy. It feels like a history painting and looks in some measure like an altarpiece (compare it with the Titian on page 72). When it was smashed on its way back home from an exhibition, Duchamp welcomed chance's further contribution to the work, but spent many hours putting it together again.

145

Kandinsky   Klee

VASSILY KANDINSKY born in Moscow in 1866; died at Neuilly, Paris, in 1944

PAUL KLEE born at Münchenbuchsee near Berne in 1879; died at Muralto in 1940

Composition IV looks abstract and even random: coloured patches, some with firm and some with soft edges, long and short brushed lines in black. It looks personal and private, a matter of handwriting and instinctive gesture rather than a public statement in paint. Yet it is quite a large painting, and we know that Kandinsky worked his way towards it slowly and deliberately, through studies made specifically for it as well as through his wider research.

We know that he was deeply moved by the colour in the landscape by Monet and that it moved him although the subject of the picture seemed indecipherable. His years in Munich had convinced him more and more that subject matter was secondary in art – that the all-over expressive character of a picture, the 'sound' of its colours and forms is its message, in that this strikes the beholder first and most deeply. Shortly after he painted this picture he was to become known as the great champion of abstract art.

His book *Concerning the Spiritual in Art,* published in 1912, was the first substantial argument for abstraction and remains the most persuasive one. It was very influential, becoming almost instantly available in four

languages: German, Russian, French and English. People in several countries quoted from it and argued with it, adopted some of its points as their own and also tended to oversimplify its message. For Kandinsky was not really arguing for abstract as against figurative art. He was arguing for an art of the spirit, of the imagination and the soul, as opposed to an art wedded to representing the real world and deriving its value from the objects it represents. He claimed that good art had always been primarily of the spirit, and that it was the industrialized, urban and middle class world of the nineteenth century that had forced art to adopt false, materialist values.

Composition IV is not abstract, but then it is not descriptive either. It mingles nameable objects, shown in rather shorthand ways, with abstract changes of colour and form, i.e. with pictorial objects that are there to convey emotion, not to suggest objects in the world. Look at the right-hand corners for example: the top corner is blue and is probably meant to suggest sky, but the blue and red in the bottom corner do not mean anything other than what such blueness and redness together can mean.

146

We can all see the rainbow between hills in the left half of the painting. Above them are two horses and riders leaping against each other. To the right of the horses is a black line outlining a shape on top of the blue hill: a fortress. The two tall black lines are lances; they are held by two or three soldiers standing in front of the blue hill wearing red caps. Two figures recline diagonally in the right half of the picture where the yellow and the relative absence of black lines and jarring shapes make for an air of relaxation.

The painting seems to be about war and peace, hell and heaven. But what if we cannot read the meaning of the objects Kandinsky puts into it? He believed with Delacroix that 'the musical part' was what communicated. Like Seurat, but much more thoroughly, he studied and pressed further the scientists' research into normal human responses to colour and form, and this encouraged him to use form and colour as a self-sufficient system of communication. Our inability to share his shorthand signs for this and that would merely make the meaning of the picture more general, more universal. On the other hand, for him consciously to avoid putting into the picture symbols and other significant objects lest we find them difficult, or so that his art should be purely abstract for some theoretical reason, would be to falsify the urge to communicate. It was not an abstract art he was championing but an art in which the spirit would operate freely, untrammelled by thoughts of naturalism and practical common sense.

Klee who had come to Munich to study art at much the same time as Kandinsky, was part of Kandinsky's circle in the years leading up to World War I, and was his colleague as professor at the progressive art and design school set up in Germany in 1919, the Bauhaus. His painting *Around the Fish* belongs to the Bauhaus years,

but Klee's work varied widely in style and character. It has to be seen in some quantity before we can begin to feel what kind of an artist he was.

Around the Fish was produced slowly, concurrently with other paintings of quite other sorts, all of them in much the same spirit of discovery. Klee worked with his pictorial materials as Brancusi did with his sculptural ones: he worked with and through them and let them lead him on. He improvised like a musician, starting perhaps with some little formal motif, or with some idea of a colour pattern, and then letting the work grow out of the suggestion he saw in it.

KANDINSKY
Composition IV 1911 (left)
oil on canvas
160 x 250 cm (63 x 98½ in)
Kunstsammlung Nordrhein-
Westfalen, Düsseldorf

KLEE
Around the Fish 1926 (right)
tempera and oil on canvas
46 x 63 cm (18⅜ x 25⅛ in)
Museum of Modern Art, New
York (Abby Aldrich
Rockefeller Fund)

A picture like *Around the Fish* may have started from a few graphic marks, perhaps those straight lines and arches that end by being the scales of the fish. Some of the objects and signs that circle around the fish have in common a particular linear device, a triangle, square or pentagon drawn with each of its sides extended in one direction beyond the angle. The mood of the picture is more or less playful and this is normal for Klee's work during most of his life. He was not an Expressionist if to be one means only to use the power of art primarily to persuade the world of the strength of one's feelings.

For both Kandinsky and Klee the essential source of art was internal. Their work shows a progressive exploration of a new visual language, with or without reference to the visible world but devoted to very direct communication from artist to spectator. As we look at their work we unconsciously re-enact its making. Klee said: 'The work of art is above all a creative process; you never experience it as a mere product'. Thus the process, always important, becomes a key element in the artists' presentation to us. The unities, which the Cubists shattered, are totally ignored as belonging only to one particular tradition of art.

Beckmann

MAX BECKMANN born in Leipzig in 1884; died in New York in 1950

FERNAND LÉGER born in Argentan, Normandy, in 1881; died in Gif-sur-Yvette in 1955

BECKMANN
The Dream 1921
oil on canvas
180 x 89 cm (71 x 35 in)
Morton D. May Collection, St
Louis, Missouri

Beckmann is sometimes grouped with the Expressionists and sometimes with a new tendency, noted by critics in the early 1920s, towards realism. Both associations make some sense but what makes them interesting is that they point to a powerful duality in Beckmann's work.

Beckmann's paintings certainly reflect reality in very telling ways. He does not address us through expressive brushwork and his colour is not planned to engage our emotions by itself. We can read his figures and their settings fairly easily. We see what each of them is doing. Neither does he address us in terms of inner urges or sensations: his feelings are given objective form. In other words, he addresses us not in musical terms but in dramatic terms. He puts before us a scene or an action that is a vehicle for his thoughts and feelings.

But he is neither a David delivering to us a message and an exhortation that could also be delivered (more boringly) through words, nor a Delacroix feeding personal intuitions into a well-known Biblical theme. Beckmann invents his own dramas and they are dramas without a precise script. The title of the picture shown here suggests all too clearly that we should not be satisfied to read his pictures in terms of realism. He peoples his pictorial world with figures from the real world but it is a dream that they belong to here and the pictorial space they inhabit has all the instability and the closeness of a nightmare.

The figures he shows are themselves disturbing and we feel that each of them symbolizes something: the hand-less man carrying a fish up a ladder, the beggar with his hand organ and monkey, the crippled clown, the maid rolling about amid the musical instruments – all of them blind or at least unseeing, except for the girl on the trunk who seems to be a new arrival in that terrible place.

Beckmann's clear vision of a deeply disturbed world was personal, yet not of course his alone. What faith the western world had in its institutions and beliefs had been shattered by that extraordinary war (1914-18), so eagerly entered into on all sides, so dismal an experience for them that fought it, so painfully regretted by victors and losers alike. Kafka's novels and stories, parts of Joyce's *Ulysses,* Eliot's poem *The Waste Land* – many of the major works of the post-war years sound the same note of deep disturbance and of insanity feared and half-expected. Beckmann's first title for this painting was *Madhouse.*

France expressed this post-war sense of human crisis in less direct ways. Some Paris artists returned to classicism and used it in elegant and persuasive ways;

they were consciously playing with the past. Others organized an assault, through the arts, against the ideals and institutions that could produce a world war; they were the Surrealists, and we shall consider their work on pages 154 to 157. But there were also artists like Léger, by no means insensitive to the tensions of their time but determined to use their art positively, to emphasize harmony between people and between people and their environment.

Léger had been part of the Cubist circle, like Delaunay. Like him too, but in the hard post-war days and not as part of the self-confidence of the pre-war years, he wanted to celebrate modern life in his pictures. In that sense he is the opposite of Beckmann. If we wanted to find parallels for the art of each in the earlier pages of this book, we might well pick Bosch for Beckmann (page 68) and Van der Heyden for Léger (page 82).

It was precisely the war that had given Léger his view of art and life. For all the horrors he experienced, he was touched most of all by the sense he had of human kinship and also of the visual splendour of even the machines of destruction. For the rest of his life he produced pictures of which ordinary men and women are the anonymous heroes, seen in their ordinary but sup-portive settings, at work, at home, on Sunday outings into the country, and most of all possessing, making and using the modern city.

To convey this he does not paint part of an actual city. That would not suggest the complexities and rhythms of city life. He composes city fragments, using the idiom if not the actual process of collage. We can identify some of his bits and pieces: people, steel girders, buildings, steps, railings, posters, a cinema screen. Other bits, in themselves abstract, contribute to the liveliness of the whole and suggest the multiplicity of the experiences we have in a city. So the picture is a semi-abstract invention.

Both painters use reality for their visions, yet neither offers us a naturalistic picture. Is it significant that the painter with a positive view of the world should need to adopt a post-Cubist language of fragmentation and semi-abstraction, whilst the painter with the grim view of the world uses the relatively traditional language of convincing figuration?

LÉGER
La Ville 1919 oil on canvas
231 x 298 cm (91 x 117½ in)
Philadelphia Museum of Art
(The A. E. Gallatin Collection)

Tatlin   Rodchenko

VLADIMIR TATLIN born at Kharkov (Russia) in 1885; died in Moscow in 1953
ALEXANDER RODCHENKO born in 1891; died in Moscow in 1956

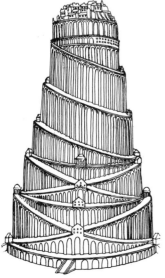

TATLIN
Model for the *Monument
to the Third
International* 1919
wood, iron and
glass

The Tower of Babel (left), as
shown in a book of 1679 by
the Jesuit scholar Athanasius
Kircher. Like other
Renaissance thinkers,
Kircher used mystical as well
as historical and scientific
knowledge. Tatlin was
stimulated by images of this
sort and the all-embracing
thought behind them.

The positive, anti-nostalgic attitude to modern life taken by Léger was in Russia a necessity and a conscious programme. After the Russian Revolution of 1917 all energies had to go into building a new society as well as a new state. War, revolution and the chaos and false starts that entailed, then civil wars and foreign invasions: Russia was a country in social turmoil and economic crisis – and a gigantic country at that, largely illiterate, industrially backward, a patchwork of many races, climates and ways of life that lacked all unity.

Lenin's slogan for progress was 'Communism = workers' councils + electricity'. Progressive artists in Russia, influenced by modernist developments in the West but also stirred in their sense of national identity by a new enthusiasm for old traditions of icon painting and folk art, had for some years been pursuing a revolution of their own. They had experimented with their own versions of Expressionism, Cubism and abstract painting, in many instances bringing to their work a spiritual emphasis and an element of mysticism comparable to that which Kandinsky took from Russia into western art.

When the Revolution came it lifted several of these adventurous artists into commanding positions in the cultural life of the country. Yesterday's hotheads became today's directors of museums, art schools and broader educational programmes. Modern art became a leading factor in modern society. New kinds of architecture, advertising design and typography, stage design and stage action, film and photography were given governmental backing; the new painting and sculpture were seen as laboratory experiments leading to the formal languages and the inventive use of material that gave all this work true novelty. Unfortunately it did not last long. By the end of 1920s the government was demanding a return to traditional idioms in art and design and encouraging a pretentious form of neoclassicism which soon was to become the preferred idiom also of fascist Italy and Germany.

It remains impossible for us to imagine a world built along rational and humanitarian lines for a classless society. But sometimes we feel we can at least glimpse something of the vision that led these artists on and brought them an enthusiastic response. It was a vision that combined faith in technology with something of the brave and necessarily innocent trust that the founders of new religions have for the world opening before them. The most eloquent expression of this double confidence is to be found in Tatlin's tower.

150

The painter and sculptor Tatlin was charged in 1919 with creating a monument to international Communism. He decided to make it a functional building as well as a monument. His tower was to stand 400 metres (1312 feet) high, bridging the river Neva at Leningrad, the old St Petersburg. The Eiffel Tower in Paris, 300 metres (984 feet) high, was built for an exhibition and remains more or less functionless. Tatlin's tower would be the headquarters of international Communism. Within its spiralling steel structure would hang three steel and glass buildings: a debating chamber (cylindrical), an office unit or secretariat (a pyramid on its side), and a media unit (a tall cylinder topped by a semi-sphere) from which news and instructions would be issued to the world by all known means, including images projected on to clouds. These units would rotate – once a year, once a month, once a day respectively – making the tower a vast clock and also setting it into an evident relationship to the solar system from which we derive our calendar. It would also resemble an observatory; the sloping girder that seems to carry the structure like a spine is aimed directly at the pole star. It would also resemble the ziggurats built in the Near East in ancient times. But this one would be the answer to the most famous or infamous ziggurat of them all, the Tower of Babel, because it would be dedicated to bringing understanding and companionship back to the planet Earth.

It could not be built in the Russia of those desperate times, as Tatlin must have known, but the model he and his assistants made achieved great fame, in Russia and beyond. News of it reached the West almost at once, and in 1925 a model of it was exhibited in Paris as part of a great international exhibition. In Russia a stamp was designed featuring the tower, and simpler models of it were carried about in processions.

Tatlin himself went on to immediately useful work, putting aside his work as a pure artist to engage his sensibilities and knowledge in solving everyday problems.

He and his disciples worked on such things as effective but simple clothing, stoves for heating, furniture, kitchen utensils and other equipment. He himself worked for many years also on a simple flying machine. Based on long studies of bird flight and of lightweight materials, this machine was intended to be equivalent to the bicycle, mass-produced and commonplace, so that everyone who wished might one day possess one and experience the joy as well as the utility of flight. Tatlin believed, rightly perhaps, that the invention of the mechanical aeroplane would merely end our centuries-old dream of being able to fly by depriving us of the experience of flight.

Rodchenko was Tatlin's most gifted and effective follower and is best known for his work as a typographer and photographer. In 1923 he made a set of illustrations for a long poem by the great Russian revolutionary writer, Mayakovsky. The poem is about many aspects of

RODCHENKO
Photomontage for Pro Eto
1923
photomontage
24 x 16 cm (9½ x 6 in)
British Library,
London

modern life as well as about Mayakovsky's love for Lily Brik. Rodchenko's illustrations echo its richness. His technique is now known as photomontage, that is making a collage of parts of photographs. He took portions of reality, captured via the camera, and constructed from them images that are in themselves unreal. The example illustrated here in some ways comes curiously close to Delaunay's picture *The Cardiff Team* (page 142). Not only the image but the spirit seems similar, but Delaunay had produced a unique and expensive art object while Rodchenko's image could easily and cheaply be reproduced by printing.

In Russian films of the 1920s, especially the work of Vertov and Eisenstein, we find the same process and much the same intention: reality captured and restructured to put before the masses ideas and information conveyed in vivid, living terms. This was the essential aim of Russian Constructivism.

151

Mondrian

PIET MONDRIAN born in Amersfoort (Netherlands) in 1872; died in New York in 1944

Is it wrong for artists to want to change the world through their work? The Romantic writer Shelley spoke of poets as 'the unacknowledged legislators of the world'. His contemporary, David (page 110), had engaged in government directly and through his paintings. Many an artist since David had committed his art to campaigning for social change and to protesting against injustice and inequality. During the first world war a group of artists and designers formed in neutral Holland, and their

canvas. One example, seen by itself, looks neat and harmonious but also arbitrary. A number seen together show that there is meaning and something like individual personality in each of them. Mondrian was not just concerned with making nice, modern-looking pictures. He had a message, and roughly it was this. Each of us lives in a state of inner conflict: we live in the present but dream of the past: we live in cities and long for nature; we live amid dirt and confusion and dream of clarity and

MONDRIAN
Study of Trees I 1912 (left)
black chalk
65 x 89 cm (25½ x 35 in)
Gemeentesmuseum, The Hague

MONDRIAN
Composition with Yellow and Blue 1929 (right)
oil on canvas
52 x 52 cm (20½ x 20½ in)
Boymans-van Beuningen Museum, Rotterdam

ambition was not only to change art and taste but also to guide the world, through their work, towards the peace and harmony which at that time it so blatantly lacked. Mondrian was the most important artist in the group.

In 1917 he was 45. He had started as a painter of landscape and still life, and occasionally also portraits. The flat Dutch landscape and the verticals in it – trees, towers, windmills – may have led him to emphasize verticals and horizontals in his work. Traditional Dutch painting sometimes implies a similar emphasis (pages 82 and 83). Mondrian's drawing of 1912, done at a time when he was beginning to abstract his images more and more under the influence of Cubism, shows how beautifully and effectively he could use the visual world as a source for dynamic linear structures.

Composition with Yellow and Blue is just one out of a long series of paintings Mondrian did from 1921 until his death, using the same basic ingredients and finding in them an endless range of expressive compositions. Primary colours, vertical and horizontal bands, a white

peace. All right then: shed the negative, the nostalgic, the painful; seize the permanent and the positive in order to shape the future.

It is often said that Mondrian and his art were against nature. The drawing shown here is a partial answer but the real point is more complex: Mondrian neither turned away from nature nor felt himself separate from it. He made human-type images, natural to people and in no way challenges to nature. The feeling we get from his images, with their relationships of form and colour, ever-varying and always effective, is in no fundamental way different from the sensations that form and colour give us when we stand before nature. He has used basic elements because they are clear and devoid of sentimental associations or other nostalgic overtones, and also because they do not belong only to art but are universal elements of construction.

In fact a lot of modern architecture and design has taken its character from the simplified language employed by Mondrian's group, which attracted wide membership after the war. Some of its members formed an alliance with Russian followers of Tatlin and worked very effectively with them to bring visual clarity and material efficiency into many aspects of design. Mondrian said that once the environment had become sane and confident, paintings would no longer be needed. Meanwhile they would function as signposts towards this world and as models of it.

Is it all theory and foolishness? If we stand in front of a Mondrian and give it our full attention, the following happens. The vertical-horizontal structure of the painting seems to take possession of the wall on which the picture hangs. It addresses itself also to us, drawing from us a physical as well as a spiritual response. I find that I instinctively stand more upright, straightening my back.

I become a taller, fitter, more balanced person. The colour chord – which includes the black and white – resounds through me, just as the harmoniousness of a fine old-master painting and the awesome nobility of a great one resound through me and strengthen me. (I am thinking of Vermeer and Michelangelo, pages 83 and 60-61, 64-65.)

When you experience that, you also find that the problem of abstraction versus figuration has completely disappeared. We do not read a Mondrian the way we read a David of even a Cézanne; we receive it like sunshine or splendid music. And if you still ask what the place of the human image is in this kind of art, the answer of course is that you are it. We ourselves are the figurative component in Mondrian's world.

Ernst   Magritte

MAX ERNST born at Brühl, near Cologne, in 1891; died in Paris in 1976

RENÉ MAGRITTE born at Lessines (Belgium) in 1898; died in Brussels in 1967

ERNST
Two Children are threatened by a Nightingale 1924 (left)
oil on panel and assemblage
46 x 33 cm (18¹/₈ x 13 in)
Museum of Modern Art,
New York

MAGRITTE
The Use of Words I 1929
(right)
oil on canvas
62 x 81 cm (24¹/₂ x 31⁷/₈ in)
Private Collection

Ernst and Magritte were two of the most important artists associated with the Surrealist movement; two others were Dali and Miró, discussed over the page. Even more than Expressionism, Surrealism is the opposite to Impressionism: it dives deep down into dark areas of fears and desires and fantastic images, and revels in their unreality, whereas Impressionism was all out-turned, looking at the face of nature under nature's light as innocently as it is in an artist's power to do. That unreality, the Surrealists claimed, is the true reality that occupies our waking and nocturnal dreams, and which we push aside to operate as the rational beings we tell each other to be – a super-reality more real than what we are used to calling reality, hence Surrealism.

Among modern art movements, these two extremes are the most popular. In the 1920s and '30s when Surrealism got a lot of notice as a movement, primarily in literature and film and secondarily in painting, people found it thoroughly offensive. It was, literally, against good social behaviour. It was anarchistic. Anarchism

was a political movement particularly active and feared towards the end of the nineteenth century. It was opposed to all forms of government, putting its trust in voluntary co-operation and holding the oppression exercised by all forms of government responsible for all crime. In much the same way, the Surrealists held that civilization itself oppresses people by forcing us all to pretend to be what we are not. We are forced to behave and even to think in an orderly way, and to keep our real feelings and thoughts to ourselves; only in our dreams or when we are specially stimulated do our fantasies take command, with all their horrors and illicit joys. The arts should reveal this world of fantasy as the real, and shared, world it is.

The Surrealists were echoing the findings of modern psychology, but they rejected them in one essential respect: they did not want people cured and made to fit easily into the social pattern; they wanted the social pattern broken and people freed to live fully and without fear. So they wrote anti-logical poetry and prose,

154

as well as diatribes against morality and law. They also sent letters insulting eminent public figures to the newspapers, and themselves published journals rich in abusive and indecent material. They made a public performance out of insulting the clergy; they held a mock trial of a leading literary figure. Their exhibitions were made scandalous as much by the way they were presented as by the work on show. The anarchists had thrown bombs; the Surrealists threw the cultural equivalent of bombs at the forms of civilization the public of their day valued most.

Has their art lost its sting? The popularity of Surrealism suggests that perhaps it has, but we can recapture at least the feel of it, if not the wound, by giving it proper attention. Ernst's picture-relief combines painting with real things, 'fine art' with rubbish. The little wooden gate and hut, and also the frame on which the painter has written the work's title and to which he has fixed a wooden knob and other bits too, all jar our notion of what a painting should be, and they do so more sharply than a Cubist collage because of the contrast between all that stuff and the painted panel. This resembles early Italian Renaissance painting with its deep perspective and luminous sky, and even hints at a religious subject, but what is the picture about? There is a bird in it; there are figures, one rushing about, one slumped on the ground, another tiptoeing mysteriously on the hut and apparently reaching out to the wooden knob. Very mysterious, yet not mysterious because it is evident nonsense, yet not nonsense either because in its poetic way it seems to mean something if only we could focus on it. Do nightingales threaten children? Perhaps we are all threatened by everything, especially by anything we associate with night and love and beauty.

Magritte's painting, also known as *The Betrayal of Images,* is painted very plainly like a shop sign and, like a shop sign, has lettering on it: 'This is not a pipe'.

Not a pipe? All right, Magritte, we see what you mean: this is a picture, an image, an arrangement of paints on canvas. But if we are not to think 'pipe' what is art for? Are we to go back through the gallery and through memories, unhitching our responses from the many images art has faced us with? Magritte makes us sharply aware of our hunger to be given illusions to value and to invest our emotions in. The very dullness of his way of painting tells us to read his picture in a common-sense way, and we rather wish he was more like a Watteau or a Rubens, inviting us to play along. But then why do we so often criticize art when it refuses to be sensible? We prefer art to lift us out of a prosaic world into a world of poetic fancies. All right, says Surrealism, we will show you your true fantasies.

155

JOAN MIRÓ born in Barcelona in 1893

SALVADOR DALI born in Figueras in 1904

MIRÓ
Le Gentleman 1924
oil on canvas
52 x 46 cm (20¹/₂ x 18 in)
Kunstmuseum, Basle

Some of the Surrealist writers were convinced that art would never be able to bring out the dreams and fantasies that are the subject matter of Surrealism without killing them dead. Fixing them in paint would surely deprive them of the resonance that made them shocking and real.

Surrealist artists had to find ways of meeting this problem. They could look back at the art of a Bosch, heaped up with awful little images (page 68), or at Romantic painters like Turner and Friedrich for the emotional charge they could give to pictures of nature (pages 118-119). Or they could use the work of art itself as a disturbance, forcing us to confront problems where we would rather confront pictures.

Miró and Dali opened up other ways of being a Surrealist in art. Both came from Catalonia, the northeast corner of Spain. Both became part of the Paris art world and thence also of the international art world of notoriety and influence. Both have pointedly maintained their roots and their homes in Spain – and there all similarities end. For a while Dali was influenced by Miró's example, but he went on to develop a kind of Surrealism that wholly contradicts the older man's, and also to build an image of himself before the world that few artists would want to share.

Miró's *Le Gentleman* is rather like a blackboard with something written and drawn on it, or like graffiti on a city wall. It looks slight, temporary. He has loosely brushed the canvas with one colour and then painted on it lines and shapes that do not immediately look like anything at all. The word 'Yes' is clear enough, but what does it say yes to? We can read the Roman figures, and we see a jokily painted foot. To get the rest we have to apply our imaginations.

Perhaps this is easier for us today than it was in 1924: cartoon films and comic strips have taught us to read rather than reject this kind of image. We soon make out a moustache, eye, eyebrow, pursed mouth and long nose, and there we have our 'gentleman'; perhaps the rest of it says things like 'Noon: time to get up'. So that is it, but we must not lose track of what Miró has done. Accepting some of the liberties introduced by Cubism, echoing also the verbal plus visual form of communication which graffiti share with some ancient kinds of writing, he has ignored the problems as well as the rewards of traditional

well-known puzzle image that switches back and forth between being a rabbit's and a duck's head; Dali has borrowed that from a German humorous weekly.

Dali called pictures of this kind 'hand-painted dream photographs'. He evaded the issue raised by Surrealist writers by combining nightmarish effects with the instability of meaning we find in our dreams. As we look at his paintings we get something of that sense of being victims of irreconcilable forces battling within us. We may wonder whether it is right to trigger deep fears in this way. The plain fact is that people like it, just as they like horror films and macabre stories.

Dali's work has the added attraction of being modern and shocking and at the same time old-fashioned and safely entertaining. We need not take too seriously his appointment of himself as the great defender of the traditions of Raphael and Vermeer; I doubt that either

DALI
Apparition of a face and fruit dish on a beach 1938
oil on canvas
114.8 x 143.8 cm
(45¼ x 56 in)
Wadsworth Atheneum,
Hartford, Connecticut
(The Ella Gallup Sumner and
Mary Catlin Sumner
Collection)

painting. Graffiti desecrate but also humanize overbearing walls; Miró's art mocks artistic pretensions whilst making art our friend.

Dali's painting announces its deliberateness and cleverness. The title of his picture helps us to see what he is conjuring with in it: a nightmarish beach, some of it too empty for comfort, some of it too packed with uncertain goings-on; the beach can turn into a face; the face can turn into a stemmed fruitbowl filled with pears. But there is also the large dog of which he does not warn us. And that nauseating, impossible drop on the right that turns the beach into a table top. And those frighteningly long shadows that some of the objects on the table/beach have and some not. The dog's foot turns out to be a

would want to be associated with him. But his careful development of a public image of himself is significant. I suggested earlier that Duchamp's implied pointing to himself as the essential art-ingredient is merely an extension of Romanticism's high valuation of the idea of genius. Dali's gradual development of himself as his chief work of art is an extension of it beyond even Surrealism's hopes for publicity and scandal: he has attained the glory of film stars and of aristocratic playboys.

Miró's art evades this self-regard and also the lugubriousness which is Surrealism's handicap. He has kept his art lyrical and fluid, and in doing so he has enlarged the range of image-making.

JOHN HEARTFIELD born in Berlin in 1891; died in East Berlin in 1968

PABLO PICASSO see pages 134-135

'We see the great new task: partisan art, in the service of the revolutionary cause'. These words are from an article written and published in Berlin in 1925, when new realistic tendencies were being encouraged by some galleries and critics as the antidote to Expressionism. Its authors were not joining in that battle. They were saying that art had to become openly political and join in the struggle against oppressive political and economic systems, or cease to have any validity. They entitled the article 'Art in Danger'.

The authors were the artist Georg Grosz and the writer and publisher Wieland Herzfeld. Herzfeld's brother Helmut had in the middle of the war changed his name into John Heartfield, anglicizing it in protest against the hate campaign then being led by the German government against Britain. It was a characteristic act of defiance. Heartfield was to spend much of his life avoiding police arrest or political assassination in post-

HEARTFIELD
This is the salvation that they bring! 1938
photomontage, printed in a newspaper, *Volks-Illustrierte*

Das ist das Heil, das sie bringen!

war Berlin. When the Nazis took over in Germany he fled to Czechoslovakia and continued to attack fascism from there; then he had to flee to England where he was interned for a time.

He had collaborated with Grosz on making photomontages in 1918-19, and it was probably their example that led Rodchenko into his work in that medium (page 151). Heartfield in the '20s became the master of photomontage as a political weapon. Where others drew cartoons, he built photographic images into powerful and memorable visual propaganda. These were reproduced in large quantities in the illustrated newspapers of the period and reached thousands of people. Others were made into posters or book jackets.

The skeletal hand and the word 'Heil' in the photomontage illustrated here refer to the Nazi salute and to Nazi propaganda about the glories of the new empire Germany was building under Hitler's leadership and extending over Europe. The word 'Heil' suggests health, welfare, salvation. The image shows what the Nazis were actually bringing. German forces were deeply involved in the Spanish Civil War and helped the fascists to turn Spain from a republic into a dictatorship. German planes bombed Spanish towns, meeting no opposition from the republican forces. Heartfield juxtaposes the hand that turns into aeroplanes and vapour trails with news photographs of dead children and bombed buildings.

He does not pretend that the whole thing is a piece of reality: he lets us see that he put the image together out of separate elements. Yet it tells like reality. Today perhaps what it shows has become appallingly commonplace; our sympathies are dulled by the daily onslaught of photographs and films of destruction. Then it was quite new and Heartfield's treatment of it struck home.

Picasso's famous painting *Guernica* is on the same theme. He had been commissioned by the Spanish republican government to produce a large painting for the Spanish space in an international exhibition in Paris. At a loss what to paint, he hesitated. Then came news of the bombing of Guernica, a small but historically significant town in northern Spain. Picasso worked rapidly during the weeks that followed. Today his mural reminds the world of the town and what happened there.

He has painted an allegory, not an account of the event or a collage of facts as offered by Heartfield. *Guernica* is above all a statement about terror. More obliquely it refers to war: the broken sword, the lance piercing the horse. There is screaming; the shapes seems to scream at

PICASSO
Guernica 1937 (detail below) oil on canvas
349 x 777 cm (137$\frac{1}{2}$ x 305$\frac{1}{2}$ in)
on extended loan from the estate of the artist
to the Museum of Modern Art, New York.

us. A burning woman leaps from a burning house. Another woman holds a dead child. The horse is dying. A head and limbs lie on the ground. A bull looks on sternly: we are not certain whether he is an aggressor or an image of a country's anger and resolution.

So the meaning of the painting is not very clear, except in the most general way. Why, then, is it so effective? I have three suggestions. One is that Picasso here proves his mastery by finding the line that divides distortion for tragic impact from distortion of the sort that produces caricature, and he has stayed just on the side of tragedy and emotional conviction. Another is that he has relied on contrasts of tone and texture rather than on colour. The painting is in dark blues and purples, and off-whites and creams, that reproduce badly but look very strong, especially in the context of a busy exhibition. In doing this, he has avoided the decorative attractions a large colour composition would almost certainly involve. Thirdly, needing to make a strong and lasting pictorial statement, he has, perhaps consciously, availed himself of a tradition that no one would expect to see operating in this context. He has given it the formal character of a traditional altarpiece in three panels: a large one flanked by two narrower ones, hinged so that they can be closed like doors. You can see something like vertical breaks in the picture to the right of the bull and the left of the falling woman; the central area is composed on pyramidal lines.

Picasso's source could well have been the Grünewald altarpiece, reproduced on page 69 – a particularly famous instance of the type, and one Picasso had been studying through reproductions during the late 1920s. Grünewald's influence can probably be also seen in the way Picasso has painted the very prominent hands and feet. Their poignancy here helps us to understand Cézanne's suppression of them in his painting of peace (page 131).

Moore   Giacometti

HENRY MOORE born at Castleford, Yorkshire, in 1898

ALBERTO GIACOMETTI born at Stampa (Switzerland) in 1901; died in 1966 at Chur

MOORE
Reclining Figure 1939
elm
205 cm (81 in) long
Institute of Arts, Detroit
(Gift of Dexter M. Ferry Jr.
Trustee Corp.)

So strong was the hold of figuration on sculpture, so firmly was sculpture identified with representations of human beings, that abstract sculpture did not become at all common until the 1950s and '60s. But figure sculpture itself saw some astonishing developments before then.

The English sculptor Henry Moore steeped himself in primitive work of many kinds, as well as in the broad history of western sculpture. The example of Brancusi was especially important to him as a carver: from him he learned the poetic and constructive value of working with the material as against imposing a form upon it.

Moore's favourite theme, of the reclining woman as a metaphor for landscape and vice versa, is not found in Brancusi but is as old as human thought. It cannot be an accident that the earth was so often identified with and as a female goddess. For Moore, the son of a coalminer and born close to the hills and valleys of the Yorkshire Dales, there was also a more personal meaning in the ancient theme. He used it from the early '30s on and it is the subject of several of his finest sculptures.

The example shown here, more than life-size and particularly richly tunnelled, shows well how the sculptor could respond both to his developing figure/landscape idea and to the demands made and the suggestions tacitly put forward by the block of elm he was carving. The shapes flow into each other, deflecting all thoughts of front and back, inside and outside. The eye moves through and round, and our tactile imagi-

nation goes with it, reading the forms and the surfaces more tellingly than actual touch could. There is strength in the forms as well as softness, a grace of a noticeably feminine sort as well as the monumentality of mountains. Anatomy becomes wood and landscape without our being aware of any act of metamorphosis or any sense of abandoning one meaning for another.

Michelangelo, whose reclining figures in fresco and in marble have certainly been in Moore's mind, would have asked what the meaning of such a sculpture might be. Our answer is the one discovered by the Romantics: that nature herself is a sufficient theme, her forms carrying in them all possible meanings, especially those we associate with piety and meditations upon life and death. It was Turner's generation that established this reliance on generalized content, and Moore's forms are indeed more like Turner's than Michelangelo's. I stress this because we accept this too as a norm and have learned not to ask for more specific meanings. Modern art, too often discussed only in terms of movements and styles, should also be questioned for its content. The undeniable beauty of a Moore sculpture would not be thought a sufficient reason for making it by a Heartfield or a Beuys (pages 158 and 171).

They would probably be more appreciative of Giacometti's standing figure: it is active and appears to be speaking to us. Giacometti long worked in Paris, where he was associated with the Surrealists. In the mid-'30s he

160

began making figures again. During the war, when he lived in Geneva, he made tiny figures a few centimetres high; later they became amazingly tall for their width – long, thin figures of remarkable presence.

There are different ways of understanding and interpreting that thinness. Modelling with plaster on a steel rod skeleton or armature, the sculptor has to predetermine the height of his figure; he may not feel the need to build it up laterally with clay but the height is there from the start. (Similarly a carver may feel it right to leave his figure massive, to bring out its blockishness as we saw in the case of Brancusi, page 140). Also, in working from the model – studying the posed living body whilst pressing the clay on to the sculpture – he may feel reluctant to let the modelled figure become a barrier between him and the model. Often Giacometti worked also from memory, but that memory was rooted in modelling directly from the model.

Giacometti was also keenly aware of the space around his figures, of their use of space, their possession of it. Paradoxically, a thin sculpture makes us aware of an engagement with space; perhaps our attention is less held by mass and surface. And this expressive relationship with space gives Giacometti's sculpture its meaning. What precisely it says is unclear. Since 1948 it has been taken to represent a pessimistic view of humanity – noble yet powerless, lonely and anxious, a victim of an arbitrary universe and of the anonymity that afflicts individuals in a mass society. That was an interpretation put on the work by a writer in a catalogue introduction, and it fitted the post-war mood of the time; there is no evidence that Giacometti himself saw his sculpture in such terms.

He has always spoken of seeing, and of making his sculpture match the way things look. His tiny figures suggest a particularly acute sense of sight, that by-passes the allowances our perceptual processes make for distance: far away figures *are* small for him, they don't just look small. If we stand close to his tall figures, at the kind of distance at which the sculptor stood in making them, we quickly lose all sense of their thinness. It is their individuality that strikes us then, the sense by which they are particular people, quite unanonymous. There is perhaps more hint of what his sculpture is about in the following quotation than in the interpretations usually offered: 'In having half a centimetre of something, you have more chance of getting some feeling of the universe than if you have a pretension to do the whole thing'.

GIACOMETTI
Man pointing 1947
bronze
178 cm (70 in) high
Tate Gallery, London

Matisse

HENRI MATISSE born at Le Cateau-Cambresis, in northern France, in 1869; died at Vence, in southern France, in 1954

MATISSE
The Red Studio 1911 (left)
oil on canvas
181 x 219 cm
(71¼ x 86¼ in)
Museum of Modern Art,
New York (Mrs Simon
Guggenheim Fund)

MATISSE
The Snail 1953 (right)
gouache and paper
286 x 287 cm
(112¾ x 113 in)
Tate Gallery, London

Matisse is usually dealt with earlier than this in surveys of art. Around 1905 he became known in Paris as the leader of a young group of amazingly barbaric and rough-mannered painters. They were known as the Fauves (wild beasts) and Matisse was seen to be the wildest of them. This gave him prominence, but also deprived him of it later, when his art became much more obviously careful and calm. In fact, it was never wild, nor extravagant, but it was capable of great energy at some times and at others of a gentler sort of strength which people mistook for conservatism. Yet in his last years, when his health was far from good, Matisse produced some of the most vigorous art of the century in terms of rare boldness and novelty, and this seems even more remarkable than his pioneering beginnings.

After his early phase, which could be described as being Expressionist in a cool way, Matisse soon simplified his means. In *The Red Studio,* for example, line does almost everything. It tells us where everything is and provides an unusually lucid space for everything to find its place in. Yet the almost unmodulated red which is his colour for nearly everything in the picture seems to deny the existence of space. The colour speaks to our senses of flatness; the line speaks to our minds, through our understanding of perspective, of space and objects.

If line predominates in *The Red Studio,* it has no role in *The Snail.* Here blocks of colour make the painting – almost literally so in that it is constructed of pieces of paper, coated with colour first and then cut into their shapes with scissors and fixed on to the paper ground. The only lines here are those made with the scissors, but if that makes scissors into a drawing instrument they also function like a carver's chisel. Matisse said, 'Cutting directly into the colour reminds me of the direct action of the sculptor carving stone'. Colour here is a material, not an attribute. Painting and line, colour and mass – all become one in this amazing work.

It marks the culmination of a career which, for all the variety of work it was responsible for, stood by some basic truths that Matisse recognized early on. One of them is, 'The simplest means are those which enable an artist to express himself best'. What earlier looked like roughness and aggressiveness in his work was merely an experimental approach and an unwillingness to repeat one experiment again and again and thus give his output a coherent style. Later, too, Matisse's style varied a great deal, from decade to decade and at times from year to year. This looked like frivolousness but was in fact the deepest seriousness, because it was not a style he was after but a true and direct means of expressing his

162

sensations. 'I want to reach that state of condensation of sensations that constitutes a picture'.

His subject was always pleasurable: women, flowers, fruit, interiors, gardens. And his aim was harmony: 'What I dream of is an art of balance, of purity and serenity devoid of troubling or depressing subject matter, an art which might be for every mental worker, be he businessman or writer, like an appeasing influence, like a mental soother, something like a good armchair in which to rest from physical fatigue.' Yet the pleasure given by his work is always energetic rather than sweet. His colours tend to be strong and his linear organization lively and against the expectations of naturalism. Imagination had to work in harness with direct experience of nature, but most important for Matisse was the develop-

ment of the work itself, always changing as each touch on the canvas produces a new organization of colours and forms. 'I cannot copy nature in a servile way; I must interpret nature and submit it to the spirit of the picture'.

These quotations all come from an essay Matisse wrote in 1908 under the title *Notes of a Painter*. (It appeared in German and in Russian in 1909). They represent what the essay is about – that art is a matter of order and sensation brought into unity, not about an order derived from rules – and what it says is as applicable to old art as to modern. Matisse held a pivotal position between the old and the new, and felt no need to proclaim antagonisms and allegiances. Thus also the question of abstraction *versus* figuration could not arise. 'For me', wrote Matisse, 'nature is always present'.

Pollock   Rothko

JACKSON POLLOCK born in Cody, Wyoming, in 1912; died in East Hampton, Long Island in 1956

MARK ROTHKO born in Dvinsk (Russia) in 1903; emigrated to the USA in 1913; died in New York in 1970

World War II (1939-45) brought a shift of cultural influences as well as political power. In 1939 the USA seemed a long way from Europe, a large and busy country intent on its own life and connecting with Europe mostly through films about love and money. To Americans, Europe was the source of culture old and new, though individual American writers and artists had been showing that there were American themes needing American modes of expression. American museums and private collections were rich in modern masterpieces from Europe – many of them acquired when European public and private collectors still hesitated to take modern art seriously – but America was also increasingly conscious of native primitive traditions as well as of her proximity to the Orient.

Her leading role in the war had given America confidence before the world, and her position of world leadership to some extent forced on her a more positive relationship to the rest. In art matters, she now became a major contributor. There was new art, and there was support for this new art, even at a national level. Lavish exhibitions showed this new art off around the world, and the world recognized the 'new American painting' as a potent new force.

It was very exciting and remains a magnificent achievement. It is represented here by two artists' work, each of them a leader in his phase of what looked like one broad movement. Pollock's work became known in New York in the '40s and in Europe in the '50s. People saw in it swirls of paint, dribbled from a stick or brush or even poured from a can. It seemed violent to them, the most anti-artistic form of painting yet. It was mocked even in New York where some critics gave intelligent support to Pollock early on.

In 1947 Pollock wrote an account of how he worked that soon became widely known and was used in arguments for and against his work. He said that he had his canvas on the floor so that he could move around it and 'literally be *in* the painting. This is akin to the methods of the Indian sand painters of the West'. His previous work had been full of images suggestive of a Surrealist aim. Here he was referring to a primitivist influence, from the magical rituals of the American Indians. After some years of completely abstract painting, in the early 1950s vague imagery again appeared in Pollock's paintings.

A tough he-man image of the pioneer American obscured the real character of Pollock's work even from his admirers. His way of painting was meditative rather than wild, ballet-like rather than aggressive. Working all

round the canvas tended to produce a balanced, centralized result, a thicket of elegant lines of paint of varying hues and densities, floating in front of a shallow white space – more the vestigial account of a movement than an image.

Rothko's work became known a little later than Pollock's and at first looked like an answer to it, being so

much more orderly and stable. Even those who still denied abstract art any possible meaning could not fail to be struck by the solemnity and even the religious feeling coming from those beautifully worked colour surfaces. The typical Rothko is a vertical image consisting of two or three soft colour areas hovering above each other before a ground of another colour. The areas are like clouds; the ground functions like a colour mist out of which the clouds appear. The colours themselves change as we look at them, hinting at other colours beneath them, and the different colour areas shift in relationship to each other as we look at them. The longer we look, the more mobile and insubstantial or immaterial the painting becomes.

All this makes such paintings resemble a modern, abstract icon, a portrait of the unknowable, unnameable god perhaps. One recalls Rothko's Russian origin; also that he was a Jew and profoundly interested in mysticism. He believed that all art should strive to be mysterious and miraculous; the only question, he said, was whether it could be that in an age without shared beliefs. His fame suggests that it can.

POLLOCK
Cathedral 1947
(left)
enamel and
aluminium paint
on canvas
180 x 89 cm
(71 x 35 in)
Museum of Fine
Arts, Dallas

ROTHKO
Green and Maroon
1953 (right)
oil on canvas
230.5 x 138.3 cm
(91 x 54¹/₂ in)
Phillips Collection,
Washington

Martin   Caro

KENNETH MARTIN born in Sheffield in 1905

ANTHONY CARO born in London in 1924

The painting reproduced here shows nothing but red lines on a white canvas – bundles of red lines, lying this way and that, some of them going over or through each other, in a tidy and controlled yet somehow random-looking way. Its title gives us a clue. Chance plus order have produced this work: an element of chance invited by the painter, and a system chosen by the painter.

The system is a grid, its intersections numbered. Martin then picked pairs of numbers at random and drew lines linking the intersections bearing those numbers. The number of lines in a bundle is determined by throwing a die. The rest is planned or decided on intuitively: the size of the canvas, the red and white paint, the diagonal relating of the grid to the square of the canvas. He could have other materials altogether, other systems, other colours, other forms than lines, another scale of grid, and so on.

Many people see artistic expression and intellectual control as opposites. They equate art with a disclosure of temperament, not to say temper, and associate intellect only with science and logic as processes that exclude feeling. The opposition is a false one. Historically, it would exclude a man like Leonardo from consideration as an artist – obviously so, since he made his interest in science, and his use of scientific knowledge in his art, so patent. And it would exclude Seurat, who claimed that his art was all method and not poetry at all. But it would exclude also all thinking, planning artists – all intelligent artists, in short, and I suspect that it is not possible to be an artist and unintelligent.

Martin has been a figurative painter and then an abstract painter; he became known through his metal constructions based upon simple numerical series. Then he returned to painting. Many of his sculptures were 'mobiles', moving sculptures that turned as they hung. His *Chance and Order* paintings imply sequence and therefore time; there is also a sense of instability coming from our knowledge that chance might have dictated another structure. This brings into his art an element of drama – not human drama but something more like the drama of nature, as when we are excited by a waterfall or by the way clouds move across a valley. Martin's discovery of the infinity of structures available through such and similar means is akin to the Greeks' recognition of the wider validity of proportional relationships: it plugs his art into the cosmos, or, to be more exact, it plugs his art into the mathematics invented by man in order to understand his place in the cosmos and the cosmos's actions in relation to himself.

Historically this kind of art is linked to Russian Constructivism, and also to Cubism and the idea of constructing a work of art, literally or metaphorically, rather than deriving an image from something seen or imagined. In adapting a constructive process to the art of painting, Martin, like Matisse in *The Snail*, is proving the extraordinary staying power of an art form often announced dead.

Caro's sculpture is constructed out of pieces of steel and aluminium – as produced industrially for engineering and building purposes – all painted red. Here the artist's sensibility dominates: each element in the sculpture is placed in relation to the others and to the whole and is justified by its effectiveness. To know such a work fully we have to walk round it and experience it over time. It is a little like an abstract painting, and looking at the photograph you may feel that its elements are not so different from lines and bars of red paint; in fact, the work yields many pictures and, more important, is not related to a wall surface but to the floor and the space on and in which we stand too.

This is, I think, one of the reasons why people find sculpture generally more difficult to engage with than painting. A painting can be said to belong to another world: its physical presence is slight and experiencing it is like thinking or dreaming. Sculpture, especially large sculptures set directly on the ground, is factual and obtrusive. It threatens our sense of territory. We graze our mental shins on it.

Yet this accords it a particularly compelling physical communication. I spoke on page 152 of experiencing a painting by Mondrian. In its way, a sculpture like this one compels a physical response from us, almost as though it was performing for us and inviting participation. This particular one reveals itself to be a light, joyous thing, and it suggests a debt to Matisse as well as to the painting that came from Pollock's example.

MARTIN
Chance and Order 5 (Red)
1970 (left)
oil on canvas
121.9 x 121.9 cm
(48 x 48 in)
Arts Council Collection,
London

CARO
Early One Morning 1962
steel and aluminium painted
red (right)
366 x 620 x 335 cm
(144 x 244 x 132 in)
Tate Gallery, London

Warhol

Cottingham

ANDY WARHOL born in Philadelphia about 1928

ROBERT COTTINGHAM born in Brooklyn, New York in 1935

WARHOL
Triple Elvis 1963 (left)
silkscreen enamel and
acrylic on canvas
208 x 122 cm (82 x 48 in)
Leo Castelli Gallery,
New York

COTTINGHAM
Joseph's Liquor 1980 (right)
oil on canvas
81.2 x 81.2 cm (32 x 32 in)
O.K. Harris Gallery,
New York

Hardly had the world begun to accept Abstract Expressionism as an important and serious development in modern art – it actually seemed that a wide public had begun to see that abstract art could have significance – when new upheavals threatened from the USA and from England. By the early 1960s they were unmistakably happening: they had become a movement, Pop art.

Pop suggests popular. The movement got a lot of publicity from the media who saw that it was news, easy to enjoy and easy to write about. It was the time when pop stars like Elvis Presley and the Beatles were emerging, and this art in many instances was responding to that world rather than the world of deep human feelings and problems. Its idiom was in many cases borrowed from the media; whereas art normally proceeded by taking ideas from art and making something new of them, this came from commercial art and so was speaking a language created by experts to reach the whole consumer society. For the same reason many commentators, especially in the United States, hated it. It denied, or seemed to deny, all seriousness and attach itself to commonplace fantasies and the hard sell. The contrast with Abstract Expressionism was too extreme, so that Pop implied a total rejection of everything Pollock, Rothko and their fellow workers had stood for.

One of the impulses towards Pop art was in fact a scholarly one: in England a group of critics and artists had begun to investigate popular culture (from fairground decoration to films and the architecture of cinemas) and of advertising, especially the highly developed art of car and fashion advertising, where high technical skills and elaborate symbolism gave persuasive force to each innovation and obsolescence.

Warhol soon showed himself to be more than a leading maker of Pop art: he was and remains a brilliant manipulator of the media. He has established himself as a superstar among artists whilst giving the impression that he does very little beyond saying yes to everything. He has surrounded himself with friends to whom he accords starlet status – literally so in the sense that he uses them in films, but also in the more general sense that he reflects publicity on them. They form his court but also his 'Factory' from which Warhol's productions emerge. No Warhol work has depended on the master's personal touch. Perhaps it depends on the master's direction and selection of themes, but since this gives equal glamour to soup cans, dollar bills, film and pop stars, criminals and car crashes, we are again foxed by a choice lacking personal character.

Warhol delivers images of stars, as of soup cans etc., in multiples: rows and rows of Marilyn Monroe or Jackie Kennedy or himself. Here out of a long series of Elvis images we see one triple image, copied from a film still. Films and film stills are themselves endlessly multipliable according to need, and so the star himself is multipliable, a mass-produced commodity whose true

personality is the more hidden, the more famous he is. Warhol works from photographs, but, unlike the Russian Constructivists and Heartfield, he seeks the unreality of the glamour shot and the as carefully selected newspaper photograph. When he adds colour, it is essentially theatrical, hiding the subject's individuality even more.

Cottingham represents a broad tendency that became a publicized movement in the late 1960s, known by various names including Photo-Realism. The paintings and sculptures associated with it were openly dependent on photographic images as their motif or model, but not in Warhol's way: not as part of an ambiguous commentary on the mass response to stardom and the art world's nervousness before the whole issue of mass-produced glamour, but merely as a way of holding an image in a more or less objective form.

As in the case of Martin (page 166) it is the dependence on this material that strikes one first, and it is easy to underrate the painter's input into work of this kind. He takes his photographs, selecting this subject and not that, and this photo of it instead of another: he chooses his angle, light conditions and coverage. Cottingham has long specialized in lettering on buildings, more particularly lettering designed to invite the passer-by, put up outside bars, cinemas, restaurants and other such places, and he likes to show them in strong sunlight.

The camera does not see the way we see, and painters know that more thoroughly than we do. It produces a two-dimensional image of a particular sort, unselective except in so far as the film itself responds in particular ways to light and colour and the lens affects focus and space relationships. Cottingham chooses, controls all that and works selectively from the photographed image, censoring details that may work against the effect he wants.

Long   Beuys

RICHARD LONG born in Bristol in 1945

JOSEPH BEUYS born in Krefeld (Germany) in 1921

LONG
Somerset Willow Line 1980
willow sticks
165 x 200 cm (65 x 79 in)
Anthony d'Offay Gallery,
London

I like simple, practical, emotional,
quiet, vigorous art.
I like the simplicity of walking,
the simplicity of stones.
I like common means given the
simple twist of art.
I like sensibility without technique.
My art has the themes of materials, ideas,
movement, time. The beauty of objects, thoughts,
places and actions.
My work is about my senses, my instinct, my own
scale and my own physical commitment.
My work is real, not illusory or conceptual.
It is about real stones, real time, real actions.
A good work is the right thing in the right
place at the right time. A crossing place.

Richard Long's own words about his work are so clear
and so sparing that they remove the need for much
commentary. The sentences I have quoted come from a
text prepared for the exhibition in which he showed the

work illustrated here. Ideally I should quote them all,
but space is limited and Long does not of course say
everything there is to be said about his work. The art
historian, impressed by the strong though quiet character
of his work, asks himself how it relates to art before
Long and around him in order to understand better his
own response and other people's too.

He has arranged willow sticks on the floor of the
gallery: he has selected those sticks and that place, that
area and that density of sticks to area. Again, we
confront an act that seems random and may even seem
like mindless sensibility and control. The artist takes
matter and makes a significant statement out of it, and in
Long's case it is a statement about people in nature, and
also perhaps about people's non-possession of nature.
We use, we despoil, we are by far the most destructive
creatures on this planet, but so far nature takes little
notice of us, and Long's sticks remain inviolate, innocent. Long walks in England or in remote and deserted
places, and records his walks in various ways, and also
the marks he leaves on the face of nature – simple marks,
as when he walks up and down along a line across a
Peruvian plateau until his boots have drawn a line, or
rearranges the stones by a river until they form a modest
sculpture. Animals make their marks, in pursuit of food
and water or protection, functional marks; Long's are
unfunctional except as art.

Long's action is in part an act against the art world: he does not want to make objects of the usual art-commerce sort. Few artists are happy to see their work as merchandise; the fact that only a few artists do well out of it must sharpen their dislike of the art market. But they want to be able to make their art and live from making it (very few actually do!) and so they need the art market. Long's generation has included many artists who have stayed outside the gallery system, some of them producing works that are not sellable – an unrepeatable performance of some kind, a mark made somewhere. Photographs can record such things and can themselves become the commercial object. Long makes very good photographs of some of the things he does, but he also uses galleries where he can:

Mountains and galleries are both
in their own ways extreme, neutral, uncluttered;
good places to work.

The impact of such a piece as this is much more powerful than that of the best photograph, because the piece is now, the photograph shows what was.

Both Long and Beuys were trained as sculptors, but Beuys has become more and more the performer and soothsayer. He is older and a German; he was nearly killed in the war in which he served as a pilot. Since the 1960s he has used the world more and more, and his works less and less, in order to change it.

How to explain pictures to a dead hare was a three-hour performance given at the opening of one of his exhibitions. Beuys, his head smeared with honey and decked with bits of gold leaf, walks around the show carrying the hare, showing it the pictures, letting its paws touch the exhibits, and then sits with the hare in his arms, saying to it silently 'what cannot be said to his fellow man'. This is easily understood as a satirical performance, mocking the blinkered attitudes of even art-lovers. But there is more to it – and again we are reminded that artists work with intelligence as well as feeling. The hare is prominent in German folk lore, a marvellously alive being that lives in and with the earth and has very sharp senses. The honey and gold draw attention to a basic human strong point, the ability to think and to imagine beauty and health. The performance was also a ritual, and we are reminded of the witch-doctor and the medicine man drawing power from nature through magical means.

Beuys has acted more and more publicly, like a politician. He has founded a non-party party, he has used court cases to establish his right to a professorship at the Düsseldorf academy, he uses exhibitions more and more as occasions for oratory and debates. But he is also a spiritualist. Like Kandinsky, Mondrian, and other modern artists, he is trying to lead us all away from our materialist habits and values. 'Marcel Duchamp's silence is overrated' he has stated (in the form of words painted on a picture-like board): for him Duchamp's radical questioning of the artist's activity was too limited and too in-turned. Beuys uses art and also the channels and the occasions of art to confront us like a religious leader, a guru. Repeatedly, in this century especially, art has tried to take on the religious identity it once had and thus to be again a guiding force and not an ornament in the form of a private enquiry. We sense, in Beuys especially, and especially also amid the post-war *Wirtschaftswunder* (economic miracle) of Germany, an attempt to return to art's primeval roles.

BEUYS
How to explain pictures to a dead hare
performed on 26 November 1965 at Galerie Schmela, Düsseldorf

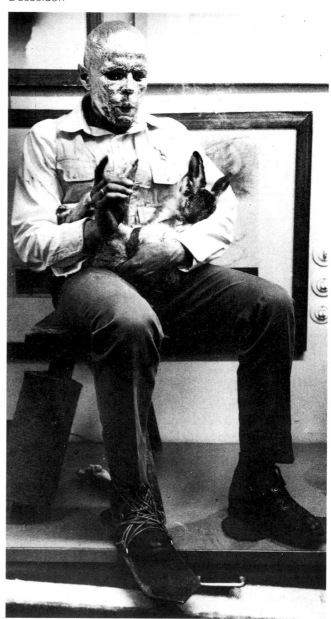

Figurative art or **Representational art** Art that is not abstract or non-representational but shows, in a more or less recognizable manner, objects and scenes from the visible world or from the world of the imagination.

Fresco A technique of painting with liquid paints into moist plaster, developed especially in Italy from about 1300 onwards. For major examples see pages 34, 44, 61, 62, 64 and 74. The colours tend to be paler than those of oil painting; also the technique does not allow for very minute detail.

Genre painting The painting of scenes showing unspecified people, often of the lower classes, going about their unheroic but sometimes amusing lives.

Gothic The style of the later Middle Ages in Europe, developed in northern France from about 1200 on, still flourishing in some places in the seventeenth century, rediscovered in the eighteenth century as a quaint style for garden buildings or pleasure houses and soon promoted as a truly Christian and, in some countries, national style. In architecture the Gothic style is associated with tall pointed arches and a skeletal structure; in painting and sculpture it is associated with an increasingly naturalistic style and with marked grace and ease after centuries of severe and sometimes expressively distorted figures.

History painting means story painting (from the Italian, *istoria*) and is the term used for the most highly valued form of painting in the Renaissance period: important subjects relating to religious doctrine or to history or great themes in literature presented in a suitably dignified manner. The academies maintained a firm scale of values: history painting was the top category, and below it came portrait painting, genre painting, still life painting and landscape painting. This scale was still upheld in academic teaching at the end of the eighteenth century, but by that time the popularity of lower forms of painting had made the scale itself less important, and had also led artists to attempt to mix categories, as when they associated a landscape scene with an important historical event or with religious symbolism.

Icon The image of Christ or a saint on a panel, developed in the Byzantine Empire as a form for devotional representations in the fifth and sixth centuries and still produced in Russia in the nineteenth. Icons were usually painted in simple, clear forms and strong colours, sometimes with a gold background, and showed little concern with suggesting three-dimensionality or space.

Impressionism A movement in painting, developed in and around Paris in the 1870s, and concerned primarily with the recording of temporary effects of light on landscape and towns through touches of paint on a (usually small) canvas. See pages 124-125.

Landscape painting Known to the Greeks and the Romans as a form of decorative painting for private houses, and valued again in the sixteenth century in Italy and the north. The Dutch painters of the seventeenth century were the first to make a habit of painting portrait-like pictures of sketches of their country without, as other landscape painters did, giving them subject matter of the history sort (see pages 83, 88 and 90).

Mosaic An image or pattern produced by setting little cubes of stone or clay (with one coloured and glazed side) into a floor, wall or vault. The Romans used stone mosaic a great deal, especially for floors; the Byzantine period used glazed mosaic for murals and decorative areas in their churches. Like fresco, mosaic does not allow for minute detail or much depth of tone, but glazed mosaic permits very rich colours from black to white including gold and also reflects natural and artifical light according to the particular angles at which the mosaic cubes are set into the surface. See pages 25 and 31.

Mural A painting, usually a large one, on a wall.

Narrative art Art which tells a story, either by showing successive moments from it in one composition (see pages 44-45) or by focusing on one significant moment in the story from which the rest of the story can be deduced – the latter being the practice demanded by history painting.

Naturalism Following the actual or assumed appearance of things in a representation.

Neoclassicism *see* Classicism.

Oil painting was developed by northern painters, notably Van Eyck (page 54), in the fifteenth century and was soon influential in Italy. There the Venetian school of the sixteenth century turned oil painting into a richly expressive art, poetic in its use of colour and tone and expressive also in its handling of the actual material, so that the brushstrokes and the texture of the paint contribute to the appeal of the painting.

Pastel Powdered pigments ground into a resin or gum binding medium. See page 127.

Perspective A system by which three-dimensional objects and the spaces in which they exist can be shown on a two-dimensional surface. There have been many such systems from the Roman period on, some rough and ready, some more precise. The system invented in Florence at the beginning of the fifteenth century enabled and encouraged painters to use space and three-dimensionality as elements contributing to their story-telling and naturalism, and perspective remained one of the bases of Renaissance painting, and also of relief sculpture, until it was challenged in the nineteenth century. See especially pages 44-49. Perspective is still used for many purposes. The Surrealist painters of the twentieth century found it one effective way of suggesting nightmarish experiences (see page 157).

Photomontage 'Montage', from the French, means things put together, mounted, and photomontage means putting photographic images together to form one image. This is the way many advertisements are made today. In the 1920s it was developed as a way of illustrating books and magazines (see page 151) and also as a form of political cartoon, gaining power from its use of realistic fragments (see page 158).

Photo-Realism Paintings, sometimes also sculptures, drawings and the like, derived from a photographed subject. The artist openly, though selectively, accepts the single-eye vision of the camera (see page 169).

Pop art A broad movement in painting, and sometimes sculpture, which emerged in Britain and the USA in the early 1960s, though some of its methods and themes were explored in the 1950s. Pop artists used subjects and idioms taken from advertising and the media (magazines, newspapers, television and so on). Their art seemed insistently low-brow and shallow in its reliance on this unworthy material; they valued it because it had life and impact and because it could be used to reach people not familiar with art. If at first they seemed to support its values it was soon clear that some of them combined enthusiasm for its persuasiveness with critical views of the society it was designed to persuade. The leading artists were Warhol (page 168), Lichtenstein and Oldenburg in America; Hamilton and Hockney in Britain.

Post-Impressionism The name given to varieties of painting, primarily of the 1880s and 1890s, done by artists who had been influenced by the Impressionist way of capturing natural appearances but had gone on to develop more personal, more meaningful and also more consciously constructed kinds of painting. Most notably these include the works of Seurat, Gauguin, Van Gogh and Cézanne (pages 126-131), and then also the works of younger artists influenced by them.

Pre-Raphaelite Brotherhood A group formed in England in 1848 by three young painters: Millais, Holman Hunt (page 122) and Dante Gabriel Rossetti. Their aim was to bring significant moral subjects and painstaking naturalism back into painting. They used subjects from religion, history and literature. They worked with bright colours on white grounds, and disliked the darkening of pictures with elaborate *chiaroscuro* and the rich classicism associated with Raphael (pages 62-63). They preferred the brighter and more apparently innocent art of the earlier Renaissance, before Raphael, for example Fra Angelico (page 48). Hence the name for their group, which they often shortened to PRB.

Primitive art The art of so-called uncivilized societies, such as African tribes and American Indians (pages 42-43 and 136). The term is also used for folk art, the art of children, the mentally sick and of unsophisticated amateur painters – all in contrast to the learned, practised and conscious art of the professional.

Primitivism refers to the use of *primitive art* sources by artists, including the return to the early, undeveloped forms of accepted art traditions, for example, to very early forms of classical art. Neoclassicism was primitivist in its search for plain, even awkward forms of classicism, and the Pre-Raphaelites were primitivist in their rejection of the fully developed Renaissance style. Modern art has seen more extreme primitivism in borrowings from African, Oceanic and other remote cultures. An outstanding example of a European primitive, an untutored but serious painter several steps removed from both the academic and the anti-academic art of his time, was Rousseau, the former customs clerk (page 137).

Realism In art generally a concern for the accurate recording of the visible world and thus close to naturalism, but a distinction is sometimes usefully made between the naturalistic treatment of surface appearances as in late Gothic art (pages 38-39 and 54-55) and a realistic attention to structure as well as surface (anatomical structure, relationships in space and so forth) as in Renaissance art. In the nineteenth century a movement named *Realism* was not only realistic in this sense but gave its attention to the life and harsh realities of peasants and workers. Courbet was a champion of Realism in the 1850s (page 120), offering his art as a counter to the emotional, poetic and sometimes dreamy inventions of Romanticism.

Relief In sculpture a three-dimensional work developed from one vertical plane, by carving into it or, more usually, by carving or modelling forms projecting from that plane in varying degrees (pages 22, 30 and 45).

Renaissance means rebirth. The term Renaissance is used to refer to developments in learning and the arts from the fourteenth century on, first in central Italy, then in northern Italy and the rest of Europe. An important aspect of this was the renewed close study of Greek and Roman authors and ancient architecture, art and other objects, in so far as they could be found. Hence rebirth: the reconnecting of civilization to the great tradition from which invading barbarians were thought to have sundered it.

Rococo The name of a style in interior decoration and ornament, developed in France in the early eighteenth century. It is also used to describe the often light-hearted and decorative art produced during the same decades and mostly for the same homes – all in reaction against the grandeur of late seventeenth century (Versailles pages 96-97). Watteau (page 104) is associated with Rococo in art but the tragic vein running through his art distinguishes him from it.

Romanesque art European art of the late eleventh and the twelfth centuries. (English Romanesque art is often called Norman.) The name rightly points to the influence of Roman architecture; there are signs of Roman influence also in sculpture and painting but more often their character is dominated by northern forms and patterns. See pages 28-29.

Romanticism A broad western movement in ideas and the arts that emphasized the value of emotions as against reason, individualism against well-established themes and idioms, overwhelming size or implied scale as against an easy relationship between mankind and the world, and energy and change as against security and stability. Thus landscape paintings might be devoted to nature's grandeur and violence rather than to serene panoramas (page 118), portraits to the inner drama of an individual's existence rather than to a confirmation of that person's standing in society. Many of Romanticism's assumptions still affect our thinking about art, not least the idea that an artist's work represents his own personality and mood before anything else.

Still life A category in art having inanimate objects as subject matter, often with symbolical meanings. Known in later Greek art, still life painting was frequent in Dutch seventeenth century art and gained a wider European public in the eighteenth. Still life, like landscape, often provided painters of the nineteenth and twentieth centuries with opportunities for exploring new methods. See, for example, Courbet (page 120), Picasso (page 139), Magritte and Dali (pages 155 and 157).

Surrealism A movement in literature and art, developed in Paris in the 1920s and after, dedicated to exploring and making public human desires and responses not admitted to by polite society. For a time the movement was allied to Communism; generally it has tended to extreme positions politically, on the left or the extreme right. See pages 154-157.

Symmetry Usually the left/right echoing of forms as suggested by the human figure standing straight and seen frontally. There are more complex forms of symmetry, as in crystals, and these are often used in patterns.

Tempera Paint in which the binding liquid is egg, used most frequently in the Renaissance and pre-Renaissance period in Italy for painting on wood. See pages 36-37.

Three-dimensional This means having depth as well as height.

Triptych *see* altarpiece.

Tympanum in medieval architecture the semi-circular wall surface between the doorway and the arch rising over it, sometimes carved with Biblical subjects. See pages 31 and 32.

Index

178

Acknowledgements

The publishers wish to thank the following photographers, agencies, galleries, museums and other institutes for their help in supplying photographs for this book.

Front cover *top left* Collection Amsterdam Historical Museum, *top centre left* Wadsworth Atheneum, Hartford Connecticut. The Ella Gallup Sumner and Mary Catlin Sumner Collection, *top centre right* SCALA, Florence, *top right* The Metropolitan Museum of Art, Bequest of Jospeh H. Durkee. Gift of Darius Ogden Mills, and Gift of C. Ruxton Love, by Exchange, 1972, *centre top* Courtauld Institute Galleries London, *centre right* Narodni Gallerie, Prague, *centre bottom* Collection Van Abbemuseum, Eindhoven, *bottom left* Bildarchiv Preussischer Kulturbesitz, *bottom centre* John Webb/National Gallery, London, *bottom right* SCALA, Florence; Back cover SCALA, Florence
2-3 *see* cover; 4-5 *see* 21, 48, 131, 149; 9 *see pages* 62, 64, 68, 104; 11 *see pages* 124, 138, 146; 12 Giraudon, Paris; 13 © ARCH.PHOT.PARIS/S.P.A.D.E.M; 14 Courtesy, Museum of Fine Arts, Boston; 15 bottom Michael Holford/British Museum, London; 16 *right* The Metropolitan Museum of Art, Bequest of Jospeh H. Durkee, Gift of Darius Ogden Mills, and Gift of C. Ruxton Love, by Exchange, 1972; 17 Ronald Sheridan; 18-19 *top* Ekodtike Athenon S.A.; 19 *bottom right* Ronald Sheridan; 20 Giraudon, Paris; 21 *left* Museo Pio Clementino Vaticano; 22-25 SCALA, Florence; 26 St Gallen, Stiftsbibliothek; 27 The Board of Trinity College, Dublin; 28 Michael Holford; 29 Bibliothèque Nationale, Paris; 31 *top* SCALA, Florence *bottom* Sonia Halliday; 32-33 Sonia Halliday; 34-37 SCALA, Florence; 38 British Library, London; 39 Lauros-Giraudon; 40 Museum of the American Indian, New York; 41 The Metropolitan Museum of Art, The Michael C. Rockefeller Memorial Collection of Primitive Art, Purchase, Nelson A. Rockefeller Gift, 1968; 42 Courtesy of the Denver Art Museum, Denver, Colorado; 43 British Museum, London; 44-46 SCALA, Florence; 47 Musée des Beaux-Arts de Lille; 48-49 SCALA, Florence; 50 Cliche Musées Nationaux Paris; 51 *top* Cliche Musées Nationaux Paris *bottom* British Museum, London; 52-53 copyright The Frick Collection, New York; 54 John Webb/National Gallery, London; 55-56 SCALA, Florence; 57 Kunst-Dias Blauel/Alte Pinakothek; 58 SCALA, Florence; 59 *left* Royal Collection, Windsor Castle, reproduced by Gracious Permission of Her Majesty the Queen *right* SCALA, Florence; 60-62 SCALA, Florence; 63 *left* Ashmolean Museum, Oxford; 64-65 SCALA, Florence; 66 Fotomas/British Museum, London; 67 Mansell Collection; 68-72 SCALA, Florence; 73 John Webb/National Gallery, London; 74-75 SCALA, Florence; 76 *left and right* Cliche Musées Nationaux Paris; 77 *top* Bildarchiv Preussischer Kulturbesitz *bottom* Courtesy, Museum of Fine Arts, Boston; 78 © Lichtbildwerstaate Alpenland Graphischen Sammlung Albertina; 79 Kunsthistorisches Museum, Vienna; 80 John Webb/National Gallery, London; 81 Musées Royaux des Beaux-Arts de Belqique, Bruxelles; 82 Collection Amsterdam Historical Museum; 83 *top* John Webb/National Gallery, London *bottom* Rijksmuseum, Amsterdam; 84 *left* Fotomas Index/British Museum, London *right* Kobberstiksamling, Copenhagen; 85 Novosti/Hermitage Museum, Leningrad; 86-87 SCALA, Florence; 88-89 Courtesy of the Earl of Derby, Knowsley Hall, Lancs; 90-95 SCALA, Florence; 96 CFL-Giraudon; 97 Photo Bulloz; 98 The National Gallery of Canada, Ottowa; 99 *top* Collection du Musée Cernuschi; 100 Giraudon, Paris;

101 *bottom* Victoria and Albert Museum, London; 102 *left* Courtesy of the Art Institute of Chicago *right* British Library, London; 103 Victoria and Albert Museum, London; 104 By Permission of the Governors of Dulwich Picture Gallery; 105 British Museum, London; 106 Wallace Collection/Fotomas Index; 107 Royal College of Music; 109 *top* Reproduced by Kind Permission of the Stewards of the Jockey Club *bottom* The Burrell Collection-Glasgow Art Gallery; 110-111 Cliche Musées Nationaux Paris; 113 *bottom* British Museum, London; 114 Fotomas Index/British Museum, London; 115 SCALA, Florence; 116 John Webb/National Gallery, London; 117 Giraudon, Paris; 118 The Tate Gallery, London; 119 Gerhards Heinhold, Leipzig-Molkau; 120 Mauritshuis, The Hague; 121 John Webb/National Gallery, London; 122 Walker Art Gallery, Liverpool; 123 Wadsworth Atheneum, Hartford, Connecticut (The Ella Gallup Sumner and Mary Catlin Sumner Collection); 124 SCALA, Florence; 126 Courtauld Institute Galleries, London; 127 The Lefevre Gallery, London; 128 National Gallery of Scotland, Edinburgh; 129 E. G. Bürhle Collection; 130 Kunstmuseum, Basel; 131 Philadelphia Museum of Art: Purchased W. P. Wistach Collection; 132 Victoria and Albert Museum, London; 133 Lauros-Giraudon; 134 National Gallery, Oslo; 135 Cleveland Museum of Art, Gift of the Hanna Fund; 136 *left and right* British Museum, London; 137 Narodni Gallerie, Prague; 138 *left* Kunstmuseum, Basel *right* Verlag gerd Hatje/John Hedgecoe; 139 The Tate Gallery, London; 140 Muzeul de Artă Craiova; 141 Collection, The Museum of Modern Art, New York. Given anonymously; 142 Collection Van Abbemuseum, Eindhoven; 143 Hamburger Kunsthalle; 144 Collection, The Museum of Modern Art, New York. Katherine S. Dreier Bequest; 145 Philadelphia Museum of Art: Bequest of Katherine S. Dreier; 146 Kunstsammlung Nordrhein-Westfalen, Dusseldorf; 147 Collection, The Museum of Modern Art, New York. Abby Aldrich Rockefeller Fund; 148 From the Collection of Morton D. May; 149 Philadelphia Museum of Art: The A. E. Gallatin Collection; 151 British Library, London; 152 Collection Haags Gemeentemuseum—The Hague; 153 Museum Boymans-Van Beuningen, Rotterdam; 154 Collection The Museum of Modern Art, New York. Purchase; 155 Phaidon Press; 156 Kunstmuseum, Basel; 157 Wadsworth Atheneum, Hartford, Connecticut. The Ella Gallup Sumner and Mary Catlin Sumner Collection; 159 on extended loan to the Museum of Modern Art, New York, from the artist; 160 Gift of Dexter M. Ferry, Jr. Trustee Corp. Courtesy of the Detroit Institute of Arts; 161 The Tate Gallery, London; 162 Collection The Museum of Modern Art, New York. Mrs Simon Guggenheim Fund; 163 The Tate Gallery, London; 164 Dallas Museum of Fine Arts. Gift of Mr and Mrs Bernard J. Reis, New York City; 165 The Phillips Collection, Washington; 166 The Arts Council Collection, London; 167 The Tate Gallery, London; 168 Photo Courtesy of Leo Castello Gallery, New York; 169 Robert Cottingham; 170 Anthony d'Offay Gallery, London; 171 © Ute Klophaus.

The works of Dali, Degas, Ernst, Matisse, Mondrian, Monet, Picasso, Rodin, Warhol are © by S.P.A.D.E.M., Paris 1981, and those of Brancusi, Braque, Courbet, Duchamp, Giacometti, Kandinsky, Klee, Léger, Magritte, Miró, Munch are © A.D.A.G.P., Paris 1981.

Picture research by Jackie Cookson
Line drawings by David Salariya